FODOR'S BED & BREAKFASTS
AND COUNTRY INNS

The Southwest's Best
Bed & Breakfasts
2nd Edition

Delightful Places to Stay and Great
Things to Do When You Get There

Fodor's Travel Publications, Inc.
New York • Toronto • London • Sydney • Aukland

The Southwest's Best Bed and Breakfasts

Editor: Hannah Borgeson

Contributors: Steven Amsterdam, Scott Baradell, John Bigley, Ron Butler, Stacey Clark, Daniel Gibson, Edie Jarolim, Alexander Parsons, Tracy Patruno, Paris Permenter, John Stickler

Creative Director: Fabrizio La Rocca
Cartographer: David Lindroth; Mapping Specialists
Illustrators: Alida Beck, Karl Tanner
Cover Design: Guido Caroti
Cover Photograph: Michael Goldman/FPG

Special Sales

Fodor's Travel Publications are available at special discounts for bulk purchases for sales promotions or premiums. Special editions, including personalized covers, excerpts of existing guides, and corporate imprints, can be created in large quantities for special needs. For more information, contact your local bookseller or write to Special Markets, Fodor's Travel Publications, 201 East 50th Street, New York, NY 10022. Inquiries from Canada should be directed to your local Canadian bookseller or sent to Random House of Canada, Ltd., Marketing Department, 1265 Aerowood Drive, Mississauga, Ontario L4W 1B9. Inquiries from the United Kingdom should be sent to Fodor's Travel Publications, 20 Vauxhall Bridge Road, London, England SW1V 2SA.

Contributors

John Bigley *and* **Paris Permenter** *updated the Texas chapter and wrote the new section on West Texas. Longtime residents of the Lone Star State, they work as travel writers and specialize in southwestern and Caribbean destinations. They have written for such newspapers and magazines as* Texas Highways, Flower and Garden, *and the* San-Antonio Express-News. *For their recent book* Texas Barbecue, *they spent six months eating almost nothing but meat and potatoes.*

Stacey Clark, *who wrote and updated the Utah chapter, is a Utah native who writes frequently about the state's people and places for a variety of local and statewide publications. She is a regular Fodor's writer and updater, with chapters of Fodor's USA, Rockies, and America's Best Bed and Breakfasts to her credit.*

Dan Gibson, *who updated the Santa Fe and Albuquerque sections, is a writer and editor whose work has appeared in many regional and national magazines and newspapers. Though he loves his native New Mexico, he sometimes feels that the "Land of Mañana" has dropped off America's literary map.*

Edie Jarolim *edited the first edition of this guide, wrote its Albuquerque and Southern New Mexico sections, and contributed to the Arizona sections. For this edition she updated the Prescott, Arizona, listings. She is a regular contributor to Fodor's guides and has also been published in the* Wall Street Journal, The New York Times, *and the* London Guardian. *She lives in Tucson, Arizona.*

Alexander Parsons, *who updated the Taos and Southern New Mexico sections, was raised in the northern part of the state. After attending college on the East Coast and then working at Random House and in Fodor's New York office, he headed back to Santa Fe where he's now a freelance writer. In addition to taking Fodor's assignments, he writes for the Associated Press and* The Santa Fean Magazine.

John Stickler, *who wrote and updated most of the Arizona sections, is a freelance writer who has founded an ad agency, published a national magazine, and filed stories for CBS News from Seoul, Korea. He writes books and articles on business and travel topics from his adobe home in the desert northwest of Tucson, Arizona.*

Contents

Foreword

While every care has been taken to ensure the accuracy of the information in this guide, the passage of time will always bring change and, consequently, the publisher cannot accept responsibility for errors that may occur.

All prices and listings are based on information supplied to us at press time. Details may change, however, and the prudent traveler will avoid inconvenience by calling ahead.

Fodor's wants to hear about your travel experiences, both pleasant and unpleasant. When an inn or B&B fails to live up to its billing, let us know and we will investigate the complaint and revise our entries where the facts warrant it.

Send your letters to the editors of Fodor's Travel Publications, 201 East 50th Street, New York, NY 10022.

Introduction

You'll find bed-and-breakfasts in big houses with turrets and little houses with decks, in mansions by the water and cabins in the forest, not to mention structures of many sizes and shapes in between. B&Bs are run by people who were once lawyers and writers, homemakers and artists, nurses and architects, singers and businesspeople. Some B&Bs are just a room or two in a hospitable local's home; others are more like small inns. So there's an element of serendipity to every B&B stay.

But while that's part of the pleasure of the experience, it's also an excellent reason to plan your travels with a good B&B guide. The one you hold in your hands serves the purpose neatly.

To create it, we've handpicked a team of professional writers who are also confirmed B&B lovers: people who adore the many manifestations of the Victorian era; who go wild over wicker and brass beds, four-posters and fireplaces; and who know a well-run operation when they see it and are only too eager to communicate their knowledge to you. We've instructed them to inspect the premises and check out every corner of the premier inns and B&Bs in the areas they cover, and to report critically on only the best in every price range.

They've returned from their travels with comprehensive reports on the pleasure of B&B travel, which may well become your pleasure as you read their reports in the pages that follow. These are establishments that promise a unique experience, a distinctive sense of time and place. All are destinations in themselves, not just spots to rest your head at night, but an integral part of a weekend escape. You'll learn what's good, what's bad, and what could be better; what our writers liked and what you might not like.

At the same time, Fodor's reviewers tell you what's up in the area and what you should and shouldn't miss—everything from historic sites and parks to antiques shops, boutiques, and the area's niftiest restaurants and nightspots. We also include names and addresses of B&B reservation services, just in case you're inspired to seek out additional properties on your own. Reviews are organized by state, and, within each state, by region.

In the italicized service information that ends every review, a second address in parentheses is a mailing address. A double room is for two people, regardless of the size or type of its beds. Unless otherwise noted, rooms don't have phones or TVs. Note that even the most stunning homes, farmhouses and mansions alike, may not provide a private bathroom for each individual. Rates are for two, excluding tax, in the high season and include breakfast unless otherwise noted; ask about special packages and midweek or off-season discounts.

What we call a restaurant serves meals other than breakfast and is usually open to the general public.

The following credit card abbreviations are used throughout this guide: AE, American Express; D, Discover; DC, Diners Club; MC, MasterCard; V, Visa.

Where applicable, we note seasonal and other restrictions. Although we abhor discrimination, we have conveyed information about innkeepers' restrictive practices so that you will be aware of the prevailing attitudes. Such discriminatory practices are most often applied to parents who are traveling with small children and who may not, in any case, feel comfortable having their offspring toddle amid breakable bric-a-brac and near precipitous stairways.

When traveling the B&B way, always call ahead; and if you have mobility problems or are traveling with children, if you prefer a private bath or a certain type of bed, or if you have specific dietary needs or any other concerns, discuss them with the innkeeper. At the same time, if you're traveling to an inn because of a specific feature, make sure that it will be available when you get there and not closed for renovation. The same goes if you're making a detour to take advantage of specific sights or attractions.

It's a sad commentary on other B&B guides today that we feel obliged to tell you that our writers did, in fact, visit every property in person, and that it is they, not the innkeepers, who wrote the reviews. No one paid a fee or promised to sell or promote the book in order to be included in it. (In fact, one of the most challenging parts of the work of a Fodor's writer is to persuade innkeepers and B&B owners that he or she wants nothing more than a tour of the premises and the answers to a few questions!) Fodor's has no stake in anything but the truth. If a room is dark, with peeling wallpaper, we don't call it quaint or atmospheric—we call it run-down, and then steer you to a more appealing section of the property.

So trust us, the way you'd trust a knowledgeable, well-traveled friend. Let us hear from you about your travels, whether you found that the B&Bs you visited surpassed their descriptions or the other way around. And have a wonderful trip!

Karen Cure
Editorial Director

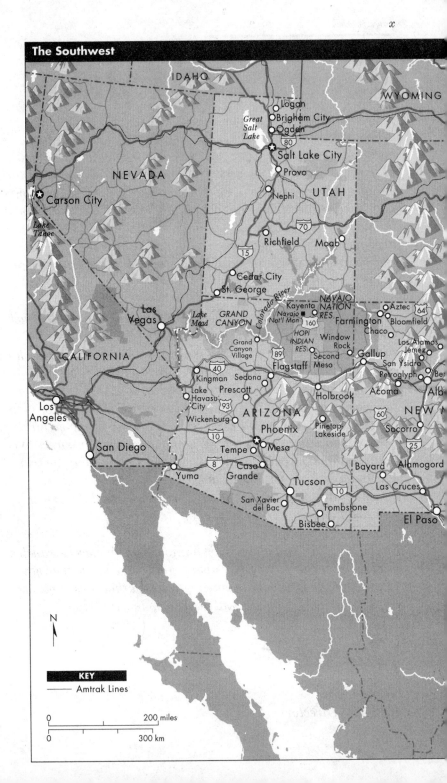

The Southwest

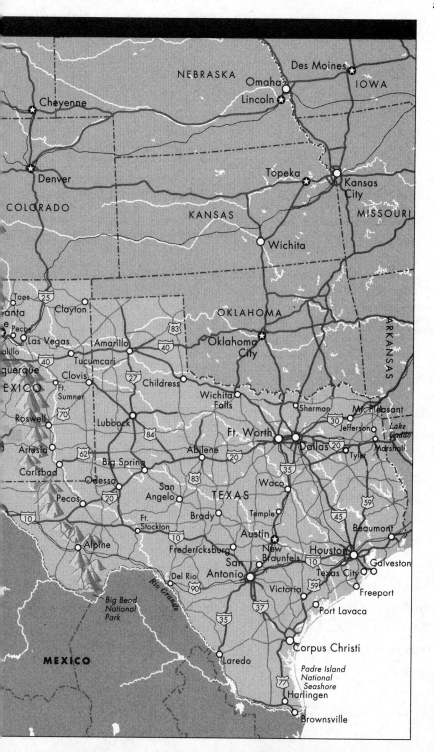

Special Features at a Glance

Name of Property	Antiques	On the Water	Good Value	Car Not Necessary	Full Meal Service	Historic Building	Romantic Hideaway	
ARIZONA								
Bartram's White Mountain Bed & Breakfast							✓	
Billings' Country Retreat	✓		✓				✓	
Birch Tree Inn			✓			✓		
The Bisbee Grand Hotel	✓					✓	✓	
Briar Patch Inn		✓				✓	✓	
Bright Angel Lodge			✓		✓	✓	✓	
Buford House B&B	✓					✓	✓	
Canyon Country Inn						✓		
Canyon Villa Bed & Breakfast Inn							✓	
Casa Alegre Bed and Breakfast Inn	✓					✓	✓	
Casa Sedona							✓	
Casa Tierra Adobe Bed & Breakfast			✓				✓	
Cathedral Rock Lodge							✓	
The Clawson House	✓					✓	✓	
"The Coldstream" Bed & Breakfast						✓		
Copper Queen Hotel					✓	✓	✓	
The Cottages at Prescott Country Inn			✓					
Country Elegance Bed & Breakfast							✓	
Coyote Pass Hospitality					✓			
Cozy Cactus Bed & Breakfast	✓						✓	
The Duquesne House Bed and Breakfast						✓	✓	
El Presidio Bed & Breakfast Inn	✓					✓	✓	
El Tovar Hotel	✓				✓	✓	✓	
Elysian Grove Market			✓			✓	✓	
The Graham B&B Inn							✓	

Luxurious	Pets Allowed	No Smoking Indoors	Good Place for Families	Near Arts Festival	Beach Nearby	Cross-Country Ski Trail	Golf within 5 miles	Fitness Facilities	Good Biking Terrain	Skiing	Horseback Riding	Tennis	Swimming on Premises	Conference Facilities
		✓	✓				✓			✓	✓			
	✓	✓	✓				✓			✓	✓			
		✓		✓						✓				
		✓		✓										
		✓	✓	✓										
			✓								✓			
		✓		✓										
		✓					✓							
✓		✓		✓			✓						✓	
		✓		✓			✓				✓		✓	
✓		✓		✓			✓				✓		✓	
		✓												
		✓	✓	✓							✓			
		✓		✓			✓							
								✓						✓
				✓			✓						✓	✓
		✓	✓	✓					✓					
		✓	✓	✓										
	✓	✓	✓								✓			
		✓	✓	✓			✓							
		✓	✓											
✓		✓		✓			✓							
			✓								✓			✓
				✓			✓							
✓		✓	✓	✓			✓		✓				✓	

Special Features at a Glance

Name of Property	Antiques	On the Water	Good Value	Car Not Necessary	Full Meal Service	Historic Building	Romantic Hideaway	
Grand Canyon Lodge	✓		✓		✓	✓	✓	
Grapevine Canyon Ranch					✓			
Greer Lodge		✓			✓	✓	✓	
The Guest House Inn	✓		✓			✓		
Hassayampa Inn	✓		✓		✓	✓		
Horizons Bed and Breakfast							✓	
The Inn at Four Ten	✓					✓	✓	
The Judge Ross House	✓					✓	✓	
Juniper Well Ranch	✓						✓	
Kelly's Whistlestop Bed and Breakfast			✓					
La Posada del Valle	✓					✓	✓	
Lantern Light Inn Bed & Breakfast	✓						✓	
The Little House Bed and Breakfast	✓					✓	✓	
The Lodge at Sedona							✓	
Lynx Creek Farm	✓	✓					✓	
Main Street Inn			✓			✓		
Maricopa Manor Bed and Breakfast Inn	✓		✓			✓		
The Marks House	✓					✓	✓	
The Meadows					✓		✓	
The Mine Manager's House Inn						✓	✓	
Mt. Vernon Inn	✓		✓			✓		
Noftsger Hill Inn	✓		✓			✓		
The OK Street Jailhouse						✓	✓	
Olney House Bed & Breakfast	✓		✓			✓	✓	
Paisley Corner Bed & Breakfast	✓					✓	✓	
The Peppertrees Bed and Breakfast Inn	✓					✓	✓	

Luxurious	Pets Allowed	No Smoking Indoors	Good Place for Families	Near Arts Festival	Beach Nearby	Cross-Country Ski Trail	Golf within 5 miles	Fitness Facilities	Good Biking Terrain	Skiing	Horseback Riding	Tennis	Swimming on Premises	Conference Facilities
			✓								✓			
							✓				✓		✓	✓
✓				✓		✓				✓	✓			✓
		✓					✓							✓
				✓					✓					✓
✓		✓							✓		✓		✓	
✓		✓	✓	✓			✓	✓		✓				
		✓		✓			✓							
	✓	✓	✓						✓		✓			
	✓	✓	✓						✓					
		✓		✓			✓							
		✓	✓	✓			✓							
		✓												
		✓		✓										✓
	✓	✓	✓	✓					✓					
		✓	✓	✓			✓							
✓			✓	✓			✓							
✓		✓		✓					✓					
		✓				✓	✓		✓	✓				
		✓					✓							
	✓	✓	✓											
		✓	✓	✓			✓							✓
		✓	✓	✓			✓							
		✓		✓										
		✓								✓				
		✓	✓	✓			✓							

Special Features at a Glance

Name of Property	Antiques	On the Water	Good Value	Car Not Necessary	Full Meal Service	Historic Building	Romantic Hideaway	
The Pleasant Street Inn Bed & Breakfast						✓	✓	
Priscilla's Bed & Breakfast	✓					✓	✓	
Quail's Vista Bed and Breakfast	✓							
Ramsey Canyon Inn	✓	✓					✓	
Rimrock West Hacienda			✓				✓	
Saddle Rock Ranch	✓					✓	✓	
San Francisco Street B&B						✓		
School House Inn Bed & Breakfast			✓			✓		
Tanque Verde Ranch					✓	✓	✓	
Thunderbird Lodge					✓	✓		
Tombstone Boarding House	✓					✓		
The Triangle L Ranch Bed & Breakfast	✓					✓	✓	
Victorian Inn of Prescott Bed & Breakfast	✓					✓	✓	
White Mountain Lodge		✓	✓			✓	✓	
NEW MEXICO								
Adobe Abode	✓			✓		✓	✓	
Adobe & Pines	✓					✓	✓	
Adobe and Roses			✓				✓	
Alexander's Inn	✓			✓		✓	✓	
American Gallery Artists House	✓		✓				✓	
Bear Mountain Guest Ranch					✓			
The Black Range Lodge						✓		
The Blue Door	✓						✓	
Bottgër Mansion	✓			✓	✓	✓	✓	
Brooks Street Inn	✓			✓			✓	

Luxurious	Pets Allowed	No Smoking Indoors	Good Place for Families	Near Arts Festival	Beach Nearby	Cross-Country Ski Trail	Golf within 5 miles	Fitness Facilities	Good Biking Terrain	Skiing	Horseback Riding	Tennis	Swimming on Premises	Conference Facilities
✓		✓		✓					✓					
		✓		✓										
		✓	✓				✓	✓			✓		✓	
		✓												
													✓	
✓		✓											✓	
		✓		✓			✓			✓				
		✓		✓			✓							
			✓				✓	✓			✓	✓	✓	✓
		✓	✓								✓			✓
		✓		✓										
		✓	✓								✓			
✓		✓		✓					✓					
	✓		✓							✓				
✓		✓		✓		✓	✓		✓	✓	✓			
✓		✓		✓		✓	✓		✓	✓				
	✓	✓	✓	✓		✓	✓		✓	✓				
		✓	✓	✓		✓	✓		✓	✓				
✓		✓		✓		✓	✓		✓	✓				
	✓	✓					✓		✓					✓
	✓	✓	✓						✓					
		✓	✓	✓		✓	✓		✓	✓				
		✓	✓	✓			✓		✓	✓				
		✓	✓	✓		✓	✓	✓	✓	✓				

Special Features at a Glance

Name of Property	Antiques	On the Water	Good Value	Car Not Necessary	Full Meal Service	Historic Building	Romantic Hideaway	
The Carter House	✓					✓		
Casa de las Chimeneas	✓					✓	✓	
Casa del Granjero						✓	✓	
Casa del Rio	✓						✓	
Casa de Milagros	✓					✓	✓	
Casa de Patrón	✓					✓		
Casa Escondida	✓					✓	✓	
Casa Europa	✓					✓	✓	
Casas de Sueños	✓			✓		✓	✓	
Casita Chamisa	✓		✓			✓	✓	
Dos Casas Viejas	✓						✓	
Dunshee's	✓		✓				✓	
Eaton House	✓					✓	✓	
Elaine's	✓		✓				✓	
The Ellis Store & Co. Bed and Breakfast	✓		✓		✓	✓		
El Paradero			✓	✓		✓		
El Rincón	✓			✓		✓	✓	
The Enchanted Villa	✓				✓	✓		
Enchanted Vista			✓					
Grant Corner Inn	✓			✓		✓	✓	
The Guadalupe Inn							✓	
Hacienda del Sol	✓					✓	✓	
Hacienda Vargas	✓					✓	✓	
Harrison's Bed and Breakfast			✓					
Inn of the Animal Tracks						✓	✓	
Inn on the Alameda				✓				

Luxurious	Pets Allowed	No Smoking Indoors	Good Place for Families	Near Arts Festival	Beach Nearby	Cross-Country Ski Trail	Golf within 5 miles	Fitness Facilities	Good Biking Terrain	Skiing	Horseback Riding	Tennis	Swimming on Premises	Conference Facilities
		✓	✓				✓		✓					
✓		✓	✓	✓			✓	✓	✓	✓				
		✓	✓	✓			✓		✓	✓				
		✓				✓			✓	✓				
		✓	✓	✓			✓	✓	✓	✓				
		✓	✓						✓	✓				
		✓	✓	✓		✓			✓					
✓		✓	✓	✓			✓	✓	✓	✓				
✓		✓		✓			✓		✓	✓				
	✓	✓	✓				✓		✓	✓			✓	
✓		✓		✓		✓	✓		✓	✓			✓	
		✓	✓	✓		✓	✓		✓	✓				
✓		✓					✓		✓					
		✓		✓		✓			✓	✓				
		✓	✓						✓	✓	✓			
	✓	✓		✓		✓	✓		✓	✓				
✓	✓		✓	✓		✓	✓		✓	✓				
	✓		✓						✓		✓		✓	✓
	✓	✓	✓	✓		✓	✓		✓	✓				
	✓	✓		✓		✓	✓		✓	✓				
✓		✓		✓		✓	✓		✓	✓				
✓		✓	✓	✓		✓	✓	✓	✓	✓				
		✓				✓			✓	✓				
		✓	✓	✓		✓	✓		✓	✓	✓			
		✓		✓		✓	✓		✓	✓				
✓	✓		✓	✓		✓	✓	✓	✓	✓				✓

Special Features at a Glance

Name of Property	Antiques	On the Water	Good Value	Car Not Necessary	Full Meal Service	Historic Building	Romantic Hideaway
Inn on the Paseo				✓		✓	✓
La Posada de Chimayo	✓					✓	✓
La Posada de Taos	✓			✓		✓	✓
Little Tree	✓						✓
The Lodge	✓				✓	✓	✓
Lundeen Inn of the Arts	✓			✓		✓	✓
Mabel Dodge Luhan House	✓			✓	✓	✓	✓
Mesón de Mesilla		✓			✓		
Old Taos Guesthouse			✓				✓
Old Town Bed & Breakfast			✓	✓		✓	✓
Orange Street Inn	✓						
Orinda Bed and Breakfast	✓			✓			✓
Preston House	✓			✓		✓	✓
Pueblo Bonito				✓		✓	
Rancho de San Juan	✓		✓		✓		✓
The Ruby Slipper				✓			✓
Salsa del Salto							✓
Sarabande	✓		✓				✓
Sierra Mesa Lodge	✓						✓
A Starry Night	✓			✓			✓
Taos Country Inn at Rancho Rio Pueblo	✓					✓	✓
Taos Hacienda Inn						✓	✓
Territorial Inn	✓			✓		✓	✓
Water Street Inn	✓		✓	✓		✓	✓
W.E. Mauger Estate	✓			✓		✓	✓
Yours Truly			✓				✓

Luxurious	Pets Allowed	No Smoking Indoors	Good Place for Families	Near Arts Festival	Beach Nearby	Cross-Country Ski Trail	Golf within 5 miles	Fitness Facilities	Good Biking Terrain	Skiing	Horseback Riding	Tennis	Swimming on Premises	Conference Facilities
		✓		✓		✓	✓		✓	✓				
	✓	✓				✓			✓	✓				
				✓		✓	✓		✓	✓				
	✓	✓	✓	✓		✓	✓	✓	✓	✓				
			✓			✓	✓		✓	✓			✓	✓
✓	✓	✓	✓				✓	✓			✓			✓
	✓		✓	✓		✓	✓		✓	✓				
	✓		✓			✓			✓				✓	✓
				✓		✓	✓		✓	✓				
		✓		✓		✓			✓	✓				
		✓	✓			✓	✓		✓	✓				
		✓	✓	✓		✓	✓	✓	✓	✓				
✓	✓	✓		✓		✓			✓	✓				
		✓		✓		✓	✓		✓	✓				
✓		✓				✓			✓	✓				✓
		✓		✓		✓	✓		✓	✓				
		✓	✓	✓		✓	✓		✓	✓	✓	✓		
✓		✓				✓			✓	✓			✓	
✓		✓		✓		✓				✓	✓			
		✓		✓		✓	✓		✓	✓				
				✓		✓	✓		✓	✓				
✓		✓	✓	✓		✓	✓		✓	✓				
		✓		✓		✓	✓		✓	✓				
✓	✓	✓	✓	✓		✓	✓		✓	✓				
✓	✓	✓		✓			✓		✓	✓				
		✓		✓	✓				✓	✓				

Special Features at a Glance

Name of Property	Antiques	On the Water	Good Value	Car Not Necessary	Full Meal Service	Historic Building	Romantic Hideaway	
TEXAS								
The Abernathy Inn	✓		✓					
Annie's Bed & Breakfast	✓		✓		✓			
Austin Street Retreat	✓			✓			✓	
The Beckmann Inn and Carriage House	✓			✓		✓	✓	
The Bonner Garden	✓					✓		
Broadway Manor	✓							
The Bullis House Inn	✓					✓		
Caddo Cottage		✓						
Carrington's Bluff	✓							
Charnwood Hill	✓					✓		
Cleburne House	✓							
The Comfort Common	✓					✓		
Crystal River Inn	✓		✓					
Das Kleine Nest							✓	
Delforge Place	✓							
The Excelsior House	✓		✓			✓		
Fredericksburg Bed & Brew								
Galbraith House	✓							
Harrison House	✓							
The Herb Haus								
Hotel Garza	✓		✓					
The Hotel St. Germain	✓			✓				
House of the Seasons	✓					✓	✓	
Inn on the Creek	✓	✓						
Inn on the River		✓				✓		

Luxurious	Pets Allowed	No Smoking Indoors	Good Place for Families	Near Arts Festival	Beach Nearby	Cross-Country Ski Trail	Golf within 5 miles	Fitness Facilities	Good Biking Terrain	Skiing	Horseback Riding	Tennis	Swimming on Premises	Conference Facilities
				✓										
		✓												
✓		✓					✓		✓					
	✓		✓			✓								
		✓		✓			✓						✓	
		✓		✓			✓							
		✓		✓			✓							
			✓						✓					
		✓		✓			✓							
✓		✓					✓							✓
		✓					✓							
		✓					✓		✓					
		✓					✓		✓					
							✓		✓					
		✓					✓		✓					
		✓		✓					✓					
		✓					✓							✓
✓		✓	✓				✓		✓					
	✓	✓		✓			✓		✓					
		✓					✓		✓					
		✓							✓					
✓		✓	✓				✓							✓
✓		✓	✓											
		✓		✓			✓		✓					✓
		✓					✓						✓	✓

Special Features at a Glance

Name of Property	Antiques	On the Water	Good Value	Car Not Necessary	Full Meal Service	Historic Building	Romantic Hideaway	
Maison-Bayou								
Mansion on Main	✓							
McKay House	✓			✓		✓	✓	
Miss Molly's Bed & Breakfast			✓	✓				
The Nagel House	✓							
The Ogé House on the Riverwalk	✓	✓		✓		✓		
Oxford House	✓							
Parkview House								
Pride House	✓							
Schmidt Barn							✓	
The Seasons								
Settlers Crossing	✓		✓			✓	✓	
Stillwater Inn	✓				✓			
Woodburn House	✓							
A Yellow Rose								
Ziller House							✓	
UTAH								
Aunt Annie's Inn	✓		✓			✓		
Bankurz Hatt	✓				✓	✓	✓	
The Bard's Inn	✓		✓			✓	✓	
The Blue House	✓		✓					
Bluff Bed and Breakfast					✓			
Bryce Point Bed and Breakfast			✓					
Castle Valley Inn	✓				✓		✓	
The Desert Chalet			✓					

Luxurious	Pets Allowed	No Smoking Indoors	Good Place for Families	Near Arts Festival	Beach Nearby	Cross-Country Ski Trail	Golf within 5 miles	Fitness Facilities	Good Biking Terrain	Skiing	Horseback Riding	Tennis	Swimming on Premises	Conference Facilities
		✓	✓	✓			✓		✓		✓			
		✓												
		✓		✓										
		✓		✓			✓							
		✓					✓							
✓		✓		✓			✓							
		✓												✓
		✓		✓			✓		✓					
		✓		✓										
		✓					✓							
✓		✓		✓			✓		✓					
		✓	✓						✓					
		✓		✓										✓
		✓	✓				✓							
		✓		✓			✓							
✓	✓		✓			✓								
		✓	✓	✓			✓		✓					
✓		✓					✓		✓		✓			
✓		✓	✓	✓			✓		✓	✓				
	✓	✓	✓	✓					✓		✓			
		✓	✓						✓					
		✓	✓	✓		✓			✓		✓			
		✓				✓			✓					
		✓	✓	✓		✓	✓		✓		✓			

Special Features at a Glance

Name of Property	Antiques	On the Water	Good Value	Car Not Necessary	Full Meal Service	Historic Building	Romantic Hideaway	
Francisco's								
Grandma Bess' Cottage	✓				✓	✓		
Grayson Country Inn	✓					✓		
Greene Gate Village	✓				✓	✓	✓	
The Grist Mill Inn	✓		✓			✓	✓	
Harvest House	✓						✓	
Morning Glory Inn					✓			
Nine Gables Inn	✓					✓	✓	
O'Toole's Under the Eaves	✓					✓	✓	
Pack Creek Ranch					✓			
Paxman's Summer House	✓					✓		
Seven Wives Inn	✓					✓	✓	
SkyRidge Bed & Breakfast	✓						✓	
Smith Hotel	✓					✓		
Snow Family Guest Ranch								
Sunflower Hill	✓		✓			✓	✓	
The Theater Bed & Breakfast	✓							
Valley of the Gods Bed and Breakfast	✓		✓		✓	✓		
Zion House								
Zion's Blue Star	✓				✓			

Luxurious	Pets Allowed	No Smoking Indoors	Good Place for Families	Near Arts Festival	Beach Nearby	Cross-Country Ski Trail	Golf within 5 miles	Fitness Facilities	Good Biking Terrain	Skiing	Horseback Riding	Tennis	Swimming on Premises	Conference Facilities
		✓	✓	✓		✓			✓		✓			
		✓	✓			✓			✓	✓	✓			
		✓	✓			✓	✓		✓					
✓		✓	✓	✓		✓			✓				✓	✓
✓		✓	✓			✓	✓		✓					✓
✓		✓	✓	✓					✓		✓			
		✓	✓	✓					✓		✓			
✓		✓				✓			✓					
		✓	✓	✓					✓		✓			
		✓	✓			✓			✓				✓	✓
		✓	✓	✓			✓		✓	✓				
✓		✓	✓	✓		✓			✓				✓	✓
✓		✓			✓				✓		✓			
		✓							✓		✓			
		✓		✓					✓		✓		✓	
		✓	✓	✓		✓	✓		✓		✓			
		✓		✓			✓	✓	✓	✓				
		✓							✓					
		✓		✓					✓		✓			
		✓	✓	✓					✓		✓			

Glossary of Southwestern Terms

Perhaps more than any other region in the United States, the Southwest has a unique architectural style, adapted to the desert landscape and heavily influenced by the area's Native American and Spanish settlers. Southwest interior furnishings are similarly distinctive, blending eclectic elements that might include Mission chests, Navajo blankets, Mexican tinwork mirrors, and bleached cow skulls à la Georgia O'Keeffe. The brief glossary that follows explains terms frequently used in this book's bed-and-breakfast reviews, particularly in the New Mexico and Arizona chapters.

Adobe. A brick of sun-dried earth and clay, usually stabilized with straw; a structure made of adobe.

Bulto. Folk-art figures of a saint (*santo*), usually carved out of wood.

Casita. Literally, "small house." The term is generally used to describe a separate guest house.

Equipale. Pigskin-and-cedar furniture from Jalisco, Mexico. The chairs have rounded backs and bases rather than legs.

Kachina. A figure representing a spirit or god of the Hopi or Pueblo Indians. Although commonly called dolls, kachinas are used as teaching aids, not as playthings.

Kiva fireplace. A corner fireplace whose round form resembles that of a kiva; a ceremonial room used by Native Americans of the Southwest.

Latilla. Small pole, often made of aspen, used as a lath in a ceiling.

Luminaria. The term used in Arizona for a small votive candle set in a paper-bag lantern, popular at Christmas; in northern New Mexico, it is called a *farolito*.

Portale. A porch or large, covered area adjacent to the house.

Pueblo style. Modeled after the traditional dwellings of the Southwest Pueblo Indians. Most homes in this style are cube-shaped. Other characteristics are flat roofs, small windows, rounded corners, and viga beams.

Ristra. String of dried red chili peppers, often used as decoration.

Saltillo tile. Large floor tile of baked, reddish-brown clay made in Saltillo, Mexico; often used as a generic term for this type of tile.

Talavera tile. Colorful ceramic bathroom or kitchen tile with elaborate, interlocking, Moorish designs, made in Puebla, Mexico. The name derives from the pottery town in Spain where the tile originated—Talavera de la Reina.

Territorial style. Modified Pueblo style that evolved in the late 19th century when New Mexico and Arizona were still U.S. territories. The territorial home incorporates a broad central hallway and entryway and adds wooden elements, like window frames, in neoclassical style; some structures have pitched rather than flat roofs, and brick copings.

Trastero. Cupboard, china closet, or other upright cabinet.

Viga. Horizontal roof beam made of logs, usually protruding from the side of the house.

Arizona

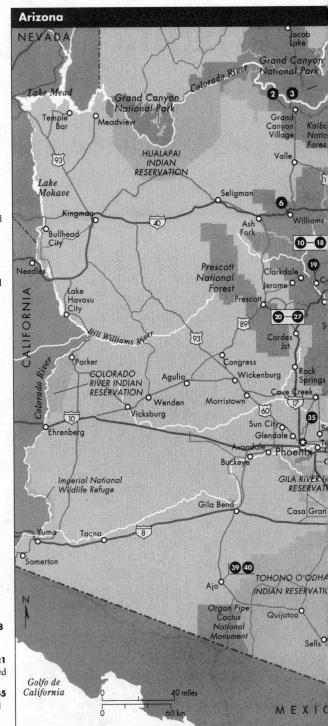

Arizona

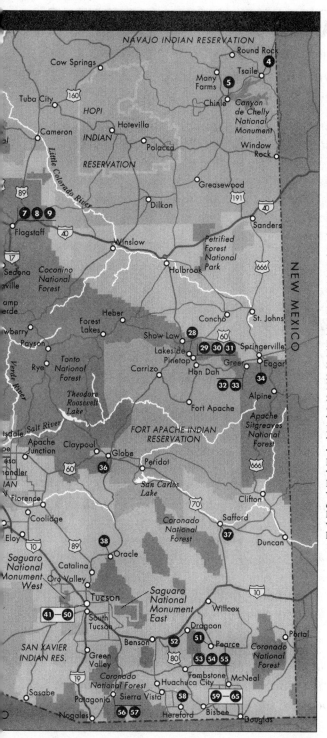

The Little House
Bed and Breakfast, **57**

The Lodge at
Sedona, **17**

Lynx Creek Farm, **22**

Main Street Inn, **64**

Maricopa Manor Bed
and Breakfast Inn, **35**

The Marks House, **23**

The Meadows, **31**

The Mine Manager's
House Inn, **41**

Mt. Vernon Inn, **24**

Noftsger Hill Inn, **36**

The OK Street Jail-
house, **65**

Olney House Bed &
Breakfast, **37**

Paisley Corner
Bed & Breakfast, **34**

The Peppertrees Bed
and Breakfast Inn, **47**

The Pleasant Street Inn
Bed &Breakfast, **25**

Priscilla's Bed & Break-
fast, **54**

Quail's Vista Bed and
Breakfast, **46**

Ramsey Canyon
Inn, **58**

Rimrock West
Hacienda, **48**

Saddle Rock Ranch, **18**

San Francisco Street
B&B, **9**

School House Inn Bed
& Breakfast, **63**

Tanque Verde
Ranch, **49**

Thunderbird Lodge, **5**

Tombstone Boarding
House, **65**

The Triangle L Ranch
Bed & Breakfast, **40**

Victorian Inn
of Prescott
Bed & Breakfast, **27**

White Mountain
Lodge, **33**

Northern Arizona
Including the Grand Canyon, Sedona, Flagstaff, and Indian Country

More than 4 million people come to northern Arizona each year to gaze into the vast, multihued abyss of the Grand Canyon. Far fewer live in this part of the state year-round: The top third of Arizona, which is about the size of Pennsylvania, has only 207,000 inhabitants—fewer than six per square mile. Much of the area is true wilderness, devoid of water, frightening and fatal to early pioneers.

The Grand Canyon is the most astonishing of the natural attractions of the region, but the many other sights have a closer-to-human scale that renders them more fathomable— and less crowded. The black-and-rust lava cones of Sunset Crater-Volcano; the subtle pastel Painted Desert; and the bold red monoliths of Monument Valley and Sedona show off the varied palette of nature, which together with manual labor created the surrealistic buff-and-blue Lake Powell. Long-abandoned ruins at Canyon de Chelly, Navajo, Wupatki, and Walnut Canyon national monuments bear testimony to the ways the original Native American inhabitants survived this often harsh, but strikingly beautiful, environment.

In the northeastern corner of the state, 25,000 square miles belong to the Navajo Nation, and in the center of that reservation is the smaller preserve of the Hopi tribe. Poor in material terms, these nations are rich in cultural traditions: At trading posts that were established in the 19th century, visitors can buy jewelry, pottery, and weavings created in the same way as they have been for hundreds of years.

A jumping-off point for visits to the Grand Canyon and Indian country, Flagstaff is rarely a destination in its own right. But this thriving university town set among the pine-covered, snowcapped San Francisco Mountains is the cultural center of the region and retains a frontier flavor despite a proliferation of fast-food places and motels. In contrast, Sedona, less than 20 miles south and reached via lovely Oak Creek Canyon, has come to rival Santa Fe in its number of tony art galleries and chic visitors. New Agers believe that creative energy points, or vortices, are concentrated among the region's spectacular red rock spires.

The accommodations listed for this region are as varied as the landscape itself, ranging from the rustic, historic lodges of the Grand Canyon and Canyon de Chelly to the opulent inns of Sedona, as luxurious—and as expensive—as any you'll find in large urban centers. The bed-and-breakfasts in Flagstaff are friendly, reasonably priced alternatives to the town's myriad faceless motels.

Places to Go, Sights to See

Canyon de Chelly National Monument (Box 588, Chinle, AZ 86503, tel. 520/ 674–5436). The sheer sandstone walls of the spectacular Canyon de Chelly (pronounced *d'SHAY*) on the Navajo Reservation are 1,000 feet tall in some places; more than 100 prehistoric Anasazi cliff dwellings perch under precipitous overhangs. Two paved rim drives take visitors to scenic overlooks of the two main canyons—Canyon de Chelly and Canyon del Muerto. For most hikes and all Jeep tours into the canyons, visitors must be accompanied by rangers or Navajo guides; call ahead or make arrangements at the visitor center.

Flagstaff. The largest city in northern Arizona, Flagstaff also has the most cultural attractions. The *Lowell Observatory* (1400 W. Mars Hill Rd., Flagstaff, AZ 86001, 520/774–3358), built in 1894, is the oldest in Arizona; astronomers discovered the planet Pluto here in 1930. Filled with fascinating artifacts of Flagstaff's logging heyday, the 40-room log-and-stone *Riordon House* (1300 Riordon Ranch Rd., tel. 520/779–4395) was built in 1904 by two lumber-baron brothers who married two sisters. The *Museum of Northern Arizona* (3001 N. Valley Rd., tel. 520/774–5211) is respected worldwide for its research and its collections centering on the natural and cultural history of the Colorado Plateau; a large array of Navajo rugs and an authentic Hopi kiva are among its fine, permanent exhibitions. In winter, the *Arizona Snowbowl* (Snowbowl Rd., 12 mi north of Flagstaff, tel. 520/779–1951) draws skiers of all levels of expertise to its 35 downhill trails; year-round, the skyride lofts visitors through the Coconino National Forest to a height of 11,500 feet, where they can view the North Rim of the Grand Canyon.

Grand Canyon National Park (Box 129, Grand Canyon, AZ 86023, tel. 520/ 638–7888). The most visited attraction in Arizona and one of the Seven Natural

Wonders of the World, the vast erosion-carved canyon is 1 mile deep, 277 miles long, and just over 2 billion years old. The view into its ever-changing vastness is awe-inspiring—but if you go to the South Rim in summer, you'll have to share it with thousands of others. *Trip Planner*, available from the address above, is a useful guide to the national park. A fun way to visit is via the *Grand Canyon Railway* (518 E. Bill Williams Ave., Williams, AZ 86046, tel. 520/635–4000 or 800/ 843–8724), which recreates the steam train run from Williams to the South Rim of the canyon inaugurated in 1901 by a subsidiary of the Atchison, Topeka & Santa Fe Railway; the museum at the Williams depot displays many interesting artifacts of the era.

Hopi Reservation. In the center of the sprawling Navajo Reservation are 4,000 square miles of land belonging to the Hopi. About 10,000 members of the tribe live here in 12 villages on top of three mesas; to the west of Third Mesa, the town of Oraibi is widely believed to be the oldest continually inhabited community in the United States, dating from around AD 1150. Some of the Hopi dances and ceremonies are open to the public; contact the *Hopi Tribe Office of Public Relations* (*see* Tourist Information, *below*) for information. Cameras, recorders, and sketch pads are prohibited in all cases. Another good resource for information is the *Hopi Cultural Center* (Second Mesa, tel. 520/734–2401), which has a group of shops, a pueblo-style museum, a good restaurant serving American and Native American dishes, and an immaculate motel.

Hubbell Trading Post National Historic Site (AZ 264, 1 mi west of Ganado, tel. 520/755–3475). Established in 1878 by John Lorenzo Hubbell, this is the oldest continuously operating trading post on the Navajo Reservation. Exhibits at the visitor center illustrate the post's history, and Hubbell's house, now a museum, contains fine examples of Native American artistry. Beautifully crafted Navajo rugs are expensive, but you won't find a better selection than the one here.

Lake Powell. With more than 1,900 miles of shoreline, Lake Powell, which stretches through northern Arizona and southern Utah, is the heart of the 1,255,400-acre Glen Canyon National Recreation Area. The jade-green lake, created by the construction of the Glen Canyon Dam in 1953, is encircled by immense red cliffs and extends through an otherworldly landscape of eroded canyons nearly devoid of vegetation. The most popular destination on the lake is *Wahweap*, a vacation village 5 miles north of Glen Canyon Dam; for information on boat rentals and other water sports, contact ARA Leisure Services (Box 56909, Phoenix, AZ 85079, tel. 800/528–6154) or Glen Canyon National Recreation Area (Box 1507, Page, AZ 86040, tel. 520/645–2471). Well worth booking is the half-day boat trip from Wahweap to *Rainbow Bridge National Monument*, where the world's largest natural stone bridge, a massive 290-foot red sandstone arch, straddles a cove of the lake. Information about, and a view of, the 710-foot *Glen Canyon Dam* is available at the Carl Hayden Visitor Center (U.S. 89, tel. 520/ 645–2511).

Monument Valley Navajo Tribal Park (3½ mi off U.S. 183, 24 mi north of Kayenta, tel. 801/727–3287). You'll recognize the soaring red buttes of Monument Valley from such westerns as *Stagecoach, She Wore a Yellow Ribbon*, and *How the West Was Won*. You can take a 17-mile self-guided tour through the heart of the 30,000-acre Monument Valley Navajo Tribal Park, but the road is unpaved and rutted; consider booking one of the many guided van tours. There are operators in and around the visitor center, which also has a crafts shop and exhibits devoted to the Native American history of the area.

Navajo National Monument (HC 71, Box 3, Tonalea, AZ 86044, tel. 520/672–2366). The largest Native American ruins in Arizona, two 13th-century Anasazi pueblos, Keet Seel and Betatakin, stand under the overhang of soaring orange-and-ocher cliffs. During the summer, national park rangers escort tours to these sites, reached via AZ 564 off U.S. 160; call 520/672–2367 for reservations and information.

Navajo Reservation. Some 100,000 members of the Navajo Nation live here on the largest Native American reservation in the United States, spread over the northeastern corner of Arizona as well as parts of Utah and New Mexico. In Window Rock, the tribal capital, located near the New Mexico border, visit the *Navajo Tribal Museum* (AZ 264, next to Navajo Nation Inn, tel. 520/871–6673), a small space devoted to the art and culture of the region, with an excellent selection of books, and the adjoining *Navajo Arts and Crafts Enterprise* (tel. 520/871–4090), which sells local creative works. Among the other attractions on the reservation are Canyon de Chelly, Hubbell Trading Post, Monument Valley Navajo Tribal Park, and Navajo National Monument, all detailed above.

Oak Creek Canyon. The winding, wooded 16-mile stretch along Rte. 89A, following Oak Creek through the red cliffs north from Sedona to Flagstaff, is among the most scenic routes in the country. Seven miles north of Sedona, you'll see a sign for *Slide Rock State Park* (tel. 520/282–3034), a good spot for a picnic and hike back into the forest. Take along an extra pair of old pants if you'd like to plunge down a natural rock slide into a swimming hole.

Petrified Forest National Park (Box 2217, Petrified Forest, AZ 86028, tel. 520/524–6228). Some 225 million years ago, this stark desert was the floor of an ancient sea; now there are tree trunks fossilized into colorful pieces of petrified wood here. The park covers nearly 100,000 acres; the section north of the highway contains the *Painted Desert*, a moonscape of warm pastels and earth tones. Drive about 25 miles east of Holbrook on I–40 to reach the visitor center.

Sedona. A stunning setting—red sandstone formations with clear blue sky and dark green forests as a backdrop—has drawn visitors to Sedona in droves in the past decade. The most popular way to explore the region is on a Jeep tour along U.S. 89A, one of the two main drags; this section of Sedona, called Uptown, also has a number of tacky souvenir outlets and New Age shops. More expensive boutiques and art galleries are concentrated along AZ 179. Two miles west of Sedona on U.S. 89A is the turnoff for the 286-acre *Red Rock State Park Center for Environmental Education* (tel. 520/282–6907), an ideal spot to enjoy the red rock formations and beautiful Oak Creek. The five park trails, all fairly short, are well marked.

Sunset Crater Volcano National Monument (Rte. 3, tel. 520/527–7042). Twenty miles north of Flagstaff, off U.S. 89, a loop road leads east to a black-and-rusty-red, 800-square-mile volcanic field created in AD 1065 when Sunset Crater erupted; it's particularly beautiful in winter when the many pine trees are topped with snow. Drive 20 miles north of the visitor center along AZ 545 to reach the entrance of the associated **Wupatki National Monument** (tel. 520/527–7040). Some 2,700 identified sites—including an ancient three-story structure with more than 100 rooms—contain evidence of Native American settlement from AD 600 until AD 1300 in this area; families from the Sinagua, Anasazi, and perhaps other Indian cultures are believed to have lived here harmoniously.

Walnut Canyon National Monument (take I–40 east of Flagstaff for 7 mi to exit 204, drive 3 mi south, tel. 520/526–3367). Sinagua Indians built nearly 300 cliff dwellings in this peaceful pine-dotted gorge more than 1,000 years ago. Paved trails lead right up to the ruins.

Tourist Information

Grand Canyon National Park (Box 129, Grand Canyon, AZ 86023, tel. 520/638–7888). **Flagstaff Visitors Center** (1 E. Rte. 66, Flagstaff, AZ 86001, tel. 520/774–9541 or 800/842–7293). **Hopi Tribe Office of Public Relations** (Box 123, Kykotsmovi, AZ 86039, tel. 520/234–2441). **Navajoland Tourism Department** (Box 663, Window Rock, AZ 86515, tel. 520/871–6659 or 520/871–7371). **Page/Lake Powell Chamber of Commerce** (Box 727, Page, AZ 86040, tel. 520/645–2741). **Sedona–Oak Creek Canyon Chamber of Commerce** (Box 478, Sedona, AZ 86339, tel. 520/282–7722 or 800/288–7336). **Williams Chamber of Commerce** (820 Bill Williams Ave., Box 235, Williams, AZ 86046, tel. 520/635–4061).

Restaurants

Known for drive-through service, Flagstaff nevertheless has some sophisticated but reasonably priced restaurants. Among them are **Cottage Place** (tel. 520/774–8431), which offers classic Continental cuisine with many innovative touches in a series of pretty, intimate dining rooms, and **Sakura Restaurant** (tel. 520/773–9118), catering to the town's many Japanese tourists, with excellent sushi and *teppan* grill specialties. **Brix Grill & Wine Bar** (tel. 520/779–5117) is popular with locals for its southwestern-style seafood and meat dishes, as well as its deli, baked goods, wines, and espresso. On display are the latest artistic creations from **Ann Marie Stillion's ArtTrek Gallery.** Low-key and more typically western, the **Horseman Lodge & Restaurant** (tel. 520/773–9118) serves unpretentious American fare in a room with knotty-pine beams and a stone fireplace, while the small, colorful **Café Olé** (tel. 520/774–8272) is good for homecooked Mexican food. The new **Beaver Street Brewery and Whistlestop Cafe** (tel. 520/779–0079) has quickly become known for its burgers, salads, wood-fired pizzas, and nine types of beer.

Yuppie-oriented Sedona has many good upscale eateries, including the romantic **L'Auberge de Sedona** (tel. 520/282–1667), where diners can enjoy haute French cuisine while overlooking Oak Creek, and **Canyon Rose at Los Abrigados** (tel. 520/282–7673), serving Southwestern-style dishes in a chic resort setting. More moderately priced but equally tasty Southwestern fare is available at the

Heartline Café (tel. 520/282–0785), a light-filled dining room with a rose-decked patio. Owner-chef Bernie Levy and his wife Bonnie had barely opened **Bernie's** (tel. 520/282–3378) when it was picked by *The Arizona Republic* as the best restaurant in Sedona. The critic loved the New York–deli lunches, but don't neglect the fresh, California-style evening entrées.

Spectacular views combined with good food are hard to come by, but three restaurants in northern Arizona fill the bill: **El Tovar Hotel** (tel. 520/638–2631), overlooking the South Rim of the Grand Canyon; the **Grand Canyon Lodge** (tel. 520/638–2611), facing the North Rim; and the **Rainbow Room in Wahweap Lodge** (tel. 520/645–2433), with vistas of Lake Powell, all serve a variety of well-prepared Continental dishes.

Most of the restaurants in sparsely populated Indian country are of the fast-food variety, but three places that offer good standard American fare along with some Native American dishes are the **Navajo Nation Inn** (tel. 520/871–4108) in Window Rock, **Goulding's Lodge** (tel. 801/727–3231) near Monument Valley, and the **Holiday Inn** (tel. 520/674–5000) just outside Canyon de Chelly.

Reservation Services

Arizona Association of Bed & Breakfast Inns (3101 North Central Ave., Suite 560, Phoenix, AZ 85012, tel. 602/277–0775). **Bed & Breakfast Inn Arizona-Arizona Accommodations Reservations** (8900 E. Via Linda, Suite 101, Scottsdale, AZ 85258, tel. 520/860–9338 or 800/266–7829, fax 520/860–9338). **Mi Casa Su Casa B&B Reservation Service** (Box 950, Tempe, AZ 85280, tel. 520/990–0682, reservations 800/456–0682).

Birch Tree Inn

This 1917 white clapboard house is in a residential neighborhood across the street from a grassy city park and from the Coconino National Forest. Joseph Waldhaus, Flagstaff's then mayor, lived here during the 1930s. After doing time as a fraternity house in the 1970s, the by-then well-worn property was rescued in 1988 by four friends from California, who turned it into a bright, clean bed-and-breakfast. The two couples, Donna and Rodger Pettinger and Sandy and Ed Znetko, take turns running the inn.

A wraparound porch runs the length of their spacious house. Inside, a handsome pool table and a piano fill a bay-windowed game room. Guests often lounge in the adjoining living room, which has a stained-oak floor and brick fireplace.

Upstairs are the guest rooms. The corner Wicker Room, decorated in blue and white, enjoys views of the San Francisco Peaks from both windows. The Pella Room, named for a town in Iowa with many residents of Dutch descent, has a delft-blue ceiling, a hand-stitched tulip quilt, Dutch lace curtains, a brochure for an Iowa tulip festival on the bureau, and two pairs of wooden shoes on the floor.

The Southwest Suite, occupying the northeastern corner, has a king bed with stucco headboard and large bath with separate tub and shower; wall-to-wall carpeting echoes the soft pastel color scheme. Carol's Room, facing out to the pine forest above Thorpe Park, is done in hunter green and beige, with a Shaker pine queen bed and matching bureau and end table. The Wagner-Znetko Room, decorated in soft yellow, is reminiscent of grandma's attic, with an 80-year-old rocking chair and an ancient sewing machine.

Guests enjoy afternoon refreshments—lemonade and crackers in summer, hot spiced cider and cookies in winter—in the parlor and a full breakfast in either the sunny dining room or on the long veranda. The hosts have 14 breakfast menus, all included in their 95-page bed-and-breakfast cookbook. Popular recipes include baked French toast stuffed with cream-cheese-and-pineapple filling and homemade praline sauce; or spicy ranchero-style potato casserole, made with chilies, cheese, and turkey breakfast sausage.

🏠 *824 W. Birch Ave., Flagstaff, AZ 86001, tel. 520/774–1042 or 800/645–5811. 2 double rooms with baths, 2 doubles share bath, 1 suite. Guest phone, TV in living room. $50–$89; full breakfast, afternoon refreshments. AE, MC, V. No smoking indoors, no children under 10, no pets.*

Briar Patch Inn

Shaded by a canopy of sycamore, juniper, canyon oak, pine, elm, and cottonwood trees, 16 log cabins nestle on the floor of Oak Creek Canyon, just north of Sedona. The murmur of the spring-fed creek blends with the rustle of the leaves to create a relaxing, peaceful ambience on this wooded, 9-acre property. It isn't hard to believe that the Briar Patch Inn has been called a "healing, magical oasis."

In the early 1880s, this was the site of a goat barn, and there's still a resident goat, along with a friendly sheep and some chickens. The cabins were built during the 1940s to provide a summer getaway from the heat of urban Phoenix; at an elevation of 4,484 feet, this area is always temperate. The place became a bed-and-breakfast in 1983.

June through August, guests enjoy the quiet strains of a violinist and classical guitarist who play by the creek during breakfast. Sunday afternoons bring outdoor chamber music concerts on the lawn. The library is stocked with volumes on Native American culture and the history and geography of the Southwest. Innkeepers JoAnn and Ike Olson also like to schedule small workshops on the creative arts here: Navajo weaving, Native American arts, painting, photography, philosophy, self-healing, and more.

The cabins are rustic cozy, with log walls, beam or plank ceilings, Southwestern furnishings, and private patios or decks. All except the three on the creek—Deck House, Creekside, and Kingfisher—have fireplaces, and a supply of aromatic, shaggy-bark cedar firewood is stacked outside the front door. The newest cabin, Eagle, has a Native American theme, featuring a lodgepole-pine bed, table, and chairs; polished clear-pine floors; and an armoire, paneling, and bath done in knotty pine. One windowed wall faces the tree-shaded creek. Blue Jay, the oldest cabin on the property, has the smallest windows.

Iced tea, coffee, and cookies are always available in the main building. In the morning, a heart-healthy buffet breakfast includes home-baked seven-grain bread or muffins, granola, yogurt, fresh eggs, hot apple sauce from local apples, and seasonal juices and fruits. Guests can take a tray to their room, dine at private tables in the main building, or eat at tree-shaded picnic tables overlooking the creek.

🏠 *HC 30, Box 1002, Sedona, AZ 86336, tel. 520/282–2342, fax 520/282–2399. 12 2-person cabins, 4 4-person cabins. 12 cabins have kitchens, masseuse available. $125–$135; full buffet breakfast. MC, V. No pets.*

Canyon Villa Bed & Breakfast Inn

Opened in 1992, Canyon Villa combines the personal comforts of a traditional inn with the amenities of a first-class resort. Innkeepers Chuck and Marion Yadon researched the business for 18 months, visiting B&Bs from New England to California, before distilling their knowledge into this two-story, state-of-the-art accommodation.

The site at the edge of the Coconino National Forest offers uninterrupted views of Sedona's main attractions: the red sandstone cliffs of Castle Rock, Bell Rock, and Courthouse Butte. This is prime property, and staying at Canyon Villa is very much like visiting the mansion of a wealthy Arizona rancher. Guests' spaces include a well-stocked library: a beam-ceiling, skylit modern living room with a glass-enclosed fireplace; and a 32-foot heated swimming pool in the garden. Snacks and beverages are set out each afternoon in the dining room.

A broad stairway covered with thick carpeting leads to the five upstairs guest rooms, all with large windows and glass French doors to capitalize on the breathtaking scenery; the less expensive room on the ground floor has less stunning views. All the rooms are named after the flowering cacti and shrubs found in the Sedona area and have private baths, balconies or patios, wall-to-wall carpeting, individual heating and cooling units, telephones, cable TV, 10-foot ceilings with fans, and eclectic Southwestern decor; the larger ones also offer double sinks and fireplaces.

Santa Fe–themed Ocotillo has a wrought-iron four-poster bed and a fireplace. The bed in Manzanita, done in blue, is also a four-poster. The corner Strawberry Cactus Room, with white wicker furniture and a blue carpet, boasts views from two sides and a bath with a stained-glass window. The Spanish Bayonet is perfect for honeymooners, with its fireplace and a bathtub two steps from the king-size bed.

Two long tables, each with eight purple-accented place settings, fill the huge, carpeted dining room, where Marion's catering background is revealed at breakfast time. Marion, Chuck, and hired help (there is a staff of 11) serve a nutritious breakfast of fruit, just-baked bread, and an entrée such as chili-cheese quiche, pumpkin pancakes, or sour cream waffles; a drawback for people traveling alone is that they may be assigned to a seat for the meal.

🏠 *125 Canyon Circle Dr., Sedona, AZ 86351, tel. 520/284–1226 or 800/ 453–1166. 11 double rooms with baths. Whirlpool tubs, robes, and pool towels in rooms. $125–$205; full breakfast, afternoon snacks. MC, V. No smoking, no pets.*

El Tovar Hotel

n 1540, the Spanish conquistador Francisco Vásquez de Coronado led an expedition of 1,000 men north from Mexico seeking the legendary Seven Cities of Cibola. While the main force headed east from Arizona, a scouting party split off from the Zuni Pueblo in New Mexico and headed west. Don Pedro de Tovar reached the three Hopi mesas in northern Arizona and pioneered the route to the Grand Canyon—thus the name of this historic hotel.

The challenge to El Tovar architect Charles Whittlesey was to design a building that would fit naturally, unobtrusively, on the edge of the world, and one that could accommodate 200 people without defacing or distracting from the natural grandeur of the canyon. Nine decades later, most agree that Whittlesey met the challenge superbly.

Constructed of native boulders and Douglas fir logs brought in from Oregon by rail, the hotel is four stories high on the south end and three on the north. The north wall of the structure is only 50 feet from the canyon's edge, providing many rooms with spectacular views. This place is as popular as the canyon itself; reservations are accepted up to 23 months in advance.

The lobby, with polished maple flooring, black hand-hewn columns and beams, a huge stone fireplace, copper chandeliers, and mounted animal heads, reflects an earlier era of adventure. Adjoining is the hotel's dining room, a cavernous room modeled after a Scandinavian great hall, which for decades has enjoyed a reputation for fine food. The Southwestern menu changes seasonally but includes a daily vegetarian special along with innovatively prepared fish, poultry, and meat dishes; free-range chicken breast with smoked tomato pinenut sauce or sweet corn and lobster tamale might be among the dinner options.

There are 12 different room types, each with a tub/shower bath. The furniture reflects the period: wrought-iron beds, sleigh beds, and mahogany two-posters are paired with upholstered lodgepole-pine couches and chairs.

Grand Canyon National Park Lodges, Box 699, Grand Canyon, AZ 86023, tel. 602/638-2401, fax 602/638-9247. 65 double rooms with baths, 10 suites. Phones and TVs in rooms; room service; mezzanine tea room, lounge, gift shop; concierge service; kennel available for pets. $115–$175, suites $200–$300. No meals included. AE, DC, MC, V. Pets not permitted in rooms.

The Graham B&B Inn

This luxurious lodging, designed by Bill and Marni Graham in 1985, was the first to be expressly built as a B&B in Arizona; it helped pioneer the proliferation of inns in Sedona. When Carol Redenbaugh and her husband, Roger, bought the place in 1992, they vowed to maintain the Grahams' reputation for excellence. They have.

Carol and Roger's touches include a lavish, three-room honeymoon suite. At center stage in the suite's bathroom, large enough for a game of handball, is a double Jacuzzi bathtub and a shower for two. TV/VCRs and phones are recent additions to every room. The contemporary, two-story inn also has a heated outdoor pool and spa, a walled, landscaped lawn and garden, and a broad deck for outdoor dining.

A beamed ceiling, two stories high, vaults over a spacious living/dining room carpeted in a dusty rose selected to match Sedona's red cliffs, and warmed by a double-face fireplace. In the dining area, cut-glass chandeliers hang above two round glass tables. The contemporary-style living room features a laser videodisc player and a selection of films.

The warm rose carpet leads up a staircase to the guest rooms, each with a marble bath, ceiling fan, and spectacular views of the red rocks from a private balcony. The Southwest Room has a rustic Taos bed; a Sedona-red, beige, and teal color-scheme; a fireplace; and a Jacuzzi. The corner Garden Room,

green with white wicker furniture, has a flowered, half-canopy bed. The Country Room is out of a Norman Rockwell painting, with floral wallpaper, lace curtains, and an iron bed covered with a hand-sewn quilt. The San Francisco Room is done in soft peach and gray in a contemporary art-deco style and has the largest Jacuzzi in the inn.

The most romantic of all is the newly decorated Champagne Room. A huge figure from a Sistine Chapel detail overlooks a hand-carved French king-size bed. Antiques, views, and a sitting area with wing chairs in front of a fireplace, complete the picture.

Breakfast may be savored in the dining room or outside on the deck. Popular entrées are German pancakes, maple bread pudding, and *huevos rancheros*. Fresh-baked goodies include Roger's bread or Carol's cinnamon bubble rolls or apricot/banana bread.

🏨 *150 Canyon Circle Dr., Sedona, AZ 86351, tel. 520/284–1425. 5 double rooms with baths, 1 suite. Robes, phones, TV/ VCR, videos, pool towels, guest refrigerator; bicycles. $99–$117, Sedona Suite $219; full breakfast, afternoon refreshments. D, MC, V. No smoking indoors, no pets; 2-night minimum on weekends.*

Grand Canyon Lodge

ess than five feet from the edge of America's greatest abyss, the Grand Canyon Lodge has one of the most stunning locations in the world. The grounds are heavily forested with pine, spruce, fir, and aspen. An easy ½-mile trail from the lodge to Bright Angel Point rewards strollers with breathtaking views of the canyon and a glimpse of Roaring Springs, while the gentle 1½-mile Transept Trail travels from the lodge to a campground and general store.

The first lodge on the site was completed in 1928. Built by a subsidiary of the Union Pacific Railroad, it was one of the last in a long line of elaborate railroad lodges in western national parks. Craftsmen were recruited from small Mormon communities nearby; their construction materials came from local quarries and logging camps. When the original lodge burned down in 1932, the railroad designed and erected a second (present) lodge, opened in 1936.

The vaulted ceilings of the main lobby and dining room are spectacularly crossbarred by thickset Ponderosa-pine beams; hand-hewn Kaibab stone unites the walls, floors, and fireplaces. Six carpeted steps lead down to the cavernous dining room, three stories tall. The menu, which changes every season, is surprisingly sophisticated for the rustic locale: marinated pork kebabs, grilled swordfish, or linguine with cilantro and pesto might be among the entrées, which change seasonally. A Sun Room and outdoor patio with spectacular views are equipped with lounge and rocking chairs.

Grand Canyon Lodge has a variety of cabins and motel accommodations. If you reserve two years in advance, you might be able to get a Rim View cabin with a private porch overlooking the canyon. All rooms have phones and private baths, but some have only showers. Motel accommodations are generic; the rustic Pioneer and Frontier cabins with wood-beam walls have more character. Most deluxe are the Western cabins, with two double, extra-long beds, full bath, dressing room, and private porch.

🏨 *TW Recreational Services, Box 400, Cedar City, UT 84720, tel. 801/586–7686 (reservations), tel. 520/638–2611 (lodge switchboard), fax 801/586–3157. 40 motel rooms with bath; 54 Western cabins (for up to 5 people), 84 Frontier cabins (up to 3 people), 23 Pioneer cabins (4 or 5 people). Dining room; cafeteria; bar; gift shop; transportation desk; National Park Service Information desk; nonsmoking rooms available. $58–$95; no meals included in room rates. AE, D, DC, MC, V. Closed in winter; no pets.*

The Inn at Four Ten

Now a friendly bed-and-breakfast, the Inn at Four Ten was built in 1907 by Tom E. Pollock, a wealthy banker and cattle rancher, as the manor house of his grand estate; its extensive grounds included a stable and separate quarters for the grooms. After Pollock died, the property was split up. Some years later, the main building became a fraternity house. It was in serious need of repair when Carol and Mike Householder purchased it in 1989.

After completing extensive renovations, including the installation of an all-white commercial kitchen, they opened for business in 1991. Howard and Sally Krueger bought the inn in 1993 and in 1995 began upgrading the rooms. Guests step from a broad front porch into an open living room with polished-oak floors, bookcases, door frames, and ceiling beams, as well as a flagstone fireplace and wicker chairs. South-facing windows in the adjoining dining room let in the soft morning light.

A great deal of detail went into the decoration of the guest rooms. Downstairs, Turn of the Century, which can sleep three people in two beds, is distinctly European, with a stained-glass window and a claw-foot tub. The elegant Tea Room has a mahogany bookcase wall, a wrought-iron king bed, powder-blue carpeting, and a seven-foot walnut burl armoire; polished-oak doors lead directly into the dining room. Also downstairs, The Southwest is furnished in Santa Fe style, with a Saltillo-tile floor, kiva fireplace, and lodgepole-pine bed imported from New Mexico.

Upstairs, split-level blue-and-white Sea & Sky has a nautical theme and a queen-size bed; there's a skylight and kitchenette on the upper level. Dakota, with a striking red and black color scheme, boasts a coral Pendleton blanket and bent twig furniture custom-made in New Mexico.

Guests have breakfast in the sunny dining room or under the gazebo in the garden. They're given a choice of juices and fruits daily; granola and yogurt are always available, too. All entrées are low-fat and low-cholesterol, yet very tasty. Favorites include Paul's oat pancakes and peach bread pudding.

🏠 *410 N. Leroux St., Flagstaff, AZ 86001, tel. 520/774–0088, or 800/774–2008. 6 double rooms with baths, 2 suites. Kitchenettes in 4, Jacuzzis in 2, fireplaces in 2, coffeemakers, mini-fridges. $100–$150; full breakfast, afternoon tea and snacks. AE, MC, V. No smoking, no pets.*

Bright Angel Lodge

Constructed in 1935 on the site of the original Bright Angel Camp at the head of the Bright Angel Trail, this lodge sits a few yards from the Grand Canyon's South Rim. Using logs and native boulders, architect Mary Jane Colter created an environmentally sensitive pioneer-style hotel. Times have changed a bit: During check-in, the lobby, with its dark timbers, Native American decor, and smooth flagstone floor, can be as crowded as a rush-hour bus station.

Accommodations—not luxurious but uniformly clean and comfortable—are in the main lodge or in quaint cabins scattered among the pines. A premium is charged for the Rim Cabins, which have rustic willow furniture, wall-to-wall carpeting, white pine-paneled walls, and beamed ceilings; some also have working kiva fireplaces. Many look out over the canyon and all are close to it, but a view is not guaranteed. The Historic Cabins are similar in style, but are set farther back from the rim.

🏠 *Box 699, Grand Canyon, AZ 86023, tel. 520/638-2401 (reservations), 520/638-2631 (switchboard), fax 520/638-9247. 11 double rooms with baths, 13 doubles with half-baths, 6 dormitory-style doubles, 47 cabins. Phones, TVs in rooms, some refrigerators; coffee shop, steak house, lounge, tour desk, kennels available. $55–$275; breakfast not included. AE, D, DC, MC, V. No pets.*

Canyon Country Inn

Smack in the center of downtown Williams, this attractive two-story Colonial bungalow has a wraparound porch perfect for people-watching. Built as a boardinghouse in 1927, it was completely gutted and refurbished before opening as a B&B in 1991.

As a result, the 13 guest rooms—most in the main house and some in a separate cottage—have new fittings. All also have patterned wallpaper, rose-color towels and sheets, lace curtains, dried flowers, floral quilts, and selected antique pieces; those in the main house have private entrances from the porch. The three upstairs theme rooms, Sheep, Goose, and Rose, are probably the most inviting. Sheep has a peaked beam ceiling, windows on three sides, and a border of dancing lambs, while romantic Rose is thoroughly devoted to its namesake flower.

A Continental breakfast—juice, coffee, and home-baked goodies such as apple dumplings, cinnamon rolls, and strawberry banana muffins—is served in the sitting area at the top of the stairs.

🏠 *442 W. Bill Williams Ave., Williams, AZ 86046, tel. 520/635-2349 or 800/643-1020, fax 520/635-9898. 13 double rooms with baths. Phones, TVs in rooms. $60–$95; Continental breakfast; fruit basket at check-in. D, MC, V. No smoking indoors ($100 fine!), no pets.*

Casa Sedona

An elaborately hand-carved front door with a polished turquoise inset is the first clue that this is a special B&B. In 1992, Dick Curtis and Misty Zitko turned a run-down 1982 apartment building into a luxury inn. An upstairs sundeck, where breakfast is sometimes served, has a panoramic view of the entire Sedona valley.

The elegantly decorated Southwestern-style rooms offer every amenity: separate shower *and* Jacuzzi bath; gas fireplace *and* forced-air heat; ceiling fan, evaporative cooling, *and* air-conditioning; wall-to-wall carpeting; refrigerator; and a terrace or patio with views of the red rocks of Sedona.

Guests can play board games in the red-tile Sierra Vista Room while gazing out its bay window. A geometric tile-hearth fireplace in the library/music center pays homage to Frank Lloyd Wright. A photo-display wall in the adjoining dining room documents the incredibly varied show-business career enjoyed by Dick, who looks a lot like Kirk Douglas.

🏨 *55 Hozoni Dr., Sedona, AZ 86336, tel. 520/282–2938 or 800/525–3756. 15 double rooms with baths. TV in living room. Telephones with free local calls, catered dinners. $105–$150; full breakfast. D, MC, V. No smoking anywhere on premises ($300 fine!), no pets.*

Cathedral Rock Lodge

This 1948 redbrick lodge, with its stone terraces and landscaped green lawn, resembles a rural farmhouse, but it's on an acre in the stunning red rock country of Sedona, not in a Midwest wheat field. Mature trees—elm, Arizona cypress, and cottonwood—a playhouse deck, picnic tables, and barbecue grills make this a perfect place for families to enjoy an Arizona outdoor experience.

The homey living room, furnished in comfortable contemporary style, has a picture window facing Cathedral Rock, a flagstone fireplace, wall-to-wall carpeting, pine paneling, and a beamed ceiling. Guest rooms are country cozy with family antiques, handmade quilts, and bathroom floors made of Douglas fir. The upstairs Amigo Suite has a kitchenette, TV, sleeper couch, and private deck. A cozy cabin remodeled in 1995 has a full kitchen, an African-themed bedroom, and a fantasy bath with a claw-foot tub.

Innkeeper Carol Shannon rotates six breakfast menus; all include just-ground coffee, fresh fruit and juice, and homemade bread and jam.

🏨 *61 Los Amigos Lane, Sedona, AZ 86336, tel. 520/282–7608, fax 520/282–4505. 2 double rooms with baths, 1 suite, 1 cabin. TV/VCR in living room, fresh fruit at check-in, nearby stable, homemade jam on departure. $70–$100; full breakfast. MC, V. No smoking indoors, no pets.*

Country Elegance Bed & Breakfast

A backcountry road leads to what looks like an unassuming ranch house in Cornville, 15 miles south of Sedona; not until you step inside do you discover that you're in a posh, two-story hideaway backed by a one-acre fish pond shaded by magnificent cottonwoods.

As her rooms eloquently attest, innkeeper Rita Sydelle is an interior decorator. The living room is carpeted in light turquoise and accented with an Oriental rug and wood-burning stove. Breakfast—veal frittata, perhaps, or cottage cheese soufflé with baked brie and fruits in a caramel-almond sauce—is served in the 63-foot, plant-filled solarium. Sitting on its Southwestern-print couches you have a great view of the trees and the pond.

The Empire Room features patterned wallpaper and a burl wood mirrored headboard and matching mirrored dresser. The contemporary-style Southern Pond Suite has a full kitchen, sitting area, private entrance, and covered patio. The Garden Room is furnished with white wicker and has unusual floral-pattern upholstery fabric on an entire wall.

🏨 *Box 1257, Sedona, AZ 86339, tel. 520/634–4470, or 800/634–4470, fax 520/634–3227. 2 double rooms with bath, 1 suite. TV, ceiling fan, turndown service; 24-hr beverage bar, library, dog-escorted walks. $75–$95; full breakfast. MC, V. No smoking, no pets; 2-night minimum on weekends, 3-night minimum on holidays.*

Coyote Pass Hospitality

You're not likely to encounter a more unusual place to stay than this roving bed-and-breakfast run by the Coyote Pass clan of the Navajo Nation. In northeastern Arizona, where lodging options are limited, this one also gives outsiders the chance to experience Native American hospitality.

It isn't for everyone: guests sleep on a mattress on the dirt floor of a hogan (cone-shaped log-and-earth Navajo dwelling), use an outhouse, and eat a traditional Navajo breakfast—perhaps blue corn pancakes with Navajo herbal tea—prepared by a member of the clan on a wood-burning stove. But for those who don't mind roughing it a bit, this is a rare chance to be immersed in Navajo culture in beautiful surroundings. The location of the guest lodgings depends on the season, but most of the hogans are near the Canyon de Chelly. Guided hikes, nature programs, and meals are also available; Will Tsosie Jr., the knowledgeable coordinator of the program, is happy to tailor a visit to guests' interests.

🏠 *Contact Will Tsosie Jr., Box 91, Tsaile, AZ 86556, tel. 520/724–3383 or 602/674–9655. Hogans accommodate 1–15 people. Guided tours, full meal service available. $75 first person, $10 each additional person; full breakfast. No credit cards. No smoking indoors.*

Cozy Cactus Bed & Breakfast

Set on the edge of the Coconino National Forest, this 1983 ranch-style complex looks directly up at some of Sedona's most scenic red rock formations. Guests can step through the fence and hike up about 200 yards to touch the base of Castle Rock.

The living room of the house is filled with theatrical memorabilia from the Broadway careers of innkeepers Lynne

and Bob Gillman. A 1930s grandfather clock here is typical of the family treasures scattered throughout the five cozy guest rooms. Two pairs of rooms each share a sitting room with a fireplace and kitchen. The Wyeth Room has a mahogany four-poster bed and reproductions of Andrew Wyeth paintings; the Nutcracker features an 1890s Swedish high-back mahogany bed and a display of carved nutcrackers.

Served in the open country kitchen at a knotty-pine table, breakfast might consist of red raspberry wholewheat buttermilk pancakes, made without sugar, or custard French toast with baked stuffed pears or baked apples in cranberry sauce.

🏠 *80 Canyon Circle Dr., Sedona, AZ 86351, tel. 520/284–0082 or 800/788–2082. 5 double rooms with baths. Cable TV in living room. $80–$95; full breakfast, afternoon beverages. AE, D, MC, V. No smoking indoors, no pets.*

Lantern Light Inn Bed & Breakfast

This European-flavored inn in Sedona, formerly part of a residential complex built in 1970, marked time for a while as a music museum. A new section was added before the place opened as a B&B in 1990. Hospitable innkeepers Ed and Kris Varjean live upstairs.

The inn is on one of Sedona's two main roads, but privacy is preserved by a cul-de-sac driveway fronted by a landscaped dirt mound. Etched-glass doors open into a subdued living room, with wall-to-wall white carpeting overlaid by rich Oriental rugs and bookcases lining the wall. The Varjeans serve breakfast on a large table in the adjacent dining room.

The country French-style Red and Blue rooms, both with white carpets topped with Oriental rugs, face south into a fenced, tree-shaded garden; they share a deck with a view of Cathedral Rock. Across a breezeway is the spacious Ryan Room, with white wall-to-wall carpeting, a king bed, sofa bed, tiled kitchenette, and sitting area.

🏠 *3085 W. Hwy. 89A, Sedona, AZ 86336, tel. 520/282–3419. 2 double rooms with baths, 1 triple with bath. TV, refrigerator in 2 rooms, private, locked entries, Shiatsu massage. $80–$110; full breakfast. No credit cards. No smoking indoors, no pets.*

The Lodge at Sedona

Barb and Mark Dinunzio were on a hiking trip from Phoenix when they found this abandoned Sedona home in 1991. Its rustic charm convinced them to try running a B&B. They were able to purchase the two-story Mountain Ranch-style lodge in 1993 and spent six months converting it into a cozy country inn and landscaping its 2½ acres of lawns and pine trees. Readers of *The Arizona Republic* have already voted it "Arizona's Best Bed and Breakfast Inn."

Beamed ceilings, red rock–work, and wall-to-wall oatmeal carpets give an organic feel to the library, the sitting room, and the fireside room, with its silk-covered wing chairs. The Master Suite has its own entrance, the door inset with stained glass. A massive stone fireplace, brick archways, and a king bed await inside. The corner Renaissance Room has a wrought-iron-and-brass queen bed, wall-to-wall carpeting, and a claw-foot tub in the bathroom.

One of the two dining rooms is an enclosed, carpeted porch, sunlit through skylights and a long window-wall. Breakfast is served here, prepared by a chef from the Culinary Institute of America.

🏠 *125 Kallof Pl., Sedona, AZ 86336, tel. 520/204–1942 or 800/619–4467, fax 520/204–2128. 12 double rooms with baths, 1 suite. Jacuzzi in 5 rooms, fireplace in 2 rooms, TV in parlor, library, spa. $95–$205; full breakfast, evening hors d'oeuvres. MC, V. No smoking indoors, no pets.*

Saddle Rock Ranch

Built as the base for a 6,000-acre horse ranch, this house opened as a B&B in 1988. Its original (1926) rugged red sandstone and adobe brick exterior echo the Old West, as do its beamed ceilings, polished flagstone floors, and superb Western art collection. It commands a spectacular, 17-mile-wide view out over Sedona, a panorama shared by the outdoor pool and deck.

Innkeepers Fran and Dan Bruno were executives with Ritz Carlton hotels, and their expertise shows. The Saddle Rock Suite, with its wall-to-wall gray carpet and white stone fireplace, features a king-size, English-style, white birch canopy bed. Lie here and look out the picture window at the endless valley view. The wood-paneled Honeymoon Cottage, once the ranch's bunkhouse, has flagstone floors, a braided rug, and a massive lodgepole pine four-poster bed covered with an antique white quilt.

Breakfast may be enjoyed out by the pool or in the Brunos's sunny, rock-walled breakfast room. Morning birdseed scattered outside the window attracts a covey of bold and hungry quail.

🏠 *255 Rock Ridge Dr., Sedona, AZ 86336, tel. 520/282–7640, fax 520/282–6829. 3 double rooms with bath. Terry robes and pool towels, concierge service, house phone; pool and spa. $115–$135; full breakfast, afternoon snacks and beverage. No smoking indoors, no pets, no children under 14; 2-night minimum stay, 3-night minimum during spring and fall.*

San Francisco Street B&B

Made of tan volcanic stone, with a steeply pitched shingle roof and a 25-foot chimney, this Flagstaff bed-and-breakfast looks like nothing so much as a giant gingerbread house. Built in 1937 in a quiet residential neighborhood shaded by ponderosa pines, it has a matching stone retaining wall, neatly tended lawn, garden, and flagstone patio.

Retired schoolteacher Freda Van Houten and her husband, Marvin, refinished the building and opened it as a B&B in December 1992. An immaculate living room has a flagstone fireplace, polished-oak floors, a beamed ceiling, wood-panel walls, and green wicker furniture. An oak butcher-block table dominates the dining room, which also has oak hardwood floors; brass chandeliers illuminate a collection of delicate porcelain demitasse cups.

The three guest rooms are light filled and attractive but fairly small, and they share a single bath. The Dutch-themed Tulip Room has a white wrought-iron bed, while the corner Rose Room has a beamed ceiling and windows on two sides.

🏠 *622 N. San Francisco St., Flagstaff, AZ 86001, tel. 520/779–2257. 2 double rooms and 1 single share bath. Pool table, TV, VCR in family room. $45 single, $55 double; full breakfast. No credit cards. No smoking indoors, no pets.*

Thunderbird Lodge

One of the few places to stay near the Canyon de Chelly and the only one on the grounds of the national monument, this Navajo-run lodge has a long history of hospitality. The trading post built on the site in 1902—now part of the lodge's cafeteria—was expanded over the years to accommodate the increasing number of visitors who came to see the cliff dwellings and the spectacular canyons nearby.

Low-slung stone and adobe units are spread out on a lawn shaded by cottonwood trees. The guest rooms have roughly hewn beam ceilings, rustic wood furniture, and Navajo prints and wall hangings.

About ½ mile southwest of the visitor center, the lodge is a hub for activities in the area: Jeep tours of the canyon can be booked here, and lectures and Native American performances are sometimes given in the evening. A cafeteria offers an inexpensive menu ranging from soups, salads, and sandwiches to complete meals, including charbroiled steaks and huge Navajo tacos made with native fry bread.

🏠 *Box 548, Chinle, AZ 86503, tel. 520/674–5841 or 800/697–2473. 71 rooms with baths (sleep up to 4), 1 suite. Gift shop, horse rentals nearby. $79–$84; no meals included. AE, D, DC, MC, V. No smoking indoors, no pets.*

Central Arizona
Including Phoenix, Prescott, and the White Mountains

Great desert meets great mountain range in central Arizona, providing a stunning variety of natural environments within easy touring distance. The region also combines some of the oldest dwellings in the western hemisphere with the homes of contemporary Native American tribes and America's newest, fastest-growing major urban center, metropolitan Phoenix.

In the middle of central Arizona, at the northern tip of the Sonoran Desert and ringed by mountain ranges, lies the 1,000-square-mile Valley of the Sun, so dubbed because of its 330-plus days of sunshine a year. The valley, formed by the Salt River, was farmed by the Hohokam Indians from 300 BC, but abandoned around AD 1450. It was not widely inhabited again until 1867, when a U.S. Army officer decided to reopen the canals the Hohokam had built in order to help feed the men and horses stationed at nearby Fort McDowell. The 300 people who settled here were prescient in naming their new town, which they predicted would rise "like a phoenix" from the ashes of a vanished civilization.

East of Phoenix loom the barren peaks of the Superstition Mountains, so called for their eerie habit of seeming just a few miles away and luring unwary prospectors to a dusty death. Beyond them, the White Mountains, with altitudes of 7,000 to 8,000 feet and Ponderosa pine forests, provide a cool retreat in summer and skiing on an Apache-owned resort in winter.

To the north of Phoenix, behind the dusty Hieroglyphic Mountains (misnamed for Hohokam petroglyphs found here), rises the gigantic Mogollon Rim, an escarpment almost as wide as Arizona; it got its name for posing an overwhelming mogollón (obstruction) to Spanish-speaking explorers probing northward. Here the slopes are green with pine trees, and the alpine meadows lush with grasses and aspens. After gold was found in the area in the early 1860s, President Lincoln sent the Arizona Territory's first governor to found the capital at Prescott and secure mineral riches for the union.

A number of the stately Victorian homes from Prescott's Territorial days have been carefully restored and turned into bed-and-breakfasts, and the White Mountain towns are scattered with rustic lodges and inns. Phoenix has not widely awakened to the B&B phenomenon, though a few choice lodgings are found here. Scottsdale has more than a dozen B&Bs and private home-stay accommodations, but zoning regulations prevent them from being "visible" to the public: no advertising, no phone-book listings, no signs out front. They can, however, be found through the reservation services listed below.

Places to Go, Sights to See

Arcosanti (35 mi east of Prescott, off I–17, tel. 520/632–7135). For a glimpse of the future, tour architect Paolo Soleri's visionary city, a prototype combination of architecture and ecology ("arcology") designed to one day house 5,000 people. Visitors are also welcome to the **Cosanti Foundation** (6433 Doubletree Ranch Rd., Scottsdale, tel. 520/948–6145), which operates Soleri's studio and the gallery where his famous wind-bells are cast and sold.

Arivaipa Canyon Wilderness. Eleven miles south of Winkelman on Rte. 77, an unpaved road heads east 8 miles to this designated "primitive area." The 4,044-acre wilderness includes a wild stretch of Arivaipa Creek and 6,145-foot Holy Joe Peak.

Besh-Ba-Gowah Archeological Park. An unusual stone-and-mud building with 300 rooms is the centerpiece of this ruined 14th-century village at the southern edge of Globe. A small museum explains the history of this site, occupied by the Salado Indians from 1225 to 1400. Contact the Globe-Miami Chamber of Commerce (*see* Tourist Information, *below*) for details.

Boyce Thompson Southwestern Arboretum (Hwy. 60/70, between Florence Junction and Superior, tel. 520/689–2811). Founded in the early 1920s along the riparian habitat of Queen Creek, this desert garden now offers 35 acres of unusual cacti, succulents, and water-efficient trees. The visitor center is on the National Register of Historic Sites.

Casa Malpais National Historic Landmark (2 mi northwest of Springerville on U.S. 60). The Mogollon mountain tribe occupied this rocky site ("House of the

Badlands") for some 200 years, abandoning it around 1400. In 1990, archaeologists discovered that volcanic caves here contained Indian burial places. The caves, or fissures—controversially described as "catacombs"—are sacred to Hopi and Zuni tribes and thus off-limits to visitors, but the public can observe the excavation of the 15-acre site, which includes a masonry pueblo, a steep basalt staircase, and a Great Kiva made of volcanic rock. Stop in first at the *Main Street Museum* (318 Main St., tel. 520/333–5375) in Springerville for information.

Downtown Phoenix. At the renovated east end of downtown Phoenix, from 6th and 7th streets between Monroe and Adams, *Heritage Square* is a block of turn-of-the-century houses in a parklike setting; the queen is the Rosson House (6th and Monroe Sts., tel. 602/262–5071), an 1895 gingerbread Victorian in the Eastlake style. Nearby, *The Mercado* (542 E. Monroe St., tel. 602/256–6322), a bright-colored neo-Aztec fantasy built in 1990, contains shops with Latin American handicrafts and the Museo Chicano, displaying the work of contemporary Hispano-American artists.

Fort Apache Cultural Center. Just outside the town of Whiteriver, on the Fort Apache Indian Reservation, are the remains of the U.S. military post established in 1870 to keep peace between settlers and tribes in the area. A museum housed in the three-room cabin of General George Crook provides a look back at U.S. Cavalry and Apache tribal history. For information, call the Tribal Offices in Whiteriver, tel. 520/338–4346.

Globe. In the southern reaches of Tonto National Forest and dotted with majestic cypress trees, Globe is the most cosmopolitan of the old mining towns west of Phoenix. It's a good area for antique shopping, and quilting is a local cottage industry. The Gila County Courthouse, built in 1888, now houses the *Cobre Valley Center for the Arts* (tel. 520/425–0889), an art gallery, crafts shop, and performing arts theater. Contact the Globe-Miami Chamber of Commerce (*see* Tourist Information, *below*) for pamphlets detailing a self-guided *walking tour of the historic downtown area*, and a *drive-yourself mine tour*, including six mine sites in the area dating from 1910 to the present.

Heard Museum (22 E. Monte Vista Rd., Phoenix, tel. 602/252–8848). The collection of primitive and modern Native American art in the Spanish Colonial-style adobe Heard mansion is probably the most extensive in the nation. Live demonstrations of Native American art forms are presented daily.

Jerome. When the copper mines closed in 1953, the community on the steep side of Mingus Mountain once known as the Billion Dollar Copper Camp saw its population drop from 15,000 to 50. But hippies discovered the ghost town during the 1960s and it is gradually reviving as an artists' colony. Set at 5,000 feet, the town has views 50 miles across the Verde Valley. *Jerome State Historic Park* (State Park Rd., tel. 520/634–5381), occupying the mansion of Dr. James "Rawhide Jimmy" Douglas Jr., Jerome's mining king, displays artifacts from the town's mining heyday.

Montezuma Castle National Monument (east of I–17, between Camp Verde and McGuireville, tel. 520/567–3322). Archaeologists estimate that this five-story

Indian cliff dwelling, set high into a sheer, limestone cliff face, is more than 700 years old. A visitor center provides information on the valley's natural and human history.

Prescott. Much of the 19th-century history of this former capital of Arizona Territory has been preserved, with more than 400 buildings listed on the National Register of Historic Places. Numerous Queen Anne-style homes dot the neighborhoods around the imposing 1916 courthouse. Among the town's other sights are the old taverns on Montezuma Street's *Whiskey Row,* the *antiques shops* along Cortez Street, and the *Sharlot Hall Museum* (415 W. Gurley St., tel. 520/445–3122), 3 acres of historical displays in a series of buildings including the 1864 Governor's Mansion. Three smaller galleries are also worth exploring: *The Bead Museum* (140 S. Montezuma, tel. 520/445–2431), *The Phippen Museum of Western Art* (4701 Hwy. 89 N., tel. 520/778–1385), and the *Smoki Museum* (147 N. Arizon St., tel. 520/445–1230), which focuses on Native American artifacts and crafts.

Scottsdale is shopper's heaven, its downtown filled with nationally known art galleries, lots of clever boutiques, and the huge *Scottsdale Galleria* (4343 N. Scottsdale Rd., tel. 602/949–3222), with 55 stores, 7 restaurants, and 8 movie theaters. *Old Scottsdale* is somewhat touristy, but its rustic storefronts and wooden sidewalks give visitors a taste of life here 80 years ago. The art galleries and antiques shops are concentrated on *Main Street,* and the 40-year-old stretch of *Fifth Avenue* is the place to find everything from cacti to handmade Indian jewelry.

Sunrise Park Resort (off AZ 260 on AZ 273 between Springerville and Pinetop/Lakeside, Greer, AZ 85927, tel. 520/735–7676), the state's largest ski area, has five day lodges, 11 lifts, and 65 trails on three mountains rising to 11,000 feet. Owned and operated by the White Mountain Apache Tribe, the resort is one of the most successful Native American business enterprises in the United States.

Taliesin West (108th St. and Cactus Rd., Scottsdale, AZ 85261, tel. 602/860–8810 or 602/860–2700). Frank Lloyd Wright's winter home, studio, and school in the desert, Taliesin is also one of the master architect's prototypes for "the natural house." Tours of this National Historic Landmark and its grounds are available daily.

Tonto National Monument (10 mi north of Payson, on Hwy. 87, tel. 520/467–2241). Northwest of Globe-Miami, just south of Theodore Roosevelt Lake, two important 14th-century cliff dwellings have been preserved. The 1,120-acre monument and visitor center reveal what life was like here in the rugged desert for the Salado Indians more than 600 years ago.

Tuzigoot National Monument (Camp Verde, tel. 520/634–5564). On the crest of a hill overlooking the Verde River, in the valley below the old mining town of Jerome, is the stone ruin of an Indian fortress. Its 100 rooms were constructed during the 13th century by the Sinagua Indians. A museum exhibits artifacts of the period.

Verde River Canyon Excursion Train (Box 103, 300 N. Broadway, Clarkdale, AZ 86324, tel. 520/639–0010 or 800/858–7245). Starting from Clarkdale, in the valley below Jerome, the Arizona Central Railroad runs north along the Verde River 22 miles to Perkinsville. The four-hour excursion uses old mining company tracks that once linked Jerome with Prescott and offers a leisurely, scenic round-trip. Sights along the way include eagles, Sinagua Indian ruins, old mining camps, red rock cliffs, and wildflowers.

White Mountains Trailsystem. A partnership project of the U.S. Forest Service, Arizona Game and Fish Department, Navajo County, the city of Show Low, the town of Pinetop-Lakeside, the White Mountain Horsemen's Association, and the Audubon Society of the White Mountains, the system is composed of some 180 miles of multi-use—equestrian, hiking, and mountain bike—loop trails along the Mogollon Rim. For a detailed map, send $3.95 to Chilton-Larson Publishing, Inc., Box 34, Pinetop, AZ 85935.

Restaurants

For travelers with deep pockets and a taste for fine dining, there are a number of innovative, upscale establishments in Phoenix. Vincent Geurithault is one of the handful of originators of Southwestern cuisine, and **Vincent's on Camelback** (tel. 602/224–0225) is the place to experience his art. Another leader of Southwestern cuisine, chef Mark Ching, presides at the **Compass Room** (tel. 602/252–1234), Arizona's only rotating dining room, at the top of downtown's Hyatt Regency Hotel. For more moderately priced meals in a restored Victorian home, try **Goldie's 1895** (tel. 602/254–0338), which has an eclectic menu and live music. Seven casual **Garcia's** restaurants (tel. 602/866–1850 in Phoenix; call for other locations), spread across the valley from Glendale to Chandler, serve good Arizonan versions of Mexican dishes. Inexpensive restaurants in the area include **Jasmine Café** (tel. 602/491–0797), offering a variety of Asian dishes in a ferny California-style setting; **Tradition** (tel. 602/996–2202), where homesick New Yorkers head for corned beef and sour pickles; and **Chianti** (tel. 602/957–9840), serving reliable Italian standards in a crowded but efficient poster-hung room.

Prescott has the only other concentration of decent restaurants in central Arizona, many within walking distance of the central Court House Square. For romantic and delicious Continental dining, try the lovely deco **Peacock Room** in the Hassayampa Inn (122 E. Gurley St., tel. 520/778–9434). The classy fern-and-brass **Murphy's** (tel. 520/445–4044) has an award-winning kitchen that turns out prime rib and pasta and a dozen seafood dishes. The eclectic menu at the **Prescott Brewing Company** (130 W. Gurley St., tel. 520/771–2795) includes healthy and flavorful dishes along with great handcrafted beers.

Situated in a former bordello in tiny Jerome, the **House of Joy** (tel. 520/634–5339) attracts patrons from all over the region, perhaps as much for its legendary setting as for its classic Continental cuisine. Reserve far in advance: It's open only for dinner on weekends.

Tourist Information

Arizona Office of Tourism (1100 W. Washington St., Phoenix, AZ 85007, tel. 602/542–8687, fax 602/542–4068). **Globe-Miami Chamber of Commerce** (Box 2539, Globe, AZ, 85502, tel. 520/425–4495 or 800/448–8983). **Jerome Chamber of Commerce** (Box K, Jerome, AZ 86331, tel. 602/634–2900). **Phoenix & Valley of the Sun Convention & Visitors Bureau** (One Arizona Center, 400 E. Van Buren St., Suite 600, Phoenix, AZ 85004, tel. 602/254–6500, fax 602/253–4415). **Pinetop-Lakeside Chamber of Commerce** (Box 266, Pinetop, AZ 85935, tel. 520/367–4290). **Prescott Chamber of Commerce** (117 W. Goodwin St., Box 1147, Prescott, AZ 86302, tel. 520/445–2000 or 800/266–7534). **Springerville-Eager Chamber of Commerce** (Box 31, Springerville, AZ 85938, tel. 520/333–2123). **Show Low Chamber of Commerce** (Box 1083, Show Low, AZ 85901, tel. 520/537–2326). **White Mountain Apache-Tribe** (Box 700, Whiteriver, AZ 85941, tel. 520/338–4346).

Reservation Services

Arizona Association of Bed & Breakfast Inns (3101 North Central Ave., Suite 560, Phoenix, AZ 85012, tel. 602/277–0775). **Bed & Breakfast Inn Arizona-Arizona Accommodations Reservations** (8900 E. Via Linda, Suite 101, Scottsdale, AZ 85258, tel. 602/860–9338 or 800/266–7829, fax 520/860–9338). **Mi Casa Su Casa B&B Reservation Service** (Box 950, Tempe, AZ 85280, tel. 602/990–0682; reservations only 800/456–0682).

Greer Lodge

An alpine lodge that could have come straight from the drafting board of a Hollywood set designer, this 1948 building in the White Mountains is made entirely of polished logs, exposed inside and out. The spacious lobby is replete with deer antlers, a black bearskin, wagon-wheel chandeliers, lodgepole-pine furniture, and plank floors. A stone fireplace crackles with juniper logs.

The backdrop—pine-studded Greer Valley, at an elevation of 8,500 feet, with deer and elk grazing in the meadows—is equally picture perfect. The Little Colorado River, stocked with trout and dammed here and there by beaver colonies, meanders through the grounds.

The rooms pick up the rustic theme, with knotty pine or polished log walls, oak or pine plank floors, and cheerful chintz curtains and bedspreads; each has a private bath and individual electric heat controls. First choice are the corner rooms, such as nos. 2, 4, and 5, which offer views of both the valley and the wooded mountains. On the third floor, under the peaked roof, is a romantic pine-paneled room with a clear view to the south. In addition to the accommodations in the lodge, there are similarly furnished rooms in the Little Lodge, a four-bedroom log cabin with a kitchen and a deck overlooking the river; and rooms in a variety of smaller cabins, some with kitchens and fireplaces.

Breakfast, lunch, and dinner are served in the skylit solar-heated dining room, open to the public. It's surrounded by glass, and every table overlooks the creek, three ponds, an expansive lawn populated with ducks and geese, and the wooded hills beyond. Breakfast possibilities include Belgian waffles with strawberries, biscuits and gravy, and blueberry pancakes. At lunchtime, salads, burgers, and hot and cold sandwiches are available.

No license is required to fish in the Lodge's two fishing ponds, but there is a fee. If you catch something in the larger fly-fishing pond, you have to throw it back, but you can keep whatever bites in the smaller bait-fishing pond.

🏨 *Box 244, Greer, AZ 85927, tel. 520/735-7515. 7 double rooms with baths, 2 suites in Lodge; 2 1-bedroom cabins; 5 2-bedroom cabins; 1 4-bedroom cabin. Cable TV in lounge, fruit basket upon arrival, bar, restaurant; fly-fishing classes Apr.–Oct. Lodge $120, Little Lodge $35 per person, cabins $75–$95; full breakfast included in Lodge rate only. MC, V. No pets; 2-night minimum on weekends, 3-night minimum on holidays.*

Lynx Creek Farm

here are more than 200 fruit trees, including seven varieties of apple, at this 25-acre property on a hilltop east of Prescott overlooking Lynx Creek, Lonesome Valley, and the Blue Hills; in addition, there's a menagerie of chickens, pigs, parrots, goats, cats, and dogs. At the bottom of the hill, Lynx Creek meanders through a shady grove of tall cottonwood trees. This idyllic setting is equally suited to honeymooners and families, offering privacy as well as plenty of space and activities for restless children.

Built in the early 1980s, the farm was bought by Greg and Wendy Temple in 1985 and turned into a bed-and-breakfast. Across the driveway from the main house, where Greg and Wendy live, is a guest house with two rooms; each has a wood-burning stove and there's a shared hot tub on the viewside deck. The cozy pine-paneled Sharlot Hall Room, named for a Prescott pioneer woman, is filled with antiques, books, and memorabilia. One of the room's two king-size beds is set in a low-ceiling loft reached by ladder—an ideal space to stow the kids. The White Wicker Room next door is light, lacy, and romantic, with wicker furniture and a queen bed with a soft feather comforter.

In 1992, Greg added a handsome log cabin with four inviting rooms. All have wall-to-wall Berber carpets, wood-burning stoves, king beds, and private hot tubs on outdoor decks that afford views of the valley. The Old West-style Chaparral Room is decorated with beat-up saddles, antlers, and a hand-stitched quilt, while the more romantic Country Garden Room features lots of plants and whitewashed log-beam ceilings. A living room with kitchenette can be connected to any of the rooms to create a two-room suite; two daybed couches open up into four single beds for extra family members.

Mornings bring guests to the breakfast room of the main house, decorated with blue ribbons that the Temples were awarded for their apples, or to the wide deck overlooking the creek below. Large breakfasts usually feature organically homegrown fruits, quiches made with fresh eggs, homemade yogurt, fresh-baked muffins, breads, and coffeecakes. On request, a Continental breakfast-in-a-basket will be delivered to your door.

Box 4301, Prescott, AZ 86302, tel. 520/778-9573. 4 double rooms with baths, 2 suites. Terry robes in rooms, phone and TV on request; playground, basketball, volleyball, horseshoes, hiking. $75–$140; full breakfast, afternoon refreshments. AE, D, MC, V. No smoking indoors, well-behaved pets only.

Maricopa Manor
Bed and
Breakfast Inn

Business travelers appreciate this all-suite facility, centrally located near downtown Phoenix and just minutes from the Heard Museum, the Herberger Theatre, and the America West Arena. Innkeepers Paul and Mary Ellen Kelley raised 12 children in this 1928 residence, on a quiet, palm-shaded street, before turning it into an elegant executive retreat.

The immaculate Spanish Colonial-style home is decorated with fine art and stocked with countless books. Visitors have the run of the high-ceiling family room, living room, dining room, and outdoor patio. Stressed guests can let off steam by tickling the ivories on the restored piano in the music room or soaking in the hot tub in the gazebo out back.

The accommodations have every amenity offered by the posh Phoenix resorts—fresh flowers, expensive toiletries—and even some they don't have: an array of paperbacks in each room, access to AT&T bilingual international operator service, and rubber duckies in the bathtub.

The Victorial Suite is in the main house. Set off the family room, it is done in satin, lace, and antiques; the private bath is across the hall. The other accommodations are arrayed outside in adjoining buildings. A private entrance leads to the Library Suite, with volumes of leather-bound books, a desk, and a canopied king-size bed.

In an adjoining guest house with its own carport and a gated driveway are two more spacious suites. Reflections Past offers a fireplace, antique mirrors, and king-size bed with a tapestry canopy. Reflections Future, done in black and white with a Chinese flavor, has a living room, a full kitchen with breakfast area, and a small study with a desk and phone.

A Franklin stove sets the tone for the traditional American decor in the Palo Verde Suite, which has two bedrooms, one with two canopied four-poster beds and a smaller one with a ¾ size spool bed set off the enclosed sun porch.

Breakfast—orange juice, hot coffee, a fresh fruit plate, homemade bread or pastries, and a hot cheese mini-quiche—is delivered to your door, at the hour you specify, in a wicker picnic basket.

🏠 *Box 7186, Phoenix, AZ 85011, tel. 602/274–6302. 4 1-bedroom suites (1 with private bath across the hall), 1 2-bedroom suite. Bathrobes in rooms, color TV and telephone on request. $79–$159; full breakfast. AE, D, MC, V. No pets.*

The Marks House

The mayor of Territorial Prescott and a man with successful interests in ranching, mining, and wholesale liquor, Jake Marks spared no expense when it came to building a house for his wife, Josephine. Redwood was imported from California; the glass in the turret windows was curved to match the rounded sills; the cast copper door hinges were engraved with decorative designs; and parquet floors were laid in the formal dining room. In all, it took two years to construct this two-story Queen Anne-style mansion on Nob Hill, overlooking the central Court House Square; it was completed in 1884.

Restoration on the building, which served for a time as a boardinghouse and a rest home, began in 1980; it debuted as a bed-and-breakfast in 1987. Today it is listed on the National Register of Historic Homes and owned by Beth Maitland, the young actress who plays Traci on CBS's "The Young and the Restless." Her parents, Dotti and Harold Viehweg, manage the inn and continue to improve it.

Like the rest of the house, the bay-windowed living room is furnished with antiques from the 1870s through the 1890s and wallpapered with a reproduction Victorian print; filled to the rafters with lacy doodads and knickknacks, it hosts a boutique for decorative items. The formal dining room, which enjoys a view out over Court House Plaza, has room for three linen-covered tables and matching oak sideboards.

The jewel in this B&B's crown is the Queen Anne Suite adjoining the circular turret; it's furnished in white wicker and has a claw-foot tub in the bath. The view north from the curved windows sweeps over the tall trees surrounding the Court House, across the city to majestic Thumb Butte in the distance. Princess Victoria, also upstairs, is done in mauve and lavender with floral patterns; an unusual, hammered copper tub in the bath was salvaged from an 1892 bathhouse in New York State.

Breakfast is served family style at whatever hour guests agree upon in advance. Popular entrées include blackberry dumplings made from an old family recipe, a deep-dish egg casserole with meat, and French toast.

🏨 *203 E. Union St., Prescott, AZ 86303, tel. 520/778–4632. 2 double rooms with baths (1 adjoining), 1 1-bedroom suite, 1 2-bedroom suite. Welcome mineral water in rooms; gift shop. $75–$135; full breakfast, afternoon hors d'oeuvres. D, MC, V. No smoking indoors, no pets.*

Paisley Corner Bed & Breakfast

This imposing two-story redbrick mansion occupies a corner lot on the main street of Eagar, a small town near the Little Colorado River. Innkeepers Cheryl and Cletus Tisdell worked three years to restore the 1910 Historical Landmark to its pre–World War I grandeur, and probably surpassed it. They used the hammered-tin ceilings from the old Fox Theatre in Phoenix to create wainscoting, borders, and ceilings throughout the house.

Opened as a bed-and-breakfast at the end of 1991, the mansion boasts furnishings authentic to the period. An enameled wood-burning stove and formal walnut table dominate the dining room. The two front rooms retain their original stained-glass windows. In the "ice cream parlour," across the front hall from the living room, Cletus shows off his two jukeboxes, which play 78 rpm records; his working antique Coke machine; and his collection of American memorabilia.

The names given the guest rooms, all upstairs, were popular ones for women at the turn of the century. Each room has wall-to-wall Irish rose carpeting and a lazily rotating ceiling fan. Fanny's black-and-gold wrought-iron bed fronts a three-faced dressmaker's mirror and a maple vanity in an unusual cattail design; the spacious bathroom, with a claw-foot tub and 19th-century pull-chain commode, is next door. In Miss Lily, most aptly called a boudoir, mauve wallpaper in a rose pattern wraps around a lace-covered, white-and-brass bed that reposes regally on a step-up platform with formidable wooden banisters. The bath sports a circular, rib-cage shower.

Entry to spacious Mabel Joy is through a pair of etched-glass doors with porcelain handles secured by a pink satin rope; the room has dark-green wallpaper with a hammered-tin border, as well as a massive, carved-oak canopy bed and matching beveled-glass vanity. Fontanille, a two-bedroom suite, boasts an artificial fireplace with tiger-oak columns and an ornate 1820s carved-walnut bed with an 8-foot-high headboard.

Cheryl's full breakfasts are prepared on a 1910 gas stove and served on rose-patterned china set on a lace tablecloth. Fresh-ground coffee precedes fresh juice, fruit, potatoes, and home-baked breads or muffins. The main dish may be quiche; a rich breakfast casserole of bacon, hard-boiled eggs, and sour cream; or French toast with real maple syrup.

🏨 *Box 458, Springerville, AZ 85938, or 287 N. Main St., Eagar, AZ 85925, tel. 520/333–4665. 3 double rooms with baths, 1 2-bedroom suite. TV in living room, welcome basket. $65–$75; full breakfast. MC, V. No smoking indoors.*

Victorian Inn of Prescott Bed & Breakfast

Prescott lays claim to being the only town in Arizona with an entire neighborhood of Victorian homes dating back to the 19th century. Tamia Thunstedt's blue-and-white trim Queen Anne could easily be that neighborhood's centerpiece. Built as a single-level square house in 1875, 11 years after Prescott was settled, it was purchased in 1883 by John C. Herndon, who imported milled lumber and handcrafted woodwork by train from back East and gradually remodeled it into his gingerbread dream house, adding bay windows and a second story with a conical turret.

Between 1982 and 1988, the building was restored. The small living room now looks as it must have 100 years ago, filled with formal Victorian antiques and lots of plush red velvet. The stained-glass windows and 17 chandeliers are all original to the house.

Four upstairs guest accommodations are also meticulously furnished in period style. The Victoriana Suite, done in rich burgundy and royal blue, has its own fireplace, two bay windows, and 1860s walnut pieces; it's the most spacious room and the only one with a private bath. The smallest is the Teddy Bear Room, dominated by a 19th-century mahogany four-poster bed and populated by stuffed bears of various sizes and colors.

The Rose Room, decorated in mauve with complementary linens, features a brass bed and antique lace curtains.

Eve's Garden Room has white wicker furniture and a chiffon canopy bed with raspberry satin sheets. The bathroom shared by the three rooms boasts a thick, wall-to-wall carpet, a claw-foot tub with brass fittings, and a handheld shower nozzle.

At check-in, Tamia's tour of the house and detailed briefing on guest procedures, including fire safety, lasts nearly 15 minutes. That's nothing. She says her formal breakfast for eight takes 12 hours to prepare, and it's easy to believe: It's an elaborate production, with a setting—antique, floral-patterned china, fine linens, and gold-plated utensils—and food suitable for Queen Victoria. Entrées range from blueberry buttermilk Swedish pancakes or French toast basted in orange sauce and served with Canadian bacon florets, to Swedish *strata*, layered bread pudding of eggs, sausage, and cheese, served with warm amaretto applesauce.

🏠 *246 S. Cortez St., Prescott, AZ 86303, tel. 520/778-2642. 3 double rooms share bath, 1 suite. Prebreakfast coffee, tea, and newspaper; gift shop. $90, Victoriana Suite $135; full breakfast. AE, D, MC, V. No smoking indoors, no pets.*

Bartram's White Mountain Bed & Breakfast

A road leading out of Lakeside dead-ends at the edge of a forest. Turn right and you're in the driveway of a gray 1940s-era ranch house, being greeted by Yum Yum and Shammy, the resident collie and toy poodle, and by the sound of chickens cackling contentedly in the back coop. Innkeepers Petie and Ray Bartram opened this country-comfortable inn in 1987; the house has a fresh, new feeling thanks to their expert use of cheerful colors and fabrics.

Each of the rooms features a private entrance and spotless wall-to-wall carpeting. The Blue Room has a queen bed with white wood-paneled walls, a lace-covered vanity, and a private patio. The Satin Room bed is of carved pine with his-and-hers electric blankets (with two-sided controls). In the Peach Room, double doors close off a separate children's room with two daybeds.

Petie is justifiably proud of her seven-course breakfasts; among her entrées are cinnamon toast stuffed with cream cheese, asparagus quiche, and smoked turkey eggs in puff pastry.

🏠 *Rte. 1, Box 1014, Lakeside, AZ 85929, tel. 520/367–1408 or 800/257–0211. 2 double rooms with baths, (3 more planned), 1 suite. Individual heating units, TV in living room. $85; full breakfast. Luxury pkg. $250. No credit cards. No smoking indoors, no pets.*

Billings' Country Retreat

Owners Dave and Alice Billings built this country homestay in 1993 at the edge of the Sitgreaves National Forest. Humorous tassel-eared Abert squirrels hop out of the pine trees to nibble peanuts on the porch; hummingbirds hover at the feeder outside the window. On the property line, an inviting trail leads through the trees toward Woodland Lake Park.

The Billings are antiques collectors and dealers with a shop in downtown Pinetop, and their home is a showcase for some prize pieces. Their roomy living room is filled with Americana, including delightful old toys. The kitchen has a pine plank floor, an 1880s stove and harvest table.

Two large guest rooms share a modern connecting bath with a claw-foot tub and a 19th-century pine washstand. Shades of blue in the carpets, curtains, and borders of the queen bedroom are picked up by the patchwork quilt. The bay-windowed king bedroom showcases an unusual brass and porcelain eight-poster bed.

🏠 *H.C. 66, Box 2614, 63 E. Turkey Track, Pinetop, AZ 85935, tel. 520/367–1709. 2 double rooms share bath. TV in living room; use of laundry, barbecue grill, fridge. $45–$55; full breakfast. MC, V. No smoking indoors, no pets (2 dogs in residence).*

"The Coldstream" Bed & Breakfast

You'd never suspect that this handsome two-story home was actually built 7 miles away in the 1920s. It was the residence of a lumber mill owner in nearby McNary and then the official company guesthouse before it was upped and moved to this wooded site near the Pinetop Country Club in 1980.

New innkeepers Cindy and Jeff Northrup and manager Sherry Siegenthaler have completely remodeled the inn. The decor is a comfortable blend of "north woods country" with modern amenities complementing the hardwood floors and clear pine and oak paneling. A fireplace warms the spacious, carpeted living-dining area; its view windows and billiard table are pleasantly diverting.

The rooms are named after 19th-century White Mountain lumber camps. McNary (triple) and Cooley (king-size) suites are upstairs, with pine-paneled walls and polished wood floors.

Breakfast is served in the dining room or in a sunny nook between the kitchen and the flagstone patio. A popular entrée is crêpes Romeo and Juliet with cream cheese and strawberries.

▦ *Box 2988, Pinetop, AZ 85935, tel. 520/369–0115. 3 double rooms with baths (1 across hall), 2 suites. Terry robes, TV with VCR, pool table; bicycles, enclosed outdoor spa, horse boarding. $95–$125; full breakfast, 4 PM social tea. MC, V. No smoking indoors, no pets, no children under 11.*

Hassayampa Inn

Prescott is rightfully proud of this exacting restoration of its downtown 1927 Spanish Colonial Revival hotel. Named for the nearby river where prospectors discovered gold in 1863, the three-story Hassayampa Inn underwent a $4-million makeover in 1985, which preserved its unique Western Roaring Twenties atmosphere.

The lobby is rich in glazed tile. The massive, faux-beamed ceiling is ornately handpainted, and plush tapestry chairs and couches complement the antique grand pianos and giant golden radiators set against the walls. Delicate bamboo sprouts from 3-foot-high ceramic pots, and classical music plays softly.

The rooms are furnished with original or period pieces and have wall-to-wall carpeting, brass bedside lamps, and lace curtains. Included in the room rate are a complimentary cocktail in the cozy bar and lounge and a full breakfast—whatever you like from the menu of the lovely Peacock Room, one of Prescott's finest restaurants.

▦ *122 Gurley St., Prescott, AZ 86301, tel. 520/778–9434 or 800/322–1927. 58 rooms with baths, 10 suites. TV, phones in rooms, restaurant, lounge, bar. $89–$119 rooms, $135–$175 suites; full breakfast, afternoon cocktail. AE, D, DC, MC, V. No pets.*

Juniper Well Ranch

This 50-acre horse ranch is set in a peaceful valley in the midst of Prescott National Forest, 25 minutes north of Prescott. At night, not a light can be seen in surrounding hills, which are home to some 1,000-year-old alligator-bark junipers. A distant rock outcropping hides a fort built more than 800 years ago by the Prescott Indians.

Two cozy, 22 × 24-foot lodgepole-pine cabins sit on the property. Each has a covered porch; exposed log walls; wall-to-wall carpeting; full kitchen; bath with ceramic tile tub; and a wood stove with a supply of aromatic juniper firewood. One cabin, with a western flavor, has a loft with a double bed reached by a ladder, a queen bed, and some English oak antiques. The other is decorated in a more romantic style with lace curtains and floral patterns. In 1994, the original ranch house was opened up to guests. Done in Western motifs, with a six-foot-high wood-burning stove, it can comfortably accommodate 10.

▦ *Box 11083, Prescott, AZ 86304, tel. 520/442–3415. 2 cabins, 1 2-bedroom ranch house. Hot tub; barbecue pits. Cabins: $105; full breakfast. Ranch house: $100 for 4 people, $10 per additional person; breakfast not included. AE, D, MC, V. No smoking indoors, small pets permitted.*

The Meadows

Looking just like a New England country inn, The Meadows sits in a flower-filled meadow at the edge of thick ponderosa pine woods. Completed in 1993, in a modified Victorian style, it opened in November 1994 to set a new standard of accommodations for the White Mountains. The four owners, all from Tucson, combine years of hospitality experience. Partner and Executive Chef Steve McBrayer serves three gourmet meals a day in the Dining Room, his fresh, innovative menus complemented by selections from the comprehensive wine cellar.

The interior is subdued French Country, with white walls and forest green carpeting. Juniper logs burn in the brick fireplace of the loft-ceiling living room, and the cozy upstairs library offers books, games, and cable TV. The one suite, no. 7, has a white fireplace, a brass bed, cable TV, and a kitchenette. The two upstairs rooms, no. 1 and no. 2, are corner rooms with restrained, floral-patterned quilts and wallpaper.

Guests select their breakfasts in the evening from daily menus and may enjoy them in their rooms or anywhere in the inn.

🏨 *Box 1110, Pinetop, AZ 85935, 520/ 367–8200. 6 double rooms with baths, 1 suite. Restaurant, wine bar, room service; mountain bikes. $70–$155; full breakfast. Smoking in designated area only, no pets; 2-night minimum weekends, 3-night minimum on holidays.*

Mt. Vernon Inn

A seamless series of additions has rendered this lovely Victorian residence, on a quiet street four blocks from the center of Prescott, an ideal destination for a variety of travelers.

The main house, beautifully restored to its original 1900 style, hosts four light-filled, romantic rooms, done in pretty but not overly fussy florals; two have bay windows and one has a private entrance. Guests who stay here enjoy a buffet breakfast, which always includes fresh-baked breads and muffins, in the downstairs dining room.

Of the outbuildings, both the Carriage House, with an upstairs sleeping loft and a downstairs room with queen-size bed, and the Studio, with two full baths, are fine for families. The Doll House—the name aptly describes its dimensions—is a private little aerie for two. Because there are individual kitchens in all three cottages, guests fend for themselves for the morning meal.

🏨 *204 North Mt. Vernon Ave., Prescott, AZ 86301, tel. 520/778–0886. 4 double rooms with baths, 3 cottages. Phones in all rooms, TVs and kitchens in cottages. $80; Continental buffet breakfast. Cottages $90–$110; breakfast not included. AE, D, MC, V. No smoking indoors, pets in cottages only.*

Noftsger Hill Inn

Frank and Pamela Hulme are busy these days removing wax from acres of white maple hardwood floors. They're in the process of converting the Noftsger Hill School, built in 1907 and overlooking the mining town of Globe, into a bed-and-breakfast. The inn opened in April 1993; all the accommodations are decorated with local antiques and have Western themes. The living room, formerly the school hallway, is furnished with a five-piece antique living room set, Oriental rugs, and a piano.

Three of the completed guest rooms are huge—23 × 30 feet with high ceilings, fireplaces, and the original slate blackboards, as well as panoramic views of the Pinal Mountains. In one, there's an antique king-size bed at the east end, twin beds at the west end, and space for a basketball game in-between. The smaller guest room used to be a school office.

A "miner-size" breakfast, which might include Mexican quiche with green chilies, is served in the dining room (converted from a classroom) at a formal antique oak table.

🏨 *425 North St., Globe, AZ 85501, tel. 520/425-2260. 3 triple rooms and 1 double with bath. Wheelchair ramp. $45–$75; full breakfast. MC, V. No smoking indoors, no pets.*

The Pleasant Street Inn Bed & Breakfast

The original 19th-century home on this corner lot in Prescott's Victorian neighborhood burned down years ago, but in 1990 an enterprising contractor moved a 1900 New England-style home onto the site. The B&B that Jean Urban opened here *feels* new because of the soft, gray wall-to-wall carpet, the just-plastered walls, and the contemporary style of the upholstered furnishings. It's also sunny and bright, a nice alternative to some of the Victorian inns.

But there are many traditional touches. In the comfy living room, with a bay window overlooking a lush lawn, a fireplace burns aromatic cedar logs. An oak table shares the dining room with a dark-pine sideboard. Breakfast, which always includes fresh fruit and homemade breads, is served here or on the south-facing terrace.

Rooms are pretty, with floral-print quilts. The Pine View Suite enjoys corner light, a bay window, and a fireplace. Another corner room, the Garden Room, has white wicker furnishings and lace curtains.

🏨 *142 S. Pleasant St., Prescott, AZ 86303, tel. 520/445-4774. 2 double rooms with baths, 2 suites. TV in living room, fresh flowers in rooms. $80–$120; full breakfast, afternoon hors d'oeuvres. MC, V. No smoking indoors, no pets.*

The Cottages at Prescott Country Inn

With an artful application of paint, white lattices, trees, and flowers, what was once a sterile 1940s motor court with 12 cottages has been converted into an inviting complex of one-, two-, three-, and four-room suites. The rooms are furnished in an eclectic country style, with hand-quilted gingham comforters, dried flowers, nostalgic prints, and lots of knickknacks. They all have private entrances, wall-to-wall carpeting, refrigerators, and coffeemakers. Four units offer carports, decks, or patios; 10 have full kitchens, and three have gas-log fireplaces. Only No. 25 has a full tub with shower; No. 24, a four-room cottage, faces the busy main road.

A Continental breakfast, delivered to guests in a country basket in the evening, includes juice, breads, rolls, muffins, and coffee, tea, or cocoa. A nice touch: When you get up in the morning, you'll find your windshield has been washed.

🏨 *503 S. Montezuma St., Prescott, AZ 86303, tel. 520/445-7991. 2 1-room units; 7 2-room units, 2 3-room units; 1 4-room unit. TV, phone, clock radio in rooms, Jacuzzi room; off-street parking, outdoor barbecue. $89–$119; Continental breakfast, complimentary lunch and dinner at a Prescott restaurant. D, MC, V.*

White Mountain Lodge

This 1892 landmark lodge in the tiny White Mountain town of Greer enjoys a panoramic view of Greer Valley. The Little Colorado River runs along the foot of the property, which is about 15 minutes from the Sunrise Ski area.

The living room in the main lodge has a stone fireplace, leather chairs and couches, and walls decorated with southwestern paintings and Native

American pottery and crafts. A dining room table seating 12 takes full advantage of the view a picture window affords. The full breakfast varies daily but includes homemade coffee cakes, muffins, donuts, and/or bread.

The seven guest rooms in the lodge are on the cozy side; most are pine paneled, and all have wall-to-wall carpeting, floral print bedspreads or country quilts, and individual electric heating units. Innkeepers Charlie Bast and Mary Lawrence also have three cabins with kitchens for rent, ideal for families and those who prefer to do their own cooking and housekeeping.

🏠 *Box 143, Greer, AZ 85927, tel. 520/ 735-7568, fax 520/735-7498. 4 double rooms, 2 double-doubles, 1 twin, all with baths; 3 cabins. TV with VCR in Entry room, guest fax and refrigerator; small pets welcome. $50–$70; full breakfast; $60–$95 for cabins. No credit cards. 2-night minimum weekends, 3-night minimum on holidays.*

Tucson and Environs
Including Pima and Santa Cruz Counties

The second-largest city in Arizona, Tucson is at once a bustling center of business and a laid-back university and resort town. Its year-round population of 665,000 swells in the winter, when snowbirds from the North come to enjoy the city's warm sun and warm hospitality. The town is flanked by vast preserves of huge saguaro cactus, but the desert here is literal, not cultural: Tucson is among only 14 cities in the United States that can claim a symphony and opera, theater, and ballet companies; Tucson also boasts a planetarium and one of the best photography centers in the country.

The region's earliest known citizens, the Hohokam Indians, lived in the fertile farming valley in AD 100, though other Native American artifacts in the area can be traced as far back as 2,000 years. At the end of the 17th century, Jesuit missionary Father Eusebio Francisco Kino rode north on horseback from Mexico to preach Catholicism to the peaceful Pima and Tohono O'Odham Indians who had settled along the banks of the Santa Cruz River. He noted in his diary in 1692 that he had arrived in the town of Stkjukshon, meaning "spring at the base of black mountain." The name was corrupted by Spanish explorers who built the presidio (fortress) of San Agustín del Tuguisón in 1776 to keep Native Americans from reclaiming the city.

Rebuilt by Franciscans in the 18th century, the lovely Spanish-Moorish-style Mission San Xavier del Bac still stands at the outskirts of Tucson on the site of Father Kino's original mission church and still serves the Tohono O'Odham Indians, whose vast reservation—only that of the Navajo Nation is larger—spreads out to the west of Tucson. But Father Kino's original route north has become I–19, along which the border town of Nogales, the artists' center of Tubac, and the huge retirement community of Green Valley now thrive. And the black mountain for which Tucson was named, probably the dark volcanic cone near downtown known as

Sentinel Peak, is more popularly known as "A" mountain
because University of Arizona students annually whitewash
the large "A" cut into its side.

For much of this century, Tucson was called the "Dude Ranch
Capital of the West." Dozens of the casual western resorts
surrounded the town, attracting pale visitors from the East.
There are only a few left today; the most famous, Tanque Verde
Ranch, is reviewed below. Bed-and-breakfasts are a more
recent development but are taking off rapidly. Some of the
inns in town look back to Territorial times when settlers built
elaborate Victorian homes—albeit out of adobe brick—and
tried to pretend they weren't in the desert; other, more
contemporary inns have been set deliberately in remote areas,
built with natural materials to capitalize on the landscape's
unique beauty. In summer, when temperatures can linger
around 101°F, some of the bed-and-breakfasts close; others
drop their rates.

Places to Go, Sights to See

Ajo. About halfway between Tucson and the California border, Ajo was a
thriving Phelps Dodge copper mining town for many years. It looked as though
it might be abandoned when the company shut down operations in 1985, but
many retirees are now being lured here by a temperate climate and low-cost
housing. On Indian Village Road, at the outskirts of town, the *New Cornelia
Open Pit Mine Lookout Point* provides a panoramic view of the town's huge
open-pit mine, almost 2 miles wide. The white, Santa Fe-style mansion of John
Campbell Greenway, who laid out the town in 1916 for the Calumet and Arizona
Mining Company, sits on a rocky ridge overlooking the mine and the lonely grave
where he was buried in 1926. Nearby, the *Ajo Historical Society Museum* (160
Mission St., tel. 520/387–7105), set in St. Catherine's Indian Mission, has collected
a mélange of articles relating to the town's past from locals. Some of the historical
photographs are fascinating.

Arizona–Sonora Desert Museum (2021 N. Kinney Rd., tel. 520/883–1380).
Considered one of the top 10 zoos in the world, the Arizona–Sonora Desert
Museum features birds, animals, and plants from southern Arizona and northern
Mexico, all displayed in carefully re-created natural habitats. All the desert
creatures are here, from scorpions and rattlesnakes to javelina, mountain lions,
and hummingbirds. Allow at least half a day to see it all.

Biosphere 2 (35 mi north of Tucson on Hwy. 77, tel. 520/825–6200 or 800/828–
2462). This controversial science project is a giant 3-acre greenhouse in which

eight "Biospherians" were first sealed for two years in 1991. The $150-million experiment is designed as a prototype for space colonization and environmental management. You can't go inside, but you may catch a glimpse of one of the ecologists behind the glass. A motel, a good restaurant, and many gift shops are on the grounds.

Colossal Cave (Old Spanish Trail, 22 mi southeast of Tucson, tel. 520/647–7275). The largest dry cavern in the United States, with a steady temperature of 72°F, Colossal Cave has never been fully explored. Treasure is said to be hidden in its dark recesses.

De Grazia's Gallery in the Sun (630 N. Swan Rd., tel. 520/299–9191. Admission free. Open daily 10–4). This is the museum, gallery, workshop, former home, and gravesite of Arizona's best-known and most-loved artist, Ted De Grazia, who depicted Southwestern, Native American, and Mexican life. From the metal mineshaft doors at the entrance to the polished saguaro tiles in the floor, the sprawling, single-story museum is as appealing as the paintings on the walls. Built by the artist with the help of Native American friends, it uses only materials from the surrounding desert. Adjacent to the museum is the **Mission in the Sun,** a hand-built adobe chapel covered with De Grazia murals; it was completed in 1952 and dedicated to Our Lady of Guadalupe, patron saint of the Yaqui Indians and of Mexico. Close to the chapel is the artist's grave, frontier style, covered by a mound of rocks. None of De Grazia's original oil paintings, sculptures, or watercolors is for sale, but the museum's gift shop sells a wide selection of cards, prints, lithographs, ceramics, and books by and about the artist.

El Presidio District. The area surrounding the original Spanish presidio, or fort, was the center of Tucson for a long time; now this downtown district is home to many museums, art galleries, theaters, and boutiques. The Spanish Colonial-style *Pima County Courthouse*, built in 1927 on the site of the original single-story adobe courthouse of 1869, is perhaps Tucson's most beautiful historical building. The nearby *Tucson Museum of Art* (140 N. Main Ave., tel. 520/884–7379) houses an impressive collection of pre-Columbian art and a permanent display of 20th-century Western art. Tours are offered of the historic buildings in the museum complex, including the Casa Cordova, the Fish House, and the Stevens Home.

Fort Huachuca (Sierra Vista, 80 mi south of Tucson, tel. 520/533–3536). Established as a frontier outpost by the U.S. Army in 1877 to control the Indians, Fort Huachuca hosts one of this country's finest museums of military history. Displays document the all-black units, called Buffalo Soldiers, who helped fight the Native Americans after the Civil War. Civilians may visit, but they must register at the main entrance, Buffalo Soldier Gate, and show vehicle registration and driver's license.

Golf. Pima and Santa Cruz counties offer some of the best desert courses in the country—and more than 300 days of sunshine to play on them. *The Tucson & Southern Arizona Golf Guide,* published by Tucson Guide Quarterly, Inc. (send $1 to Box 42915, Tucson, AZ 85733, tel. 520/322–0895), describes and rates all the local courses. For a personalized golf package based on your budget, interests, and experience, you might contact **Tee Time Arrangers** (tel. 800/742–9939).

Kitt Peak National Observatory (56 mi southeast of Tucson, off AZ 286, tel. 520/325–9200 for recorded tour information, tel. 520/620–5350 for visitors center). This cluster of 19 telescopes in the Quinlan Mountains, on the Tohono O'Odham Indian Reservation, includes the largest solar telescope in the world. The visitors center has films and tours of the mountaintop complex.

Mission San Xavier del Bac (Mission Rd., just outside of Tucson, tel. 520/294–2624). The beautiful "White Dove of the Desert," established in 1783 by Franciscan missionaries on the site of an older Jesuit mission and finished 14 years later, is the only Spanish mission in the United States still serving its original, Native American parishioners. Its wealth of painted statues, carvings, and frescoes has earned San Xavier the designation "Sistine Chapel of the United States."

Nogales. Many visitors to Tucson take the easy 63-mile drive down I–19 to Mexico's lively border town of Nogales, a good place to shop for souvenirs— everything from stuffed armadillos and cowboy boots to handcrafted tiles and pottery—or to have a good Mexican meal. Most Americans park in one of the many lots on the U.S. side (about $4 a day) and walk across the border.

Old Tucson Studios (201 S. Kinney Rd., tel. 520/883–0100). Built originally as a movie set in the 1940s, this Old West theme park has scheduled gunfights, live shows, rides, restaurants, and shops. It's still an active filming location with a complete sound stage; the *Young Riders* TV series and Sharon Stone's *The Quick and the Dead* were shot here. A fire in April 1995 destroyed much of the park. At press time (summer 1995) the park was closed for reconstruction; call to see if it's reopened.

Organ Pipe Cactus National Monument (visitor center 32 mi southeast of Ajo, off AZ 85, tel. 520/387–6849). The largest gathering spot north of Mexico for the many-armed cousin of the saguaro, Organ Pipe has two scenic loop drives, one 21 miles long, the other 53 miles long, both on winding, graded dirt roads; stop at the visitor center for a map. The latter trail leads to Quitobaquito, a desert oasis with a flowing spring.

Patagonia. Art galleries and boutiques coexist with real Western saloons in this little, tree-lined town some 82 miles south of Tucson, surrounded by rolling hills and choice cattle-grazing land. At the *Patagonia-Sonoita Creek Preserve* (tel. 520/394–2400), 750 acres of riparian habitat are protected along the Patagonia-Sonoita Creek. More than 260 bird species have been sighted here, along with deer, javelina, coatimundi, desert tortoise, snakes, and more.

Pima Air Museum (6000 E. Valencia Rd., tel. 520/574–0462 or 520/574–9658). The dry desert air is kind to old aircraft; they never rust. Come here to see 180 planes representing more than 80 years of U.S. aviation history. Also run by nonprofit Pima Air Museum foundation is the **Titan Missile Museum** (exit 69 off I–19, 25 mi south of Tucson, tel. 520/791–2929), the only one of 54 Titan II sites left intact when the SALT II treaty with the Soviet Union was signed. Visitors can descend into the command post, where a ground crew of four lived, and look at the 114-foot, 165-ton, two-stage liquid-fuel rocket. Now empty, it originally held a nuclear payload with 214 times the explosive power of the bomb that destroyed Hiroshima.

Ramsey Canyon Preserve (90 mi southeast of Tucson, off AZ 92, tel. 520/378–2785). Designated the first U.S. National Natural Landmark, in 1965, this 300-acre preserve with well-marked trails is home to more than 170 species of birds, dozens of species of butterflies, deer, snakes, frogs, and mountain lions.

Sabino Canyon (5900 N. Sabino Canyon Rd., tel. 520/749–2327). Part of Coronado National Forest, but filled with desert flora and fauna, this is a good spot for hiking, picnicking, or enjoying the waterfalls, streams, and natural swimming holes on a hot day. No cars are allowed; a narrated tram ride (45 minutes round-trip) takes you to the top of the canyon. Nighttime tram tours are offered when there's a full moon.

Saguaro National Park. Probably the only national park that has a city in the middle of it—Tucson separates the east section of the park from the west—this one is also unique in the United States as a habitat for the towering saguaro (pronounced *suh-WAR-oh*) cactus. These slow-growing plants—they can take up to 15 years to add one foot and may live more than 200 years—are protected by state and federal laws: Enjoy, but don't disturb them. The 21,000-acre portion on the far west side of town (tel. 520/733–5100) is the more visited one, but it's rarely crowded, and you'll practically have the scenic trails on the 62,000-acre east side (tel. 520/296–8576) to yourself if you go during the week.

Tubac. The military garrison established here in 1752 to protect early Spanish settlers and the peaceful Pima and Tohono O'Odham Indians from Apache raids is the oldest European settlement in Arizona. It was from here that Juan Bautista de Anza led 240 colonists across the desert, an expedition that resulted in the founding of San Francisco in 1776. Today, the little town is a popular art colony with more than 70 galleries, studios, and shops; contact the Tubac Chamber of Commerce (tel. 520/398–2704) for information on the annual *Tubac Festival of the Arts*, held in February. The *Tubac Presidio State Historic Park and Museum* (center of town, tel. 520/398–2252) preserves relics and history of the early colony, and the first 3 miles of the *de Anza National Historic Trail*, along the Santa Cruz River from Tumacacori to Tubac, was dedicated in 1992.

Tumacacori National Monument (50 mi south of Tucson on I–19, tel. 520/398–2341). Around 1800, on the tree-shaded banks of the Santa Cruz River, the Franciscans built the mission of San Jose de Tumacacori. The friars fled in 1848 as a result of fierce Indian raids; legend has it that the silver church bells they buried nearby have never been recovered.

University of Arizona. The original land for this 325-acre university was "donated" by a couple of gamblers and a saloon owner in 1891, but Territorial funds were used to construct the first building, Old Main. Among the many interesting museums on campus are the *Center for Creative Photography* (1030 N. Olive Rd., tel. 520/621–7968), housing one of the world's largest collections of 20th-century photographs; the *Arizona Historical Society's Museum* (949 E. 2nd St., tel. 520/628–5774), with fascinating displays of Arizona history and an excellent historical archive; the *Mineral Museum* (Old Geology Bldg., N. Campus Dr., tel. 520/621–4227), which has an extensive collection of fossils (including a huge dinosaur footprint) and minerals; and the *Grace H. Flandrau Science Center and*

Planetarium (Cherry Ave. and University Blvd., tel. 520/621–4515), where attractions include a 16-inch public telescope, a flashy multimedia show, and an interactive meteor exhibit.

Wineries. The term "Arizona wine country" may sound like an oxymoron, but the soil and atmospheric conditions in the Santa Cruz Valley, southeast of Tucson, are ideal for growing grapes. The growers in the scenic ranching region, all found near where Rtes. 82 and 83 intersect, include the kosher **Santa Cruz Winery** (lower Elgin Rd., Elgin, tel. 520/455–5375), **Sonoita Vineyards** (3 mi southeast of Elgin, tel. 520/455–5893), and **Arizona Vineyards** (2301 Patagonia Hwy., 3 mi north of Nogales on Rte. 82, tel. 520/287–7972). Most of them give tours and tastings from Thursday through Sunday; call ahead for hours.

Restaurants

Tucson's excellent range of restaurants includes everything from low-key, authentic Mexican cafés to upscale resort dining rooms. The best of the upper range include **Janos** (tel. 520/884–9426), serving cutting-edge Southwestern cuisine in an elegant historic adobe, and the **Ventana Room** (tel. 520/299–1771) in the posh Ventana Canyon Resort, where the fine Continental food is matched only by the views of the desert or of Tucson in the distance. The black-and-white art deco interior of **Daniel's** (tel. 520/742–3200) provides a classy setting for the restaurant's nationally recognized northern Italian dishes. At the end of 1994, the Tucson National Golf & Conference Resort opened an upscale restaurant, **The Catalina Grille** (tel. 520/297–2271), that serves innovative Southwestern dishes on its broad stone terrace or in the dark-carpeted dining room. At the more moderately priced **Café Terra Cotta** (tel. 520/577–8100), you can enjoy Southwest-inspired specialties on the outdoor terrace or in a colorful indoor dining room. In a similar price range, **Bocatta** (tel. 520/577–9309) has a good Northern Italian menu, with an emphasis on pasta, and a pretty dining room. Although they are different in cooking style, both the innovative **Café Poca Cosa** (tel. 520/622–6400) and the more traditional **El Charro Café** (tel. 520/622–1922) are good bets for an inexpensive Mexican meal in the downtown area. Sooner or later, all locals head for the Mexican-American enclave of **South Tucson,** where it's hard to go wrong with any of the low-priced places you'll find on Fourth Avenue south of 22nd Street.

Arizona wine country is home to two surprisingly sophisticated but moderately priced restaurants. In tiny Elgin, **Karen's Wine Country Cafe** (tel. 520/455–5282) could be straight out of Sonoma, California, with its pretty country French-style patio and innovative menu featuring salads and pasta dishes—and of course a good selection of wines by the glass. **Er Pastaro** (tel. 520/455–5821), a low-key place, serves every type of pasta imaginable, as well as a nice selection of Italian wine. Hours at both restaurants are limited; call ahead.

Tourist Information

Ajo District Chamber of Commerce (Box 507, Ajo, AZ 85321, tel. 520/387–7742). **Metropolitan Tucson Convention & Visitors Bureau** (130 S. Scott, Tucson, AZ 85701, tel. 520/624–1817). **Patagonia Community Association** (Box

241, Patagonia, AZ 85624, tel. 520/394–2400). **Tubac Chamber of Commerce** (Box 1866, Tubac, AZ 85646, tel. 520/398–2704).

Reservation Services

Arizona Association of Bed & Breakfast Inns (3101 North Central Ave., Suite 560, Phoenix AZ 85012, tel. 602/277–0775). **Bed & Breakfast Inn Arizona-Arizona Accommodations Reservations** (8900 E. Via Linda, Suite 101, Scottsdale, AZ 85258, tel. 602/860–9338 or 800/266–7829, fax 602/860–9338). **Mi Casa Su Casa B&B Reservation Service** (Box 950, Tempe, AZ 85280, tel. 602/990–0682; reservations only 800/456–0682). **Old Pueblo Homestays B&B Reservation Service** (Box 13603, Tucson, AZ 85732, tel. 520/790–0030 or 800/333–9776, fax 520/790–2399). **Premiere Bed & Breakfast Inns of Tucson** (3661 N. Campbell Ave., Box 237, Tucson, AZ 85719, tel. 520/628–1800).

El Presidio Bed & Breakfast Inn

I t's a loyal restoration," says Patti Toci of her Victorian adobe home. "We wanted it just as it was when people lived here in the 1880s." She and her husband, Jerry, labored for 12 years toward that goal and admirably achieved it by 1987, when they opened their bed-and-breakfast.

Listed in the National Register of Historic Places, the Territorial-style home has 21-inch-thick walls made of adobe brick and a 17-foot ceiling with hand-hewn beams in the *zaguan* (center hallway). Polished-oak flooring added during the 1920s and numerous antiques, including a pair of early 18th-century cherrywood corner cases and a stolid grandfather clock, all museum-quality pieces, create a more formal, Victorian atmosphere. The Veranda Room, once the mansion's back porch, is now the dining room. Broad windows look onto a cobblestone courtyard banked with geraniums, snapdragons, and rose-bushes, and are shaded by mature trees—among them Aleppo pine, fig, desert ash, and grapefruit—that attract hummingbirds and cactus wrens. The birds also like to frolic in the three-tiered fountain that Jerry found in Magdalena, Mexico.

Each of the three suites has a different theme. The Victorian Suite, in the main house, has a parlor decorated with white wicker furniture, a kiva fireplace, and a braided rug. French doors line two sides of the room: One pair leads into the zaguan living room, and the other faces a lovely, tree-shaded garden. The Gate House Suite, with a huge blue wicker bed and a private entrance, has the feel of a French country manor. The brick veranda of the Carriage House Suite is topped by a Mexican-tile roof. Inside is a kitchenette with a stocked refrigerator; a living room; a rose-themed bedroom with a pine two-poster bed; and a bath with a countertop made of imported Spanish tile.

Guests enjoy an elaborate breakfast, which varies daily, at a handsome walnut dining table that can expand to seat 10. Among the delightful possibilities are chorizo and eggs on corn tortillas; gingerbread pancakes with fresh strawberry sauce and shirred eggs; or sweet potato waffles with sautéed apples and yogurt with sunflower seeds. Patti's lemon muffins, topped with lemon streusel, are made with lemons picked from the tree outside the window.

297 N. Main Ave., Tucson, AZ 85701, tel. 520/623–6151 or 800/349–6151. 3 suites. TV, phone, bathrobes in each room; kitchen in 2 suites stocked with beverage and fruit, TV in sitting room; privileges at nearby health club. $95–$115; full breakfast. No credit cards. No smoking indoors, no pets; closed some Julys.

The Mine Manager's House Inn

When the Phelps Dodge copper mine closed in 1985, and all the miners packed up and left, everyone assumed Ajo would become a ghost town. Not Martin Jeffries. He and his wife, Faith, began buying up the vacant properties being sold off by the company. Their prize purchase was the empty 1919 mine superintendent's house and its 3 acres of neglected, terraced gardens.

The imposing, 5,000-square foot mansion overlooks the entire town from its site atop the highest hill in Ajo. The Jeffries completely refurbished the solid masonry structure, installed all new wiring, and furnished the rooms with period furniture and art. And on New Year's Day 1988, they opened a bed-and-breakfast.

The public areas include a library/sunroom, a spacious living room, and a formal dining room with a view out over the town. A hot tub in the back is wonderful for soaking tired muscles after a day of desert travel.

Each of the five individually decorated rooms has high ceilings and ceiling fans. The Greenway Suite, also called the "honeymoon suite," is the largest one and boasts a marble bathtub and vanity, an upholstered headboard with flowers and cupids, and pretty floral drapes. The Nautical Room has two queen-size brass beds and a 180° view out over the town; parts of an old schooner, including the steering wheel, are worked into the decor.

In 1990 the Jeffries sold the Mine Manager's House to a French Canadian couple from California, Micheline and Jean Fournier, who built on the B&B's early success and maintained the Jeffries' tradition of comfort and service. Each evening, for example, guests are offered a dish of gourmet English toffee ice cream or peach frozen yogurt.

Breakfasts are served on linens and fine china in the superintendent's light-filled formal dining room. The meal may feature eggs Benedict or Belgian waffles with a raspberry sauce, in addition to coffee, fresh juices, and seasonal fruits.

🏨 *1 Greenway Dr., Ajo, AZ 85321, tel. 520/387–6505 or 800/266–7829, fax 520/387–6508. 2 double rooms with baths, 3 suites. TV and VCR in living room, library, guest coin laundry; outdoor hot tub, barbecue grill, off-street parking, off-site pet boarding. $69–$99; full breakfast. MC, V. No smoking indoors.*

The Peppertrees Bed and Breakfast Inn

Early settlers who came to the Arizona Territory at the turn of the century tried to create pockets of civilization in what was then a dusty desert outpost. Some 80 years later, perhaps in a similar spirit, Marjorie Martin brought antiques from her family home in the English Cotswolds to furnish her 1905 redbrick Victorian. After a careful restoration, she opened the Peppertrees in 1988. The classic residence is two blocks from the main gate of the University of Arizona and near the Fourth Avenue shopping district.

To check into the inn, guests enter the main house. Rooms with 12-foot-high ceilings and pine floors covered with Oriental carpets highlight Marjorie's furnishings, most of which date back to the last century. The mahogany-and-glass bookcase in the living room contains the family's Royal Doulton china.

Penelope's Room has windows on three sides; the one to the south looks out on a mature pomegranate tree and landscaped patio. It's decorated in Victorian style, with a white wrought-iron bed, a frilly rose-patterned comforter, and a 150-year-old mirrored mahogany dresser.

Adjacent to the main house is a 1917 Bungalow-style home with a large, comfortable living room and two bedrooms decorated with mahogany furniture, frilly, patterned comforters, and lace curtains. Behind the main house, across a cozy garden with a splashing Mexican-tile fountain, are two fully equipped guest houses. Each duplex unit, furnished in contemporary style, has two bedrooms upstairs with a shared bath. Downstairs are a half-bath, living room, dining area, full kitchen, and private patio.

A gourmet cook, Marjorie published her *Recipes from Peppertrees Bed and Breakfast Inn.* Breakfast is served buffet-style in the dining room or, on those perfect southern Arizona mornings, outdoors on the patio. There is always fresh fruit and home-baked breads or scones and a main dish such as blue-corn pancakes or savory French toast filled with cream cheese and orange. Special diets can be accommodated with advance notice, and picnic baskets may be ordered for day excursions.

 724 E. University Blvd., Tucson, AZ 85719, tel. 520/622-7167 or 800/348-5763, fax 520/622-5959. 3 double rooms with baths, 2 2-bedroom duplex guest houses. Guest houses have phones, TV, washer/dryers. $78-$150; full breakfast. D, MC, V. No smoking, no pets indoors.

Tanque Verde Ranch

We want to get the guests involved in the desert," says Bob Cote, owner of the Tanque Verde Ranch. "Then they can see the delicate balance of nature here, the fragility of this specialized ecosystem." Viewing the flora and fauna of the Sonoran Desert is just one of the many ways in which guests at this historic lodging, built as a frontier cattle ranch in the 19th century, will find themselves immersed in the experience of the Old West. Many European visitors who'd previously seen cowboys only in the movies come back year after year for the real thing.

The first adobe building erected in Tucson, on land granted by the Spanish government, the ranch dates back to 1868. In this century, it became one of the early guest ranches in Tucson and was devoted exclusively to that purpose for many years. Recently, the 640-acre property once again became a working cattle ranch, with 300 cows and 21 bulls at last count.

More than 100 years of additions to the original small ranch house have resulted in a complex with 60 units, extensive dining areas, and a wide range of recreational facilities. There are some 120 horses to ride and many opportunities to ride them, from the daily morning trot out to a campfire breakfast cookout, to all-day pack trips into the nearby Rincon Mountains. Don't worry if you're a tenderfoot: Riding lessons are included in the room rates. Ranch activities also include daily nature walks with the ranch naturalist and evening lectures. Every Thursday morning at the crack of dawn, the ranch conducts a bird-banding program on the property.

Less nature-oriented activities can be pursued at the ranch's five tennis courts; health club with sauna and whirlpool; shuffleboard, volleyball, and basketball courts; and heated indoor and outdoor swimming pools. Although the spacious rooms are decorated in Southwestern style, with exposed beam ceilings and, in many cases, kiva fireplaces, they're hardly rustic: All have private baths, individually controlled cooling and heating units, and telephones. Nor are meals in the franks 'n' beans mode: The chef since 1971 has built an international reputation for his fine Continental and American cuisine.

🏨 *14301 E. Speedway Blvd., Tucson, AZ 85748, tel. 520/296–6275 or 800/234–3833, fax 520/721–9426. 14 double rooms, 34 deluxe (up to 3 people) rooms, all with baths, 12 suites. Private patios for many rooms; extensive indoor and outdoor recreational facilities and programs. $215–$360, including 3 meals and all recreational activities. AE, D, DC, MC, V. No pets.*

Casa Alegre Bed and Breakfast Inn

When innkeeper Phyllis Florek decided to open a bed-and-breakfast, she searched from Napa Valley to the Caribbean for the right building in the ideal climate. Her choice was a 1915, stuccoed, bungalow-style home near the University of Arizona in Tucson. In 1991, after thoroughly renovating it, she opened her "Happy House."

The home features a volcanic stone fireplace in the living room, hardwood floors, Oriental rugs, dark-wood door frames and cabinets, and a swimming pool in the back garden. The most spacious accommodation is the corner Saguaro Room, with its own fireplace, windows on three sides, a lodgepole-pine bed, and saguaro rib curtain rods. The bed in the Hacienda Room has a headboard originally hand-carved for a Mexican priest and a handsome Mexican wood armoire. In 1994 Phyllis added the 1923 Buchanan House, next door. It has one bath and two bedrooms.

A full breakfast—perhaps hot bread pudding with strawberries or green chili quiche—is served in the dining room or on the covered back patio.

🏠 *316 E. Speedway Blvd., Tucson, AZ 85705, tel. 520/628-1800 or 800/628-5654. 3 double rooms with baths, 1 2-bedroom suite with kitchen. TV with VCR in Arizona Room; pool and hot tub, fireplaces. $80-$95; full breakfast. D, MC, V. No smoking indoors, no pets.*

Casa Tierra Adobe Bed & Breakfast

You won't find a better place to experience the magic of the Sonoran Desert than Tucson's Casa Tierra (Earth House), an environmentally conscious B&B near Saguaro National Monument and the Arizona–Sonora Desert Museum. The last leg of the trip here is via dirt road. Innkeeper Karen Hymer-Thompson reports that guests often arrive asking, "Why don't you get that road paved?" They leave saying, "I'm glad you're a little hard to reach."

The adobe hacienda that Lyle Hymer-Thompson built on the couple's 5 acres couldn't be more suited to the landscape, with its vaulted brick entryways, central courtyard, viga and latilla ceilings, handmade ceramic lights, Mexican furniture, and brightly painted Talavera tiles. Three colorful Southwestern-style guest rooms all have private entrances and patios. A short path leads to an outdoor Jacuzzi ramada (a roofed structure without walls), where guests can watch the sun set or the moon rise. Huge picture windows in the dining room allow them to enjoy Karen's fresh-ground coffee and home-baked goodies while gazing at saguaro cactus and desert critters.

🏠 *11155 W. Calle Pima, Tucson, AZ 85743, tel. 520/578-3058, fax 520/578-3058. 3 double rooms with baths. Microwaves, minifridges in rooms; outdoor Jacuzzi, access to barbecue and coffeemaker. $75-$85; full breakfast. No credit cards. No smoking indoors, no pets; closed June-Aug.*

The Duquesne House Bed and Breakfast

Don't be startled when you enter this gracious, tree-shaded Eden in tiny Patagonia and see a 21-foot-long snake. Innkeeper Regina Medley is an artist who works with textiles; her reptile and other soft sculptures and paintings enliven various parts of her tin-roofed adobe inn, as do the creations of other local artists.

New buttresses and plastered Santa Fe benches have been added to the B&B, built as a boardinghouse for miners more than 90 years ago, and burned adobe bricks replaced the original wood floors, but the 17-inch-thick adobe walls, narrow doors, and lintels are all original. The Western period furniture throughout the house was collected in the Patagonia area. Each of its three high-ceiling guest units has its own private street entrance. The interior bedrooms are windowless and somewhat spare, but this just adds to their Old Southwest feel.

Regina's breakfasts, served buffet style, may be enjoyed in your room, on the flower-filled screen porch, or at the hostess's table in the dining room, part of a Santa Fe-style great room.

🏠 *357 Duquesne St., Box 772, Patagonia, AZ 85624, tel. 520/394-2732. 3 suites. Radios in all rooms, woodburning stove in 2 rooms, ceiling fans. $65; full breakfast. No credit cards. No smoking, no pets.*

Elysian Grove Market

In 1924, Jose Trujillo built his grocery store in Barrio el Hoyo, at the shady, downhill end of this typical Mexican neighborhood. During the 1960s, the stuccoed, Territorial adobe shop was converted to residential use, and in 1993 the B&B opened. (In 1994, this was a location for the film *Boys on the Side*.)

Innkeeper-decorator Debbie LaChapelle lives in one unit, and the other two comprise her Mexican barrio–flavored B&B. Her collection of 18th–20th-century Mexican and American fine art, folk art, and antiques furnishes the inn.

Both suites have sleeping quarters on two levels: in a wine-cellar type area and on the ground floor opening onto the garden—a mix of verbena, lantana, aloe vera, and prickly pear shaded by mature mesquite and tamarisk trees and a chinaberry. The rooms have 12- to-16-foot ceilings with hammered tin (one patched with an old license plate), brown stucco walls, oak floors, and

Mexican tile baths with showers and pull-chain toilets.

Debbie brings Colombian coffee and a Mexican-style breakfast to each room at the hour requested. She also will conduct a walking tour of the historic neighborhood, now gradually being restored.

🏠 *400 W. Simpson, Tucson, AZ 85701, tel. 520/628–1522. 2 2-bedroom suites, 1 with full kitchen. Fireplace, fridge, microwave, phone, radio, and tapes. $65–$75; full breakfast. No credit cards. No pets, no smoking indoors, children discouraged.*

The Guest House Inn

Like virtually every other building in Ajo, this one was built by the Phelps Dodge Corporation; it was designed in high style in 1925 to accommodate executives visiting the copper mine. Abandoned when the mine closed in 1985, the inn was purchased three years later by Norma Walker, who used to work here as a housekeeper.

The four original VIP guest rooms, now remodeled, all have different themes. The Ajo Room features Santa Fe-style decor, while the Old Pueblo Room emphasizes Ajo's Spanish Colonial heritage. The Bisbee Room has twin brass beds and Victorian furnishings, and the Prescott Room boasts a four-poster bed and fittings reminiscent of Arizona's Territorial days.

The B&B's pride is the stately dining room with its formal, 20-foot table where breakfast is served; one specialty is pecan waffles with berries and cream. A longtime Ajo resident, Norma can direct you to all the best places for bird-watching in the area.

🏠 *3 Guesthouse Rd., Ajo, AZ 85321, tel. 520/387–6133. 4 double rooms with baths. Individual heating/cooling controls in rooms, fireplace and TV in common room; patio. $49–$69; full* breakfast. DC, MC, V. No smoking, no pets.

Horizons Bed and Breakfast

With a view spanning 3,500 square miles—"Equal to half the state of Connecticut," says innkeeper Sallie Sperling, who hails from the East Coast—Horizons Bed and Breakfast is aptly named. Sallie and her husband Peter built this luxurious contemporary home in 1991 amid acres of pristine desert in northeast Tucson in the foothills of the Santa Catalina Mountains. Their private road ends at the mouth of the Agua Caliente Canyon, ideal for hiking.

The guest suite, furnished in contemporary Southwestern style with a queen-size bed, enjoys windows on three sides, a private entrance, and a sky-lit, terra-cotta tile private bath; the sitting room features a writing alcove and a private library. Guests have breakfast in the equally striking main house; in addition to fresh coffee, fruit, and juice, they might enjoy baked pancakes with hot lingonberry preserves or Yampa Valley eggs, Sallie's special Western recipe made with cheddar cheese, tortillas, and salsa. Special diets are happily accommodated.

🏠 *5050 N. Indian Horse Trail, Tucson, AZ 85749, tel. 520/749-2955 or 800/723-2955, fax 520/749-8876. 1 suite. TV, VCR, phone, fresh flowers, terry robes, daily fruit basket in suite; pool, telescope. $110; full breakfast. No credit cards. No smoking, no pets.*

La Posada del Valle

Built as an elegant residence in 1929 by Southwestern architect Josias T. Joesler, who combined Santa Fe Territorial with Spanish Colonial elements to create his signature style, La Posada del Valle (Inn of the Valley) sits on the edge of a quiet neighborhood near the university. This classic adobe is surrounded by walled, landscaped flower gardens and an abundance of orange trees. Innkeepers Karin and Tom Dennen, and their daughter Claudia, are originally from South Africa.

The high-ceiling living room is dappled with sunlight; a tall white bookcase, filled with books on Southwestern history, art, and culture, lines one wall. Afternoon tea is served here, in front of the copper-hooded adobe fireplace. The dining room, where guests enjoy a full breakfast, has a picture window facing north to the Santa Catalina Mountains.

Each of the five guest rooms is named after a famous woman of the Roaring Twenties: Karen Blixen, Isadora, Sophie, Claudette, and Pola. Decor and furnishings successfully re-create the ambience of the period.

🏠 *1640 N. Campbell Ave., Tucson, AZ 85719, tel. 520/795-3840. 4 double rooms with baths, 1 cottage. Each room has private entrance, 2 have phones, TV in living room and cottage; Tucson Racquet Club privileges available. $90–$125; full breakfast. MC, V. No smoking, no pets.*

The Little House Bed and Breakfast

Opened in early 1986, the Little House was the only bed-and-breakfast in Santa Cruz County. Even with some recent local competition, it continues to draw many of the birders who come for the abundant avian activity in the nearby Patagonia-Sonoita Creek Sanctuary. Don and Doris Wenig, retired schoolteachers from Tucson, bought two old adobes in 1980 and reconstructed them, turning the larger into their home and the smaller into guest rooms.

Shaded by tall trees, the Little House has two rooms, each with a corner fireplace and private patio. Both are furnished in contemporary Southwestern style with original local art on the walls. A lush courtyard separates these two units from the innkeepers' tin-roofed home.

Breakfast is served on the porch overlooking the garden or in the dining room. Don grinds coffee beans for the freshest brew and uses eggs laid by local hens. The breads and sausages are homemade and served with fresh juice or in-season fruits.

🏠 *341 Sonoita Ave., Patagonia, AZ 85624, tel. 520/394-2493. 2 double rooms with baths. Audiocassette and CD players in rooms, Southwestern library. $55-$70, full breakfast. No credit cards. No smoking, no pets.*

Quail's Vista Bed and Breakfast

Built in 1987 on the brow of a hill looking out on the rugged west face of the Santa Catalina Mountains, Quail's Vista enjoys one of the most spectacular views in southern Arizona. Among the other nice features of this Santa Fe-style solar adobe B&B are a cactus garden, a flagstone terrace where families of quail gather, and a redwood deck. Innkeeper Barbara Jones, a licensed tour guide, can direct guests to all the best places to see in Tucson.

Inside the house, peeled spruce columns support the beamed ceiling and low, rounded walls; brick floors, a kiva fireplace, Native American pottery, Mexican blankets, and local artworks in the public areas are also in keeping with the Southwestern theme. Guest rooms feature Saltillo-tile floors, white-oak closets, and bright, Mexican-tile baths. Grandma's Room has a Victorian theme, with an antique queen-size bed and framed heirloom portraits. The largest room, the Queen Master Suite,

offers a lodgepole bed, a kiva fireplace, and a spectacular view of the mountains. Breakfast is a Continental buffet of cold cereals, pastries, and coffee.

🏠 *826 E. Palisades Dr., Tucson, AZ 85737, tel. 520/297-5980. 1 double room with bath, 2 doubles share bath. TV, VCR, CD player in living room; outdoor hot tub, nearby country club privileges (extra). $65-$85; Continental breakfast. No credit cards. No smoking indoors, no pets.*

Ramsey Canyon Inn

Tucked into a scenic, tree-filled gorge in the Huachuca Mountains, 10 miles south of Sierra Vista, this charming bed-and-breakfast adjoins the Mile Hi/Ramsey Canyon Preserve run by the Nature Conservancy. It's a haven for birdwatchers and, at 5,400 feet, one of the most temperate spots in the nation: The annual average high is 75°; the average low is 50°.

The front section of the Ramsey Canyon Inn was built of native stone in 1963. The 1988 addition at the back of the house includes six guest rooms, named by innkeeper Shirlene DeSantis after her favorite hummingbirds. These accommodations, furnished in country Victorian style, enjoy the soothing ripple of a year-round stream, as do two separate housekeeping cottages.

The dining room, a few steps up from the rustic living room, has a picture window facing a hummingbird feeder. As guests dine on stuffed French toast or blue corn pancakes served with jam from the inn's own orchard, they can watch the tiny birds flitting about.

🏠 *31 Ramsey Canyon Rd., Hereford, AZ 85615, tel. 520/378-3010. 6 double rooms with baths, 2 housekeeping cottages. Fireplace in living room, hummingbird gift shop. $90-$105; full breakfast, evening dessert. No credit cards. Smoking on patio only, no pets.*

Rimrock West Hacienda

Scenery—a panoramic view of Tucson—and solitude—20 acres of desert—are what innkeeper Mae Robbins and her husband Val provide for guests. Bobcats, coyote, javelina, and quail are frequent visitors to their 1960s-era adobe ranch house.

The beamed ceiling of the comfortable living room spans white-painted adobe walls, thick white carpeting, over-stuffed couches, and an adobe fireplace burning massive pecan logs (in winter). The art is all by Mae, Val, or their artist-son Christopher, whose studio is next door.

Both the queen room and the twin room have thick white Berber carpeting, modern pastel Southwestern decor, and mountain views. They open onto a sunny brick courtyard land-scaped with oleander, aloe vera, and a splashing Mexican fountain. A kidney-shaped pool occupies its own walled and landscaped enclosure.

Breakfast is usually served on the patio's cowhide Mexican tables and chairs. Mae offers a choice of cereals, eggs, pancakes, and fruit with her specialty hot muffins.

🏠 *3450 N. Drake Pl., Tucson, AZ 85749, tel. 520/749-8774. 2 double rooms with baths, 1 cottage with kitchen. Ceiling fans, TV, air-conditioning; pool. $85–$130; full breakfast. No credit cards. No smoking, no pets, no children under 16.*

The Triangle L Ranch Bed & Breakfast

Buffalo Bill is said to have been a regular visitor to this cattle and sheep ranch, homesteaded in the 1890s. The original 2,700 acres have been reduced to 80, but innkeepers Tom and Margot Beeston got the best part of the land, at a temperate elevation of 4,500 feet and with the largest oak trees in Oracle—a town 35 miles north of Tucson and now best known as home to Biosphere 2.

Guest accommodations are in four private cottages, dating from the 1880s to the 1920s and restored and furnished with period antiques. The Guest House is an ivy-covered adobe with a screened sleeping porch shaded by giant oaks. The three-bedroom Hill House has a front deck and views of the Santa Catalina Mountains as well as wrought-iron beds, a fully equipped kitchen, and a bath with a claw-foot tub and a shower.

Activity is centered in the main ranch house. Breakfast is prepared in a large, turn-of-the-century kitchen and includes eggs from the ranch hens. The 15-foot table in the formal dining room and the matching sideboard are early 19th-century pieces that Margot inherited from her great grandmother.

🏠 *Box 900, Oracle, AZ 85623, tel. 520/896-2804. 4 cottages. Kitchens in 2 cottages, fireplace in 1 cottage. $80–$95; full breakfast. D, MC, V. No smoking indoors, no pets.*

Southeastern Arizona
Cochise and Graham Counties

Cochise County. The name alone evokes every dime-novel image of the Wild West—ferocious Indian wars, vast land grants, huge mineral stakes, and savage shoot-'em-ups. But it all really happened here in southeastern Arizona, and in a setting little different from the one visitors see today. Abandoned mining towns and sleepy Western hamlets dot a lonely landscape of rugged rock formations, deep pine forests, dense mountain ranges, and scrubby desert grasslands.

South of Sierra Vista, just above the Mexican border, a stone marker commemorates the spot where the first Europeans set foot in what is now the United States. In 1540, 80 years before the Pilgrims landed at Plymouth Rock, Spanish conquistador Don Francisco Vásquez de Coronado led one of Spain's largest expeditions from Mexico along the fertile San Pedro River valley, where the little towns of Benson and St. David are found today. They had come north to seek the legendary Seven Cities of Cibola, Indian pueblos rumored to have doors of polished turquoise and streets of solid gold.

But the real wealth of the region lay in its rich veins of copper and silver, not tapped until more than 300 years after the Spanish marched on in disappointment. Then all hell broke loose. Fortune seekers who rushed to the region to get in on a sure thing were met by the Chiracahua Apaches, led by Cochise and Geronimo; from rugged mountain hideaways, the Indian warriors fought off encroaching settlers and the U.S. cavalry sent to protect them. Prospector Ed Scheifflin, who struck a huge silver lode in 1877, had been cautioned not to prospect in the desert because "all you'll find out there is your tombstone"—thus the name he gave to his first mining claim and the settlement that grew up around it, a tongue-in-cheek "I told you so" to his detractors.

*Tombstone's boom days were over by the end of the century,
when a high water table prevented further mining there,
though "the town too tough to die"—once the county seat and
larger than San Francisco—survived both a major fire and
the loss of its main source of revenue. The nearby mountain
town of Bisbee, which found its fortune in copper, not silver,
fared much better; its mines didn't close until 1975.*

*Today the area is mining the new lode of tourism, and the
bed-and-breakfast inns springing up in Cochise County
communities, especially Bisbee, are a good barometer of the
degree to which they've hit pay dirt. Many of the places here
are not luxurious, but most are very comfortable—and where
else can you fulfill your frontier fantasies by staying in a
former four-room schoolhouse, a miner's boardinghouse, or a
branch of the county jail?*

Places to Go, Sights to See

Amerind Foundation (Dragoon, exit 318 off I-10, tel. 520/586–3666). Hidden in
the oaks and boulders of Texas Canyon is a striking Spanish-style museum
devoted to Native American culture, founded in 1937 by amateur archaeologist
William Fulton, whose collection of mostly Southwestern art is housed in the
adjacent Fulton-Hayden Memorial Art Gallery. The setting, the house, and the
quality of the displays make this well worth a short detour.

Bisbee. Dominated for many years by the Phelps Dodge Corporation, Bisbee
went into decline when its last mine closed in 1975, but was revitalized in the
1980s as an artists' community. At the edge of town, visitors can still see the huge
hole left by the *Lavender Pit Mine* and descend for a fascinating tour of the
Copper Queen Mine (1 Dart Rd., tel. 520/432–2071). Across the street, housed in
the former Phelps Dodge general office, the *Mining and Historical Museum*
(Queens Plaza, tel. 520/432–7071) houses photographs and artifacts from the
town's mining heyday. Behind the museum is the venerable *Copper Queen Hotel,*
built a century ago (*see* review, *below*), and, adjacent to it, *Brewery Gulch,* where
beer used to flow down the street and into the gutter. Bisbee's *Main Street* is
lined with appealing crafts shops, boutiques, and restaurants, many of them in
well-preserved turn-of-the-century brick buildings.

Chiracahua National Monument (Dos Cabezas Route, near intersection of U.S.
666 and AZ 181, tel. 520/824–3560). Here vast outcroppings of volcanic rock worn
by erosion into pinnacles and spires are set in a forest where autumn and spring
occur at the same time. During the last century, the beautiful but rugged
landscape was the home territory of Chief Cochise and his Chiracahua Apache

tribe, who dubbed it "Land of the Standing-Up Rocks." In 1862, U.S. troops built a fort designed to help protect stage routes from attacks by the Apache. On AZ 186, just north of Chiracahua National Monument, *Fort Bowie National Historical Site* (tel. 520/847–2500) and the *Butterfield Stage Stop* are testaments to this historical period.

Douglas. Founded in 1902 by Dr. James Douglas to serve as the copper smelting center for the mines in nearby Bisbee, Douglas doesn't seem to have changed much since the 1950s; it's often used as a location for Hollywood films set in even earlier times. There's not much yet to see inside, but the *Douglas/Williams House Museum* (10001 D Ave., tel. 520/364–7379), opened in 1991 by the Arizona Historical Society, is the 1909 home of "Rawhide" Jimmy Douglas, son of the man for whom the town is named. "Texas" John Slaughter, sheriff of Cochise County from 1886 to 1890 and U.S. marshal, retired to *Slaughter Ranch/San Bernardino Land Grant* (17 mi east of Douglas, tel. 520/558–2474) after his law enforcement adventures in Tombstone and Bisbee were over. A visit to the preserved ranch and a videotape of Slaughter's life and times provide a glimpse of the wild and woolly Old West. Neither Douglas nor *Agua Prieta*, just across the way in Mexico, fits the stereotype of border towns. It's an easy crossing to and from Agua Prieta, a clean and pleasant place to shop for well-priced Mexican goods; haggling is not generally practiced here.

Ghost Towns. A number of the smaller mining communities of Cochise County died when their veins of ore ran out, and their adobe buildings gradually melted back into the desert under the summer monsoons. Some of what are termed ghost towns in the area are only heaps of rubble, but others give strong evidence of better days. At *Gleeson*, marked by a turnoff just east of Tombstone on AZ 80, some building ruins and an old cemetery can still be seen. A few holdouts still live in the town of *Dos Cabezas*, 15 miles southeast of Willcox, enough to keep the post office open; the 1885 Wells Fargo station still stands. A tunnel through the mountaintop connects the eastern and western halves of the abandoned town of *Hilltop*, farther southeast of Willcox. The gold camp of *Pearce*, 1 mile off Rte. 191, 29 miles south of Willcox, also has a post office and one viable store; the ruins of the mill, the mine, and many old adobes are very much in evidence. There is one resident left in the former mining town of *Courtland*, 21 miles north of Douglas on Rte. 191, but he does not encourage sightseers. Six miles northwest of Portal in the Chiracahua Mountains, *Paradise* was active in the 1900s, and a few old-timers still live here. Look for the old town jail among the ruined buildings.

Texas Canyon (63 mi east of Tucson off I–10). You don't have to get off the freeway to see Texas Canyon, a striking gathering of huge boulders that appear to be delicately balanced against each other, but a rest area here with bathrooms and picnic tables is a good place to stop for lunch.

Tombstone. Every Sunday and sometimes on Saturday, the fatal 1881 gunfight between Wyatt Earp and Doc Holliday and the Clanton gang is reenacted by professional stuntmen on *Allen Street*, the main tourist drag of Tombstone. You can see the graves of some of the losing gunmen at the *Boot Hill Graveyard* at the northwestern corner of town, facing U.S. 80. At the *OK Corral* (Allen St., bet. 3rd and 4th Sts., tel. 520/457–3456), the site of the shoot-out, a recorded voice-over details the infamous event; the history of the entire town is dramatically narrated by Vincent Price at the adjoining *Historama*. You can step back into time at the *Bird Cage Theater* (6th and Allen Sts., tel. 520/457–3421), where a honky-tonk piano once played and performers such as Lillian Russell trod the creaky boards; and at the beautiful mahogany bar of the *Crystal Palace* (Allen and 5th Sts., tel. 520/457–3611). For the least touristy look at the town's history, visit *Tombstone Courthouse State Historic Park* (Toughnut and 3rd Sts., tel. 520/457–3311); the courthouse, built in 1882, is filled with fascinating artifacts of the town in the days when it was the seat of Cochise County.

Willcox, once the Cattle Capital of the country, is also the hometown of cowboy singer and actor Rex Allen, whose life and times are detailed at the *Rex Allen Arizona Cowboy Museum* (155 N. Railroad Ave., tel. 520/284–4583). Also in town is the *Museum of the Southwest* (1550 N. Circle Rd., tel. 520/384–2272), focusing on rancher and Native American life in the late 1880s and early 1900s; its Cowboy Hall of Fame salutes the Arizona cattlemen. Adjacent to the museum, *Stout's Cider Mill* (tel. 520/384–2272) is a good place to pick up some dessert for the road; with an excellent climate for growing apples at an elevation of 4,167 feet, Willcox is now the apple pie center of Arizona.

Restaurants

As Bisbee continues to be discovered by visitors, dining quality and options are steadily improving. In early 1993, a chef from Phoenix's famous Arizona Biltmore Hotel opened the excellent **Cafe Roka** (tel. 520/432–5153). The small Northern Italian-style menu in this stylish restaurant emphasizes pastas; portions are generous and the entrée price ($9.50–$14) includes soup, salad, and a palate-cleansing sorbet. Also reasonably priced, **Stenzel's** (tel. 520/432–7611), set in a wooden cabin, is known for its seafood, but its meats and pastas are well prepared too. Tombstone's restaurants are geared for the eat-and-run, modest-budget tourist trade. The bustling **Lucky Cuss** (tel. 520/457–3561) is renowned for its mesquite barbecued ribs, homemade soups, and chili. At the **Nellie Cashman Restaurant and Pie Salon** (tel. 520/457–3950)—the oldest restaurant in Tombstone, opened in 1882—the menu is basic American with a variety of burgers, hot and cold sandwiches, steaks, fried chicken, and some Mexican entrées; there are often lines to get in.

Tourist Information

Cochise County Tourist & Visitor Center (77 Calle Portal, Suite A-140, Sierra Vista, AZ 85635, tel. 520/458–6940 or 800/288–3861). **Douglas Chamber of Commerce** (1125 Pan American Way, Douglas, AZ 85607, tel. 520/364–2477). **Graham County Chamber of Commerce** (1111 Thatcher Blvd., Safford, AZ 85546, tel. 520/428–2511). **Greater Bisbee Chamber of Commerce** (7 Naco Rd., Bisbee, AZ 85603, tel. 520/432–5421). **Sierra Vista Area Chamber of Commerce** (77 Calle Portal, Suite A-140, Sierra Vista, AZ 85635, tel. 520/458–6940). **Tombstone Tourism Association** (Box 917, 5 Fifth St., Tombstone, AZ 85638, tel. 520/457–3335 or 520/457–2211). **Willcox Chamber of Commerce & Agriculture** (1500 Circle I Rd., Willcox, AZ 85643, tel. 520/384–2272).

Reservation Services

Arizona Association of Bed and Breakfast Inns (3101 N. Central Ave., Suite 560, Phoenix, AZ 85012, tel. 602/277–0775). **Bed & Breakfast Inn Arizona-Arizona Accommodations Reservations** (8900 E. Via Linda, Suite 101, Scottsdale, AZ 85258, tel. 602/860–9338 or 800/266–7829, fax 602/860–9338). **Mi Casa Su Casa B&B Reservation Service** (Box 950, Tempe, AZ 85280, tel. 602/990–0682; reservations 800/456–0682).

The Clawson House

The Clawson House sits regally atop Castle Rock, the craggy buttress of Tombstone Canyon, and surveys Old Bisbee. Once the home of S. W. Clawson, the superintendent of the Copper Queen Mine, it was built in 1895 on the only flat acre in town, an executive fortress overlooking its fiefdom.

In 1988, Californians Wally Kuehl and Jim Grosskopf purchased the proud old redwood structure and spent two years restoring and furnishing it with the art and antiques they had collected during the previous 30 years. Many of the fittings are original to the house, including the etched Italian crystal windows, glass French doors, creaky oak floors, and crystal chandeliers. The Oriental carpets in the living room, the fireplace in the grand parlor, and the white-paneled china cabinet in the formal dining room all reflect the fussy glory of the period, as do the stuffed animal heads, mounted horns, ceramics, and other assorted collectibles that fill practically every inch of surface. Nor are the walls left bare: Both public areas and guest rooms are lined with Currier & Ives prints, framed battle scenes, landscapes, and portraits of long-lost Victorians.

But if you tire of Victorian clutter, all you need do is step out to the sunporch for the world to open up. To the south you can look out over the once-wild and bawdy Brewery Gulch, past the raw, gaping, Lavender Pit Mine to the silhouette of the San José Mountains in northern Mexico on the distant horizon. To the north, the eye follows Tombstone Canyon, lined with 19th-century homes and the occasional giant cottonwood trees, to the crest of the Mule Mountains.

Upstairs, two spacious, well-lighted rooms share a bath that still has the original floor tiles and claw-foot tub. The downstairs bedroom has a 6-foot mahogany bedstead with mirrored mahogany vanity to match, a ruby-domed gas chandelier converted to electricity, and a standing lamp with a tasseled, red velvet shade.

Jim's elaborate breakfasts are served in what was originally the water tower, now a cozy dining nook attached to the modern kitchen. A fresh fruit compote with lemon yogurt might be followed by home-baked zucchini/pineapple bread and Swiss cheese and chili quiche, still hot from the oven.

116 Clawson Ave., Box 454, Bisbee, AZ 85603, tel. 520/432-5237 or 800/467-5237. 1 double room with bath, 2 doubles share bath. Cable TV, use of house phone; off-street parking. $65–$75; full breakfast. AE, D, MC, V. Smoking in designated areas only, no pets.

Olney House
Bed & Breakfast

George Olney was a sheriff of Graham County in the Wild West days of the 1870s. Unable to budget a salary, the county fathers agreed to pay him $2.50 for every arrest. Within two years he had amassed $30,000. Much of these earnings were spent on this classic, two-story example of Western Colonial Revival, completed in 1890. From the bay windows on the second floor, with a 180-degree view of Safford and the verdant Gila River Valley, Sheriff Olney could look for local desperados.

In 1988 the National Park Service announced that 20 Safford buildings had qualified for listing in the National Register of Historic Places: the 1920 Arizona Bank, the 1920 Southern Pacific Railroad Depot, a 1915 schoolhouse, a 1920 hotel, and 16 private residences. The oldest of these was the Olney House.

Innkeepers Patrick and Carole Mahoney, from San Francisco, spent four years renovating the redbrick, 14-room mansion. In 1992 they opened it as Graham County's first B&B. The home boasts 12-foot ceilings (now with circulating fans); five fireplaces with unusual, ceramic-tile detailing; polished oak and maple floors; and lots of elegant wood paneling. The bright corner dining room fills with morning light from three wide, seven-foot windows. Many of the furnishings are treasures brought back by the Mahoneys from travels in Southeast Asia. Upstairs there are three corner bedrooms.

A huge pecan tree shades two cottages in the back. Other trees on the landscaped corner lot include willows, cottonwood, Italian and Arizona cyprus, native pine, ash, and paloverdes. Each year the Mahoneys harvest fresh fruit from their apple, plum, and peach trees to make jams.

The breakfast coffee beans, ground fresh daily, are from Graffeo in San Francisco. The dill and cilantro in the omelettes and potatoes are picked from the garden. Guests have a choice of muesli with yogurt, honey, and fruit; oatmeal with pecans, wheat germ, honey, and fruit; or a cheese omelette spiced with roasted New Mexico chilies (mild, medium, or hot).

🏨 *1104 Central Ave., Safford, AZ 85546, tel. 520/428–5118 or 800/814–5118. 3 double rooms share bath, 2 cottages. TV, cable, music, fireplace in living room, spa. $70; full breakfast. MC, V. No smoking indoors, no pets.*

School House Inn Bed & Breakfast

The two-story brick Garfield School, in the Tombstone Canyon neighborhood on Bisbee's west side, was built in 1918 to educate children in grades 1 through 4. The original four large classrooms, one for each grade, were divided into apartments in the 1930s and used as a nursing home in the 1970s. Abandoned by 1981, the building was refurbished and converted to a B&B in 1989.

Like most schools of the era, this one has solid masonry walls, maple floors, and high ceilings. The large dining room downstairs is carpeted; one corner is a family room with a couch and easy chairs positioned around a television set.

Current proprietors Marc and Shirl Negus took the built-in-schoolhouse theme and ran with it. Depending on how you feel about your school days, the guest rooms, all on the second floor, may strike horror into your heart or fill you with fond memories. Here's your chance to sleep, with impunity, in the Principal's Office, the Library, the Music Room, or the History Room, among others; just pick the subject you found the most soporific. Oh yes, and a cast-iron desk hangs over the stairwell.

The spacious accommodations are country comfortable, with flowery quilted comforters, dark-wood furniture, lace curtains, and stenciled wall borders; some have writing desks, wall-to-wall carpeting, or area rugs on the maplewood floors. Those at the front of the building provide views of upper Tombstone Canyon and the Mule Mountains. All rooms offer comfortable seating areas for reading and relaxing. In the Arithmetic Suite, old math books and flashcards are available to test your skill with numbers.

When the weather is fine, guests can enjoy breakfast—pancakes, say, or a crustless green chili quiche served with walnut bran muffins—on the outdoor patio, shaded by a magnificent oak tree; birds of all kinds like to splash in the patio's gurgling fountain, and hummingbirds dart to several overhead feeders. Just below the inn, there's a large public park with volleyball and basketball courts.

▦ *Box 32, 818 Tombstone Canyon, Bisbee, AZ 85603, tel. 520/432–2996 or 800/537–4333. 6 double rooms with baths, 3 2-bedroom suites. Library; barbecue, off-street parking. $45–$65; full breakfast. AE, D, DC, MC, V. No smoking, no children under 14, no pets.*

The Bisbee Grand Hotel

This 1906, two-story rooming house for copper miners burned down in 1908 and had to be rebuilt. In 1986, an antiques dealer from Texas transformed it into a flamboyant, Old West–Victorian hotel. Bill Thomas and his late wife Gail later purchased it and opened it as a B&B in July of 1989.

Today, with its broad staircase, skylight, balcony overlooking Main Street, ornate chandeliers, red carpets, and red-flocked wallpaper, it recalls nothing so much as a historic bordello; the high-ceiling rooms heighten that impression. The Garden Suite is filled with a forest of faux plants, a trickling fountain, sinful red carpeting, and a six-foot walnut bed suitable for Adam and Eve. In the red-ceiling Oriental Room lined with black Cantonese wallpaper, the focus is on the ornate, 19th-century, carved teak Chinese wedding bed.

A full breakfast, featuring custom-blended Bisbee Grand Coffee, is served in the lobby, on the landing, or outside on the balcony.

▥ *61 Main St., Box 825, Bisbee, AZ 85603, tel. 520/432–5900 or 800/421–1909. 4 double rooms with baths, 4 doubles share 3 baths, 3 suites. Ceiling fans, sinks (in all but 1 room), claw-foot tubs in suites, house phone; off-street parking. $50–$90; full breakfast. AE, D, MC, V. No smoking, no pets.*

Buford House B&B

Built in the 1880s by George Buford, a wealthy mine owner, this modest Territorial-style adobe has seen some of Tombstone's rowdiest days. It was home to two local sheriffs and to the last stagecoach driver in Arizona.

Antiques shop owner and White House alumnae Brenda Reger renovated the house in 1990 to create five attractive themed guest rooms. The spacious downstairs Garden Room, the only one with a private entrance and fireplace, boasts an original sunken tiled tub.

Breakfast may be enjoyed in the dining room or on the veranda, overlooking the garden; one of Brenda's specialties is a rich apple French toast.

▥ *113 E. Safford St., Box 98, Tombstone, AZ 85638, tel. 520/457–3969 or 800/263–6762. 1 double room with bath, 1 twin with bath, 3 doubles share bath. Sinks in each room; barbecue. $65–$95; full breakfast. No credit cards. No smoking indoors, no children under 4, no pets.*

Copper Queen Hotel

Many consider the Copper Queen to be the only place to stay in Bisbee. Built by the Copper Queen Mining Company (which later became Phelps Dodge) in 1902, the imposing five-story brick hotel was once *the* gathering spot for politicians, mining officials, and celebrities, among them John Wayne, Teddy Roosevelt, and General "Black Jack" Pershing. More recently, it's hosted Hollywood types who've discovered Bisbee as a Wild West TV and movie location.

The rooms all have high ceilings with circulating fans, tall windows, and roomy private baths. Some are tiny, however, and the walls are thin. A modernization program is now restoring them to their original grandeur, one by one.

The white-pillared Copper Queen Dining Room, just off the lobby, serves three meals a day in an atmosphere of faded period luxury. The Copper Queen Saloon recaptures the days of World War I, when copper prices were high and Bisbee was booming.

▥ *11 Howell Ave., Drawer CQ, Bisbee, AZ 85603, tel. 520/432–2216 or 800/247–5829. 45 double rooms with baths. Telephones, radios, and color TVs in rooms, non-smoking rooms* *available, restaurant, bar; pool; gift shop. $72–$100; breakfast not included. AE, D, MC, V.*

Grapevine Canyon Ranch

You expect Jack Palance to gallop up to the gates of this guest ranch in the Dragoon Mountains, about 80 miles southeast of Tucson, and take you out to round up some dogies. You will have the chance to watch—and, in some cases, take part in—real cowboy activities at the working cattle ranch next door. This is the place to come if you've ever had fantasies of riding off into the sunset: Horses for all levels of experience are on hand. There are also lots of hiking trails on quintessential Western terrain, and the ranch is a good base from which to explore Douglas, Tombstone, Bisbee, and Chiracahua National Monument.

Accommodations, located in either cabins, casitas, or a lodge house, vary: Some are rather plain, while others have striking contemporary Southwestern furnishings. All have spacious decks and porches. Three hearty meals are served buffet style in the rustic dining room, where a fire blazes on cool evenings.

🏨 *Box 302, Pearce, AZ 85625, tel. 520/826–3185, fax 520/826–3636. 3 2-person cabins, 2 casitas for up to 3 people, 4 casitas for up to 5 people, 3-bedroom lodge for up to 9 people. Pool, hot tub, games room, TV/video room, gift shop, unscheduled live entertainment. $150–$170 per person; 3 meals included. AE, D, MC, V. No pets.*

The Judge Ross House

Bonnie and Jim Douglas renovated this two-story 1908 redbrick house in Warren, a suburb south of Bisbee where mining executives built homes at the turn of the century. The Douglases filled their homey B&B to the brim with art, knickknacks, and fine pieces from their lifelong collection of antiques.

Two guest rooms upstairs, which share a bath, are furnished in fussy Victorian style, with flowered quilts and patterned wallpaper. The larger downstairs room has a private bath and a claw-foot bathtub that sits almost in the middle of the bedroom.

Guests can read in the family room, stocked with books and magazines, or watch the TV and videos. Bonnie makes sure there are candies and refreshments readily available, and she keeps the place decked out with fresh flowers. Breakfast, which might include eggs Benedict or Dutch pancakes stuffed with baked apples, is served either in the formal dining room, on the upstairs sunporch, or outside on the tree-shaded patio.

🏨 *605 Shattuck St., Bisbee, AZ 85603, tel. 520/432–4120 or 520/432–5597. 1 double room with bath, 2 doubles share bath. Garden. $60–$65; full breakfast. MC, V. No smoking, no pets.*

Kelly's Whistlestop Bed and Breakfast

If you're coming from Tucson, you'll drive past the dramatic boulders of Texas Canyon to reach this bed-and-breakfast in Dragoon, a small community in northern Cochise County near the ruins of the 19th-century Butterfield Overland Stage Station. The road to the inn, which passes the Amerind Foundation archaeological museum, soon rises to high desert rangeland, where Kelly's Whistlestop sits on 4 acres at an elevation of 4,600 feet. The name of this rammed-earth solar structure, with walls 2 feet thick, alludes to proprietors Jim and Katy Kelly and the Southern Pacific Railroad, which runs nearby.

The guest house is a separate, 2-bedroom, rammed-earth unit with a cozy kitchen-sitting area heated by an antique woodstove.

A homemade breakfast is served in the main house dining room: perhaps sourdough pancakes, Irish scones, or breakfast burritos.

▦ *Box 236, Dragoon, AZ 85609, tel. 520/586-7515. 2 double rooms share bath. Refrigerator, coffeemaker, electric skillet, and sink in shared sitting room; sundeck, barbecue grill, horse corral. $45-$55; full breakfast. No credit cards. No smoking indoors, pets permitted with advance notice.*

Main Street Inn

A place with a history of hospitality, the Main Street Inn was built as a hotel in 1888 and later served as a boarding-house for copper miners. More than a century later, Wally Kuehl and Jim Grosskopf, who also own the Clawson House (*see above*), renovated the building and welcomed the public to it again.

All eight rooms are on the second floor, as are a living room, TV room, kitchen, and glassed-in back porch. The somewhat creaky wooden floor is covered with wall-to-wall carpeting. The high-ceiling rooms are done in Southwestern style; some have skylights and exposed brick walls, and those facing Main Street feature distinctive bay windows.

A buffet Continental breakfast is prepared up at the Clawson House each morning. Jim brings down muffins and breads fresh out of the oven, to be enjoyed with juice and coffee at the inn.

▦ *26 Main St., Box 454, Bisbee, AZ 85603, tel. 520/432-5237 or 800/467-5237. 3 double rooms share 2 baths, 4 doubles share 2 baths, 1 2-bedroom suite. House phone; off-street parking. $45-$65; Continental breakfast. AE,* D, MC, V. *Smoking in designated areas only, no pets.*

The OK Street Jailhouse

If the narrow building at No. 9 OK Street, one block from Bisbee's Brewery Gulch, looks formidable, that's because it was built in 1904 as the downtown branch of the Cochise County Jail. The first story is faced with stone blocks, the second with brick; the walls and floors are of thick, poured concrete, and the windows are barred with solid iron grilles. It took a clever entrepreneur to turn the place into a two-story suite.

The downstairs jailer's office is now the small entry area. The drunk tank, framed by floor-to-ceiling cell bars, houses a small modern kitchen, a half bath, and a contemporary-style living room with a couch that folds out into a queen bed. Upstairs, in the heavily barred cell once used for serious offenders, is a bedroom with a queen bed, small sitting area, and modern bathroom with shower and Jacuzzi tub. Guests have the entire building to themselves for the duration of their self-imposed sentence; advance arrangements are made to pick up the key from managers Reg and Doris Turner.

▦ *9 OK St., Box 1152, Bisbee, AZ 85603, tel. 520/432-7435, 800/821-0678 (message phone), fax 520/432-7434. 1 duplex suite. Telephone, TV. $100 (2 nights $150, 3 nights $200, 7 nights $350); no breakfast. MC, V. Pets accepted with advance notice only.*

Priscilla's Bed & Breakfast

At the corner of Safford and Third streets in Tombstone, behind a neat, pale green picket fence, stands a wooden Victorian home built in 1904. The architecture is restrained: a peaked roof, bay window, yellow-pillared front porch, simple board-and-batten sides.

Admiring the home's quiet New England charms, you might easily forget that you're two blocks from the site of the infamous shoot-out at the OK Corral. (Okay, the house was built 23 years later, but Tombstone still glories in its most notorious event.)

The building has been lovingly restored by innkeeper Barbara Gray who opened the B&B in 1992 and named it after her mother.

The three guest rooms all have sinks but share one bathroom. The decor is country Victorian, with double beds, floral patterns, and white lace curtains.

Breakfast, usually bacon and eggs or ham and eggs with fresh fruit, is eaten at the round, lace-covered dining room table. Sometimes Barbara bakes a loaf of fresh bread and serves it with her homemade jam.

🏨 *101 N. Third St., Tombstone, AZ 85638, tel. 520/457–3844. 3 double rooms share bath. Guest telephone. $55; full breakfast. No credit cards. Smoking in designated areas only.*

Tombstone Boarding House

Those who like the intimacy of a B&B but feel a little odd about staying in someone's house will find the best of both worlds at the Tombstone Boarding House, in a quiet residential neighborhood. Shirley Villarin's two meticulously restored 1880s adobe houses sit side by side; guests sleep in one of them, and go next door to the Villarin house to eat breakfast or watch TV.

The eight spotless rooms have refinished fir, maple, and oak floors and period furnishings collected from around Cochise County: for example, a cast-iron bed, a hand-carved wooden headboard from the 1880s, and an antique Army cot from Fort Huachuca that kids enjoy. Breakfast, served in a cheerful, pretty, blue-and-white kitchen, usually includes bacon and eggs, fresh fruits and juice, and Shirley's hot biscuits or muffins. Fresh-brewed coffee or tea is left outside the room early in the morning if a guest requests it. At check-in, arrivals are given a coupon good for a glass of wine at Don Teodoro's Mexican restaurant, just a block away.

🏨 *108 N. Fourth St., Box 906, Tombstone, AZ 85638, tel. 520/457–3716. 7 double rooms with baths, 1 1880s miner's cabin. Piano and TV in living room. $55–$70; full breakfast, evening wine. No credit cards. No smoking indoors.*

New Mexico

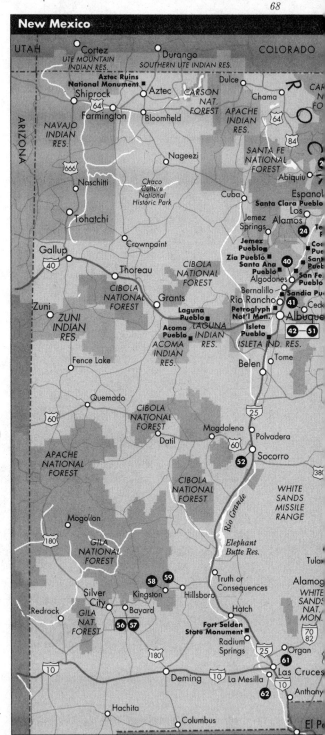

New Mexico

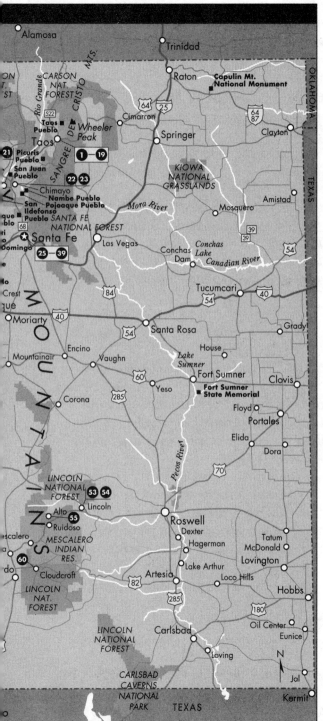

Santa Fe and Environs

Santa Fe is a beacon; the superstar attraction of the Southwest's burgeoning tourist boom. The City Different, as it is called, is a favorite vacation retreat for New York publishers, Hollywood stars, and legions of other people who are drawn to its enchanting landscape, elegant hotels and fine restaurants, cultural scene, and long, colorful history; it is the oldest capital city in the United States.

And the City Different, with its crisp, clean air and bright, sunny weather, couldn't be more welcoming. Santa Fe is perched on a 7,000-foot-high plateau at the base of the Sangre de Cristo Mountains. It's surrounded by a 2,000-year-old Pueblo civilization and characterized by its nearly 400 years of Spanish/Hispanic inhabitation.

In this age of malls and urban sprawl, Santa Fe is one of the few western cities that still radiates from its historic center—the town plaza—laid out in 1609. "Only three blocks from the Plaza," "one mile south of the Plaza," note restaurants, hotels, and bed-and-breakfasts in their advertising and brochures. Shops, galleries, and restaurants lining the Plaza pay high rents and high taxes, as any proprietor is quick to let you know in a casual, offhand moment.

Santa Fe is also characterized more than anything by its distinct Pueblo-style architecture, a predominance of adobe or pseudo-adobe that at times can be almost overpowering. But look closely and you'll see a melange of architectural styles, including Victorian and American Craftsman, each reflecting the many cultures that have helped shape modern Santa Fe. Both ancient pueblos and the Hispanic villages, with their earthen tones and rounded, flowing lines, meld into the landscape. Here the earth still rules.

Be it the architecture, the light, the ambiance, the lifestyle, or its novel residents, many visitors come back here to live. So many, in fact, that real estate prices and real estate taxes are soaring. Numerous people born in the former Spanish Colonial capital can no longer afford to live in it. Such is the price of success.

Santa Fe is among the smallest state capitals in the country and is without a major airport, but visitors pour in year-round. The city's population, an estimated 62,000, swells to nearly triple that figure at Indian Market in August. Hotel rates are on a par with those of top hotels and resorts in popular spots all over the globe. Prices charged for contemporary artwork— Santa Fe is said to be the third major art center in the country, after New York and Los Angeles—are similarly high.

Rates in the city's numerous bed-and-breakfasts reflect this pricing, as do the amenities they have. Most inns will arrange dinner and airport transfer reservations, as well as entertainment tickets for their guests. Breakfasts, whether a full gourmet or Continental-plus presentation tend to include a generous helping of regional specialties, fresh-baked breads and pastries, seasonal fruits and juices, and gourmet coffees and imported teas. By and large, no matter how high the cost, you won't feel shortchanged when you leave.

Places to Go, Sights to See

Art Galleries. Santa Fe's brilliant light, limpid skies, and timeless landscape of mountains and mesas have long hypnotized artists. The city has more than 125 galleries and no one knows how many full-time professional artists. The Santa Fe Convention and Visitors Bureau (*see* Tourist Information, *below*) offers a broad listing of galleries, and the *Wingspread Collectors Guide to Santa Fe and Taos*, available at most city newsstands, bookstores, and hotels, is a good bet for those seriously interested in buying art in Santa Fe. Standout galleries include *Copeland Rutherford Fine Arts* (403 Canyon Road, tel. 505/983–1588); *Fenn* (1075 Paseo de Peralta, tel. 505/982–4631); *Gerald Peters Gallery* (439 Camino del Monte Sol, tel. 505/988–8961); and *Horwitch-LewAllen Galleries* (129 W. Palace Ave., tel. 505/988–8997).

Canyon Road. A symbol of Santa Fe, Canyon Road once served as an Indian trail. During the early part of the century, woodcutters with their loaded burros used El Camino de Cañon as their route into town, where they sold bundles of chopped wood door-to-door. The road's 2-mile stretch from the center of town is the historic center of Santa Fe's art colony and today is lined with many of the city's finest art galleries, shops, and restaurants.

Cathedral of St. Francis (131 Cathedral Pl., tel. 505/982–5619). Founded by Jean Baptiste Lamy, Santa Fe's first archbishop, this handsome French Romanesque-style cathedral was built by Italian stonemasons in 1869. A small adobe chapel on the northeast side of the cathedral houses *Nuestra Señora de la Paz* (Our Lady of Peace), the oldest representation of the Madonna in the United States.

Chimayo. Peaceful little Chimayo, 25 miles north of Santa Fe in the Sangre de Cristo mountains, is famous for its weaving, regional food, and the *Santuario de Chimayo,* sometimes called the "Lourdes of the Southwest." Many miracles are believed to have occurred in the small, colonial-style adobe church, and mud from the *pozito* (small well) inside the chapel is reputed to have healing properties. The Santuario draws a steady stream of worshipers all year long, but over Good Friday and Holy Week, as many as 50,000 people visit.

Indian Vendors. Under the shaded *portales* of the Palace of the Governors on the north side of the Santa Fe Plaza, local Native American artisans display and sell their pottery and jewelry. All of the more than 500 vendors who are registered to sell under the portales are members of New Mexico pueblos or tribes.

Loretto Chapel (212 E. Santa Fe Trail, tel. 505/984–7971). Another French Romanesque structure, begun in 1873 and modeled after the famous Parisian church Sainte-Chapelle, Loretto Chapel is known for the "Miraculous Staircase": Many of the faithful believe that it was built by St. Joseph, who, disguised, came to the aid of the church sisters.

Los Alamos. Some 45 minutes north of Santa Fe, west of U.S. 84/285 on NM 502, the birthplace of the atomic bomb spreads over fingerlike mesas at an altitude of 7,300 feet. Research continues at Los Alamos National Laboratory (in areas such as nuclear weaponry, lasers, nuclear energy, and superconductivity). The town itself is relatively colorless but has a number of good restaurants, hotels, and museums, including the *Bradbury Science Museum* (15th and Central, tel. 505/667–4444) and *Los Alamos Historical Museum* (2132 Central Ave., tel. 505/662–4493).

Museums. The Pueblo-style *Palace of the Governors* on the north side of the Plaza is the oldest public building in the United States. It houses New Mexico's *History Museum* (tel. 505/827–6451), whose exhibits chronicle more than 450 years of territorial and state history. Almost next door is the *Museum of Fine Arts* (tel. 505/827–4455), with an impressive 8,000-piece permanent collection emphasizing the work of regional artists. New to the Plaza area is the museum of the *Institute of American Indian Arts* (Cathedral Place, tel. 505/988–6211), housed in the renovated former Federal Post Office. About a mile from the Plaza along the Old Santa Fe Trail is the *Museum of International Folk Art* (706 Camino Lejo, tel. 505/827–6350), among the town's most popular attractions. Next to it are two more excellent collections of Native American arts and artifacts: the *Museum of Indian Arts and Culture* (710 Camino Lejo, tel. 505/827–6344) and the *Wheelwright Museum of the American Indian* (704 Camino Lejo, tel. 505/982–4636).

Pueblos. Nineteen Pueblo and one Apache Indian reservations are found in northern New Mexico, where descendants of the ancient Anasazi Indians preserve their customs today. Each pueblo has its own personality, history, and specialty in art and design; those nearest to Santa Fe are Cochiti, Nambe, Pojoaque, San Ildefonso, Santa Clara, and Tesuque. To help decide which ones you want to visit, stop at the striking Indian Pueblo Cultural Center in Albuquerque (*see* Albuquerque chapter for details), or call the Eight Northern Indian Pueblo Council office (505/852–4265, ext. 23).

Santa Fe Ski Area (tel. 505/983–9155). Only half an hour from the Plaza, but 3,000 feet higher, this ski area is noted for excellent snowfall and a variety of terrain for all abilities.

Santa Fe Opera (Box 2408, Santa Fe, NM 87504, tel. 505/982–3855). Each July and August, some of the most acclaimed talents of Europe and the United States perform at the Santa Fe Opera's spectacular indoor-outdoor amphitheater, carved into a hillside 7 miles north of the city, amid the piñons of the Sangre de Cristo foothills.

Santuario de Guadalupe (100 Guadalupe St., tel. 505/988–2027). At the terminus of El Camino Real, 3½ blocks southwest of the Plaza, is the oldest shrine to Our Lady of Guadalupe (patron saint of Mexico) in the United States. Built by Franciscan missionaries between 1776 and 1795, it is now the center of the Guadalupe Historic District; adjacent Guadalupe Street is filled with colorful shops and restaurants.

Restaurants

Santa Fe is perhaps best known for its excellent New Mexican cuisine, a tantalizing array of classic regional specialties adapted generations ago from local ingredients—green and red chilies, a variety of peppers, ground and whole blue and yellow corn, pork, pinto beans, honey, piñon nuts, apples, and other native fare. Among the outstanding restaurants are the **Pink Adobe** (tel. 505/983–7712), **Casa Sena** (tel. 505/988–9232), **The Shed** (tel. 505/982–9030), **Tia Sofia's** (tel. 505/983–9880), and **La Terulia** (tel. 505/988–2769). For a change of pace, and price, there's Canyon Road's posh **Compound** (tel. 505/982–4353), the only restaurant in New Mexico where men are required to wear a jacket and tie, and **Corn Dance** (tel. 505/986–1662), which features unusual and tasty American Indian cuisine. Also, don't miss Mark Miller's award-winning **Coyote Cafe** (tel. 505/983–1615). Among its innovative northern New Mexican dishes are lobster enchiladas and ravioli filled with wild boar and goat cheese sausage.

Chimayo has one of the most classic New Mexican restaurants in the region, **Rancho de Chimayo** (tel. 505/984–2100), whose regional fare is made from centuries-old family recipes.

Tourist Information

Los Alamos Chamber of Commerce (2132 Central Ave., Los Alamos, NM 87544, tel. 505/662–8105). **New Mexico Department of Tourism** (Lamy Bldg., 491 Old Santa Fe Trail, Santa Fe, NM 87503, tel. 505/827–7400). **Santa Fe**

Chamber of Commerce (510 De Vargas Center, N. Guadalupe St., Santa Fe, NM 87501, tel. 505/983–7317). **Santa Fe Convention and Visitors Bureau** (201 W. Marcy St., Box 909, Santa Fe, NM 87504, tel. 505/984–6760 or 800/777–2489).

Reservation Services

Bed and Breakfast of New Mexico (Box 2805, Santa Fe, NM 87504, tel. 505/982–3332). **New Mexico Bed and Breakfast Association** (Box 2925, Santa Fe, NM 87504; write for brochure, and contact participating inns directly).

Alexander's Inn

Owner Carolyn Lee, the daughter of a foreign service diplomat, traveled all over the world while she was growing up. But when it came time to raise her son, Alexander, she decided to settle in Santa Fe and launch a B&B. Santa Fe is the richer for it, and Carolyn hasn't done badly either since opening in 1986. Her charming establishment, only six blocks from the Plaza on historic Palace Avenue, sees a lot of repeat business and is often booked solid.

A self-described fitness buff who loves to ski, mountain bike, dance, whitewater raft, and play tennis, Carolyn and her B&B exude a refreshing wholesomeness and youthful vitality: "You can shop anywhere in the world; I try to interest my guests in getting out and participating in some of the wonderful outdoor sports available here."

Of course, leaving the premises might be a problem, as they are conducive to laziness. The Craftsman-style two-story residence, built in 1903, is fronted by a deep veranda and covered with wooden shingles. Its spacious rooms are furnished with American country–style furniture. Fine woodworking is found throughout, as is pretty floral-patterned wallpaper. The upstairs rooms feature walk-in size dormer windows that flood the rooms with light and produce odd and delightful nooks, crannies, and angles. A downstairs bedroom, perhaps the best room, has a fireplace and original stained-glass windows.

Across a small backyard, which bursts in summer with flower gardens under the shade of some immense old trees, are two cottages. The front unit has a loft-style bedroom up a spiral staircase, a complete kitchen, and a fireplace. The rear unit has a raised kiva fireplace and Saltillo-tile floors.

In keeping with her healthy lifestyle, Carolyn's homemade granola, muffins, yogurt, sumptuous fruit salads, coffee, juice, and tea make for a hearty and delicious start for the day. In warm weather you can eat out on the rear deck; in spring an apricot tree bends its fragrant boughs over your table.

🏠 *529 E. Palace Ave., Santa Fe, NM 87501, tel. 505/986–1431. 3 double rooms with baths, 2 doubles share bath, 2 cottages. TV in cottages and in common room, fresh flowers, health club membership and mountain bikes available free of charge. $75–$140, cottages $85–$150; Continental-plus breakfast, afternoon snacks. MC, V. No smoking, some pets allowed.*

Grant Corner Inn

This is the bed-and-breakfast that innkeepers talk about when they get together over potluck dinners. It's one of the best run and most successful in the state. Owners Pat and Louise Walter couldn't be more suited to their job. He's a designer-builder who engineered the structural changes in the 1915 East Coast Colonial-style manor, the only one like it in Santa Fe; she's the daughter of Jack Stewart, who founded the renowned Camelback Inn in Scottsdale, where she grew up. Louise later studied at the Cornell hotel school. Donning chef's hat and apron, Pat now runs the kitchen while Louise runs the rest of the show.

And what a production. Located only two blocks from the Plaza in a small tree-filled lot, surrounded by a veranda and garden, the house originally belonged to the Winsor family, wealthy New Mexican ranchers. The rooms and public areas are appointed with antiques and treasures collected from around the world by the Walters. Hand-stitched quilts, brass and four-poster beds, armoires, and artwork make each room unique. The undisputed star is Room No. 8, a visual treat with its antique wood-burning stove, white brass bed, love seat, quilted bedspread, Oriental rugs, and Old World touches. The downstairs public rooms also hearken back to grander days, with overstuffed couches, ceiling fans, and crystal chandeliers.

The breakfast menu includes such treats as banana waffles, eggs Florentine, and green-chili-laden New Mexican soufflé, all accompanied by fresh-ground European coffee, fresh-squeezed juice, fruit, and homemade rolls and jellies. Small wonder the public comes clamoring on weekends when the dining room is open to one and all. Meals are served in front of a crackling fire in the dining room or, in summer, on the veranda. Guests get a complimentary glass of wine in the evening. Elaborately prepared picnic baskets are available, too.

The Grant Corner Inn also operates the Grant Corner Inn Hacienda, a Southwestern-style condominium five blocks away; it's available for parties of up to four. Rates ($205–$235 per night) include breakfast at the inn.

🏠 *122 Grant Ave., Santa Fe, NM 87501, tel. 505/983–6678. 7 double rooms with baths, 2 doubles share bath, 1 single. Cable TV and telephones in all rooms, in-house massages available, lounge with dining nook, microwave, and refrigerator; privileges at nearby tennis club. $70–$140; full breakfast. MC, V. No smoking.*

Inn on the Alameda

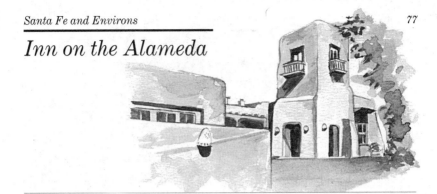

Alameda means "tree-lined lane," befitting its location alongside the Santa Fe River, which gurgles virtually through the center of town. This setting, between the historic Santa Fe Plaza and gallery-filled Canyon Road, is both tranquil and convenient: Even without a car, guests have easy access to shopping, museums, and restaurants.

Opened in 1986, this lodging was originally intended to be a bed-and-breakfast with resident managers. However, it soon blossomed into one of Santa Fe's most prestigious small hotels, combining the relaxed atmosphere of a New Mexico country inn with the amenities of a world-class hotel.

Rooms, in a contemporary adobe complex with a network of enclosed courtyards and *portales* are decorated in Southwestern colors, down to the accessories, beds, wall hangings, and wood-frame mirrors. Handmade armoires, oversize chairs, headboards, ceramic lamps, and colorful tiles all exemplify the best of local craftsmanship. Prints and posters by Armado Peña, R. C. Gorman, and other renowned local artists grace the walls. All of the inn's eight individually designed suites are appealing, some more opulent than others. Room 140, for example, features two kiva fireplaces, two TV sets, and two phones. Here and there you'll find a bleached cattle skull mounted on the wall or over a door.

Although the inn has no full-service dining room, its complimentary gourmet breakfast buffet is a wonder, with homemade muffins, bagels, creamy pastries, cinnamon rolls, fruit and fresh-squeezed fruit juices, teas, and Kona coffee, all served up by a friendly team of young Native Americans. Guests may eat at tables in the lobby's spacious library or in the Agoyo Room lounge; room service is also an option. A number of fine restaurants are nearby. The inn helps with tickets and reservations for evening entertainment and has a number of attractive package arrangements with spas, tours, and ski resorts.

▥ *303 E. Alameda, Santa Fe, NM 87501, tel. 505/984–2121 or 800/289–2122, fax 505/986–8325. 58 double rooms with baths, 8 suites. Cable TV with HBO and robes in all rooms, wet bars, refrigerators, kiva fireplaces, and patios with some rooms, massage room, exercise center, guest laundry, 2 outdoor hot tubs, patio dining, full bar; pets welcome. $140–$215, suites $200–$350; Continental-plus breakfast. AE, D, DC, MC, V.*

Preston House

This 1886 Queen Anne Victorian home, the only one of its kind in Santa Fe and with all of its angles and turrets intact, is the elegant restoration of noted artist-designer Signe Bergman, who moved from Santa Barbara to Santa Fe in 1974 to pursue a painting career. It wasn't until she was commissioned to do a large hotel mural in 1978 that she began to think of opening an inn of her own. She purchased Preston House that year and set about restoring it, later adding an adobe guest house and two Queen Anne-style garden cottages to the property.

Preston House is tucked away in a quiet garden a few blocks from the Plaza. Its guest house is just across the dead-end street, and the cottages are in the back. The main house is on the National Register of Historic Places.

The public rooms are open and sunny; fruit bowls, original, fantastically futuristic stained glass, lace curtains, and fresh-cut flowers add to the appeal. Books in the well-stocked library shed light on some of Preston House's former owners, among them three colorful characters: land speculator George Preston, who operated with a band of other charlatans in divvying up the Southwest territories after the Civil War; a man who exposed the gigantic Peralta-Reavis land-grant fraud; and a cure-all doctor.

Guest rooms in the main house are furnished in ornate late-19th-century fashion. Some have Edwardian fireplaces, ceiling fans, stained-glass windows, brass beds, Queen Anne chairs, and fringed lace tablecloths. Room 1, off the dining room, is for early risers. Rooms in the adobe guest house, in contrast, are done in the traditional Southwestern mode. Room 15, with a king and sofa bed, fireplace, and sitting room, has its own entrance. The Queen Anne-style garden cottages, with queen beds, single-size window seats, and fireplaces, couldn't be cozier.

An elaborate Continental breakfast is served at two tables in the large, pleasant kitchen. Full afternoon tea and dessert are offered as well. The owner's paintings, which hang in galleries and private collections all over the country, are displayed throughout the house and may be purchased.

🏠 *106 Faithway St., Santa Fe, NM 87501; tel. 505/982–3465. 4 double rooms with baths, 2 doubles share bath in main house; 7 double rooms with baths in adobe guest house; 2 garden cottages. TV and phones in rooms. $70–$140, suite $145; Continental-plus breakfast, afternoon tea. AE, MC, V. No smoking.*

Rancho de San Juan

Mountains, mesas, and the Ojo Caliente River valley make up the stunning vista from Rancho de San Juan, set beneath the petroglyph-dotted Black Mesa, 35 miles north of Santa Fe. Out in the middle of nowhere there is a stunning silence under a huge sky. Yet here is a spanking new, incredibly elegant Pueblo-style structure.

Conceived, owned, and run by David Heath and John Johnson, this enchanting B&B is their dream come true. David, formerly in real estate and retail—at Saks Fifth Avenue, among other fine stores—and John, a registered architect who worked extensively in the Far East, spent 10 years planning this career move. Searching for the perfect location, they stumbled upon this isolated valley and immediately knew they had found it. They bought a 225-acre tract.

When you enter the main building, an eye-dazzling painting of Navajo yeis (gods) greets you. To your left is the refined but relaxing living room, its 14-foot-high ceiling spanned by hand-peeled vigas centered by an immense fireplace. Oriental rugs, tile floors, wonderful Southwestern and Native American art and artifacts, carved-wood corbels, and antique doors are indicative of meticulous attention to detail and finely honed design sensibilities.

To your right is the 16-seat dining room, open to the public Wednesday through Saturday nights and for Sunday lunch, and to guests any night of the week with prior notice. Tiffany china, silver, and linen create a graceful impression, highlighted by the antique wooden fireplace mantel. Here John serves up full breakfasts to guests and exquisite dinner delicacies, focusing on northern Italian and French cuisine, or local specialties. A private dining room, seating up to 12, is off to one side.

The five accommodations cluster around a pretty courtyard. Each room has a different theme but all are as finely finished. The San Juan room has a Victorian motif with a crocheted lace bedspread and raw silk drapes. The Zia is the smallest room and the only one without a fireplace, but its colorful Mexican textiles lend it a festive air. The Black Mesa room has a Territorial-style fireplace, a faux canopy bed, and a small flower garden.

Box 4140, Espanola, NM 87533. 5 double rooms with baths. Each room has private entrance and patio, individual heating, ceiling fans, terry cloth robes, oversize towels, all-cotton linens, starched and ironed bed sheets, sherry in decanters on silver trays; massage, facials, and herbal wraps by appointment; public dining room; private dining room with VCR and slide machine for meetings; outdoor patio dining with fountain, picnic baskets with notification, hiking paths, hand-sculpted cave. $95–$135. MC, V. No smoking indoors, no pets.

Territorial Inn

The last of the private homes along tree-lined Washington Avenue in the heart of downtown Santa Fe—just off the Plaza—the Territorial Inn was built in the 1890s by Philadelphian George Shoch. A stylish blend of New Mexican stone-and-adobe architecture, this pitched-roof structure is surrounded by large cottonwoods, a front lawn, and a private rose garden.

In recent years, the building was occupied by a law firm. Legal secretary Lela McFerrin acquired the property in 1989, and she preserved or restored much of the century-old building. Now the inn has the gracious feel of the days when it was home to Levi A. Hughes, a well-known Santa Fe merchant who, with his wife, graciously entertained high society and visiting celebrities of the day.

The reception area and living room are large and comfortable, with overstuffed couches and chairs, fireplaces, a large bowl of jellybeans, and a set of encyclopedias. An eye-catching turn-of-the-century brick stairway leads to the upstairs guest rooms.

The 10 bedrooms range from large and luxurious to cozy and quaint; all are individually furnished with period pieces; canopy, brass, or four-poster beds; handmade quilts; and down comforters. Many of the ceilings have canopy linings, traditionally found in early adobe homes with viga beams. (They originally helped to keep dirt, twigs, and insects from falling into the soup; here, they cover the fluorescent lighting fixtures used in the legal offices of the former occupants.) The best rooms are No. 9, with its canopy bed and Victorian fireplace, and No. 3, with its private patio; the most claustrophobic is No. 7.

Breakfast—fresh pastries, strawberries and cream, juice, and coffee—is delivered to the bedrooms or, in summer, served in the rose garden. There's afternoon tea or wine and cheese, and brandy turndowns with cookies at night. Pets aren't allowed, but Mr. Shumway, a collie, keeps the guests from being lonely for four-legged companions.

215 Washington Ave., Santa Fe, NM 87501, tel. 505/989–7737, fax 505/986–9212. 8 double rooms with baths, 2 doubles share bath. Cable TV with HBO, ceiling fans, and down comforters in all rooms; fireplace in 2 rooms; gazebo-enclosed hot tub; off-street parking; laundry service available. $80–$150; Continental-plus breakfast. MC, V. No smoking, no children under 10, no pets.

Adobe Abode

Pat Harbour is an inveterate collector with a passion for primitive art. Mexican pottery and American folk art, including a collection of rare ship engine molds, are in evidence everywhere in her charming adobe compound, built circa 1907 three blocks from the Plaza. The main house, with viga beam ceilings, hardwood floors, and a living room with fireplace, adjoins casitas flanking a shaded courtyard.

Two rooms added in 1993 are based on themes—the Bronco has saddles, lariats, twig furniture, and old Western furnishings, including a wall of Western hats; the Cactus Room features Oaxacan textiles and pottery and colorful hand-carved animals. In 1994, Pat renovated a two-room suite, giving it decor from the south of France. The other accommodations are totally eclectic, combining hand-painted furniture with pencil-post beds and other antiques.

A full gourmet breakfast is served on one of Pat's 18 sets of china, including colorful dishes commissioned and handmade by local potters.

▦ *202 Chapelle St., Santa Fe, NM 87501, tel. 505/983-3133, fax 505/986-0972. 6 double rooms with baths. Cable TV, private phones, coffeemakers, custom toiletries, and terry cloth robes in all rooms. $100–$155; full gourmet breakfast, sherry and cookies always available. D, MC, V. No pets, no smoking in rooms.*

Casa del Rio

The setting is spectacular—12 acres of pastureland flanked by mountains, with the Chama River gurgling by, all in the heart of Georgia O'Keeffe country: Casa del Rio is 13 miles from Abiquiu and 27 miles from Ghost Ranch, both former homes of the artist. Eileen and Mel Vigil opened this small B&B with two separate casitas in 1988, and they are still at work on it. They recently completed patio walls, an outdoor swimming pool, a water garden, and a meditation room.

The Vigils raise purebred Arabian horses on the property (guests who want to ride are invited to bring their own horses), and racks above the door frames display part of Mel's gun collection, including a prize Winchester. The public rooms in the main house are furnished with a combination of European antiques and regional pieces—tile floors, viga ceilings, and an antique curved-glass cabinet displaying Indian jewelry (it's for sale). The guest rooms feature handcrafted Spanish Colonial-style furniture created by local carver Tim Roybal, whose work has been featured at the Smithsonian Institution.

▦ *Box 702, Abiquiu, NM 87510 (19946 U.S. 84), tel. 505/753-2035. 1 double room with bath, 1 casita. Fireplaces in both rooms, wake-up tray, fresh flowers, outdoor pool; water garden. $85–$95; full breakfast, afternoon tea. No credit cards. No smoking indoors, no pets.*

Casa Escondida

An intimate and serene adobe with pitched tin roof, Casa Escondida is set on 6 fertile acres in the sleepy village of Chimayo, famous for its Hispanic weavers. The Sangre de Cristos tower to the east, with the Truchas Peaks and Santa Fe Baldy poking above the red and brown hills. Its rural setting has made it very popular with mountain bikers. Equally inspiring is owner Irenka Taurek, who speaks several languages.

The house is decorated with American Arts and Crafts furniture, lamps, and pottery. A large hot tub is hidden in a grove behind wild berry bushes. The main house has five rooms, all with private baths. Some rooms have kiva fireplaces and packed earthen floors. Others have private patios and decks—

such as the airy, attractive upstairs Vista Room, with its great views. Also upstairs, the Kiva Room boasts a queen-size four-poster bed, kiva fireplace, and an oversize tub. The Sun Room, large and bright with a private patio, has viga ceilings and a brick floor. The separate one-bedroom Casita Escondida also has a kiva fireplace and viga ceilings, along with Saltillo-tile floors and a lovely sitting area.

A full breakfast is served in the dining room, which looks out onto a lawn and trees.

🏨 *Box 142 (off NM 76 at Road Marker 0100), Chimayo, NM 87522, tel. 505/351–4805 or 800/643–7201. 5 double rooms with baths, 1 1-bedroom cottage. Full kitchen with microwave in casita; wildflower gardens, hot tub. $75–$130, cottage $150; full breakfast, afternoon snacks. AE, MC, V. No smoking.*

Dos Casas Viejas

On historic Agua Fria Street, once part of the ancient Camino Real and right next door to the Guadalupe Inn (*see below*) is a half-acre walled compound containing Dos Casas Viejas (Two Old Houses). Dating back to 1860, they were last restored and revamped in 1990 to include such modern amenities as a 40-foot lap pool. Parts of the original portale still exist, as do the viga ceilings and Mexican-tile floors.

Once you manage to get buzzed through the security gate, you'll find this friendly, delightful place. The dining room is in the main house, the home of owners Irving Belfied, a retired dentist, and his wife, Jois, an interior designer; coffee, tea, freshly squeezed orange juice, and fresh-baked breads and muffins are served in the morning in the dining area, on the outdoor patios, or in your room. Guest rooms and suites are in two separate adobes, one of which was completed in 1993. Each room was decorated around the couple's fine art collection and features Mexican and New Mexican antiques, handsome furniture, coved viga ceilings, Saltillo-tile floors and skylights. No. 3, with its open arrangement of bedroom and sitting room, is most popular.

🏨 *610 Agua Fria St., Santa Fe, NM 87501, tel. 505/983–1636. 2 double rooms with baths, 2 minisuites, 1 suite. All rooms have cable TV, ceiling fans, minifridges, private entrances and patios, and raised fireplaces; lap pool. $145–$195; Continental-plus breakfast. MC, V. No smoking, no pets.*

Dunshee's

Dunshee's is so pretty and romantic that former Chicago *Tribune* travel editor Al Borcover was married on the patio here on his fourth visit. A great buy for Santa Fe, this B&B offers two reasonable lodging options in the quiet, historic east-side neighborhood only a mile from the Plaza and just off Canyon Road. Don't be fazed by the dirt lanes; this is as upscale as Santa Fe gets.

The first option is in the restored adobe home of proprietor-artist Susan Dunshee: a large suite that includes a living room with a cozy seating area and a bedroom with a queen bed and Mexican-tile bath; a gourmet breakfast is served. The other choice is a two-bedroom adobe casita with a patio and a full kitchen with a dishwasher and a refrigerator amply stocked for do-it-yourself breakfasts. Both the suite and the casita have viga ceilings, kiva fireplaces, decorative linens, and folk art, and both have private entrances.

The backyard offers a shady portale, terraced gardens, wisteria vines, and fruit and aspen trees.

🏨 *986 Acequia Madre, Santa Fe, NM 87501, tel. 505/982–0988. 1 casita, 1 2-bedroom suite. TV, stereo CD/tape player, microwave in each room, fresh*

flowers, art by leading local artists.
$110–$120; full breakfast in B&B,
Continental-plus in casita. MC, V. No
smoking, no pets.

El Paradero

El Paradero, set on a street five blocks
south of the Plaza, was built as a Spanish farmhouse between 1800 and 1820.
Its Territorial-style details were added
in the 1880s, its Victorian doors and
windows appended in 1912. Ouida Mac-
Gregor and Thom Allen acquired the
property in 1982 and added conveniences and the second-story rooms,
while retaining the adobe's essential
character, best described as funky or
"down-home."

A dog named Mr. Bean presides over
the main sitting room, where you'll
find a piano, fireplace with alcove seating, oversize wooden chairs, *santos*
(saints) carvings, and Indian kachina
dolls. Nine of the guest rooms are on
the ground level around the small
courtyard and three are upstairs in the
main house. The latter, flooded with
sunlight, are the more luxurious and
spacious, with Saltillo-tile floors,
Talavera-tile baths, and handwoven
textiles. Such tangy Southwestern
entrées as *huevos rancheros*, blue corn
pancakes, and breakfast burritos are
served in the sunny breakfast room.

🏠 *220 W. Manhattan Ave., Santa Fe,
NM 87501, tel. 505/988–1177. 8 double
rooms with baths, 4 doubles share 2
baths, 2 suites. Cable TV in suites,
color TV in sitting room, two fireplaces in public areas. $60–$110, suites
$130; full breakfast. No credit cards.
No smoking, pets allowed in some
rooms; closed 4 days over Christmas.*

The Guadalupe Inn

Two sisters and a brother are the
proud owners of this northern New
Mexico–flavored B&B, which opened
in 1992. One of them, Dolores Myers,
was born on the property, the site of

her grandfather's grocery store. She
speaks with authority about the many
colorful characters who have resided in
this historic area along the route of the
Camino Real.

The breakfast area and living room are
what you see when you enter the inn.
With coved viga ceilings, lots of light,
comfortable couches, Saltillo-tile floors,
and fireplace, the space is very inviting. And just around a corner is a large
indoor hot tub that looks out over a
small garden where raspberries thrive.

The rooms are each distinct, with
varying results. Some feature handmade beds by renowned craftsman
David C. de Baca, as well as tin light
fixtures, latilla ceilings, fanciful bathroom tile, and gas fireplaces. Popular
with honeymooners is the Celebration
Room, with its immense contemporary
claw-foot tub surrounded by mirrors
opening onto the bedroom. Avoid No.
6, which is smallish and has sub-
standard art.

🏠 *604 Agua Fria St., Santa Fe, NM
87501, tel. 505/989–7422, fax 505/989–
7422. 11 double rooms with baths, 1
suite. Cable TV, telephones and queen
beds in all rooms, whirlpool tubs in 4
rooms, gas fireplaces in some rooms,
covered parking. $125–$150, suite $175;
full breakfast. AE, D, MC, V. No
smoking, no pets.*

Inn of the
Animal Tracks

Three blocks east of the Plaza is this
enchanting 90-year-old restored
Pueblo-style home (it's actually brick
beneath the plaster) with beamed ceilings, hardwood floors, and handcrafted
furniture. The Inn of the Animal
Tracks is one of the most popular
B&Bs in town—people come just for
the delicious afternoon repast—open
to nonguests by reservation—when
owner Myrna Wheeler sets out anything from a dip of frijoles, black

olives, and green chili to tasty pastries and hot chocolate, coffee, or tea.

Playing off its animal theme, rooms have names like Eagle, Wolf, or Otter carefully selected to match their characters. Otter has the only tub, for instance. Rabbit is full of stuffed and terra-cotta rabbits, rabbit books, rabbit paintings; tucked under the bed are bunny-rabbit slippers. "I've always had a great love for animals," says Myrna, who allows no pets, although a mutt and two cats roam freely about the premises. The beds are all queen-size Swedish platform style, with down comforters and pillows, and feather mattresses. In the warmer months, a landscaped patio shaded by pear, apple, peach, and apricot trees is a pleasant place to relax.

🏠 *707 Paseo de Peralta, Santa Fe, NM 87504, tel. 505/988-1546. 5 double rooms with baths. Cable TV in guest rooms, fireplace in 1 guest room and in common room, fully air-conditioned. $90–$130; full breakfast, afternoon tea. AE, MC, V. No smoking indoors, no pets.*

Inn on the Paseo

In 1991, owners Nancy and Mick Arseneault won the Santa Fe Mayor's Award of Excellence for the restoration of their pitched-roof northern New Mexico-style bed-and-breakfast. Since then they've continued to refine and spruce up the turn-of-the-century Inn on the Paseo, four blocks from the Plaza and four from Canyon Road.

This contemporary Southwestern B&B is tastefully decorated with homey and modern touches. Guest rooms, some with private entrances and fireplaces, are decorated with four-poster beds or beds with hand-carved washed-pine headboards, local artwork, and handmade quilts. The upstairs suite has a whirlpool large enough for two; it's a wonderful spot

for gazing out at Santa Fe's fabulous sunsets, and also has an excellent view of the historic Cross of the Martyrs. The rooms facing busy Paseo de Peralta may be noisy. A copious Continental breakfast buffet is served fireside in winter and on the patio or deck during the warmer months. It usually includes a tasty hot dish.

🏠 *630 Paseo de Peralta, Santa Fe, NM 87501, tel. 505/984-8200 or 800/457-9045, fax 505/989-3979. 18 double rooms with baths, 1 2-bedroom suite. Cable TV, telephones in rooms, fax service. $89–$175; Continental breakfast. AE, DC, MC, V. No smoking, no pets.*

La Posada de Chimayo

New Mexico's first bed-and-breakfast, the rustic and peaceful La Posada de Chimayo opened to guests in June 1981. It is tucked away in a valley 30 miles north of Santa Fe in one of the prettiest areas of northern New Mexico—a stunning hilly region on the High Road to Taos studded with orchards and picturesque villages, where the sky explodes into a shower of stars each night.

The inn is composed of two adobe guest houses. One, built in 1981, contains two separate suites, each with a sitting room, small bedroom, and bath. The room to the west has great views. Both are warmed by fireplaces, a Trombe wall, and back-up gas heaters. Breakfast is served a minute's stroll down the dirt road at the other facility—a renovated farmhouse with double adobe walls built in the 1890s. A shady portale wraps around two sides, and the building houses a pleasant dining area and living room, as well as two bedrooms.

Rooms in both guest houses are tastefully appointed with Mexican rugs, handwoven bedspreads, comfortable regional furniture, and some good books to read. The Lizard, in the farmhouse, is light-filled and cheerful, with a free-standing Mexican terra-cotta fireplace and packed earth floor.

Owner Sue Farrington, an expert on Mexico and Mexican cooking, offers a full breakfast in a variety of south-of-the-border flavors.

⌂ *279 Rio Arriba, County Rd. 0101, Box 463, Chimayo, 87522, tel. and fax 505/351–4605. 2 double rooms with baths, 2 suites. Fireplaces in all rooms, spacious grounds, walking trails. $80–$125; full breakfast, afternoon wine. MC, V. No smoking indoors, no children under 12, pets with prior approval only.*

Orange Street Inn

A rather unremarkable 1948 wooden frame house in a quiet Los Alamos residential neighborhood, the Orange Street Inn is close to Bandelier National Monument and the Parjarito Mountain downhill ski area. Owners Susanne and Michael Paisley, formerly from Los Angeles, opened the inn in 1989 and have been revamping and improving it ever since. They plan to add two bathrooms in 1995.

There's a trim garden, and unique turn-of-the-century collectibles are found throughout the house: One room has a child's antique desk, another has a mounted rifle and a wooden rocking horse. Full breakfasts include such specialties as butternut coffeecake and cappuccino. Afternoon wine and hors d'oeuvres are served in the summer; pay-as-you-go soft drinks and snacks are always available.

⌂ *3496 Orange St., Los Alamos, NM 87544, tel. 505/662–2651 or 800/662–3180. 2 double rooms with baths, 4 doubles share 2 baths, 2 suites. Private entrance to suite, cable TV/VCR in common area, guest use of kitchen and laundry; ski packages available. $50–$85; full breakfast, afternoon wine and snacks. D, MC, V. No smoking, pet stays negotiable.*

Pueblo Bonito

Secluded behind thick adobe walls, Pueblo Bonito was built in 1873 in traditional pueblo style. Laid out in a series of charming but aging casitas connected by private courtyards, narrow brick paths, and archways, the property was once a private estate with its own stable and landscaped grounds. Owners Herb and Amy Behm acquired this National Historic Landmark in 1985 and renovated it within stringent Department of the Interior guidelines—no hot tubs or swimming pools.

Each casita is named for an area Native American tribe and is furnished with treasures from the region—Navajo rugs, baskets, Native American sand paintings, Pueblo and Mexican pottery, and carved wooden santos and other Spanish antiques. Most have traditional viga ceilings, and many have full kitchens; floors range from flagstone or brick to maple, oak, and pine.

The daily breakfast buffet includes seasonal fruits, juices, Danishes, muffins, croissants, cereal, fresh-brewed coffee, and an assortment of teas. It is served in winter before a fireplace and in summer on a patio.

⌂ *138 W. Manhattan Ave., Santa Fe, NM 87501, tel. 505/984–8001, fax 505/984–3155. 11 double rooms with baths, 7 suites. Cable TV, fireplace in all rooms; laundry facilities. $85–$130; Continental breakfast, afternoon refreshments. MC, V. No smoking, no pets.*

A Starry Night

After traveling the world, working in several professions, and writing three novels, Lee Purcell opened a B&B to finance her three granddaughters' college educations. She chose a Territorial-style adobe built at the turn of the century in Santa Fe's historic downtown, but its quiet street and its small size provide for unusual serenity. Sitting on her back patio under a vine-draped arbor buzzing with hummingbirds, surrounded by more than 500 tulips and daffodils and an herb garden, you might think you are in the country.

Inside are two charming, if somewhat crowded, guest accommodations. The Room has a bathroom with shower a few steps down a secluded hall; the Suite has French doors that open onto the patio and its adjoining bathroom features a claw-foot tub on a blond tile floor. The book-lined living room is graced with Oriental rugs on hardwood floors and comfortable couches and easy chairs.

🏨 *324 McKenzie St., Santa Fe, NM 87501, tel. 505/820–7117. 1 double room, 1 suite. Cable TV and phones in rooms, microwave and minifridge in suite. $116; Continental breakfast. MC, V. No smoking indoors, no children.*

Water Street Inn

Part of an award-winning adobe restoration, just four blocks from the Plaza, this inn has been recently redecorated and refurbished by its new owners. The large to very spacious rooms all reveal a talented interior designer at work, from reed shutters and pine antique beds to hand-stenciled paintings, claw-foot tubs, beveled glass mirrors, and a mixture of Native American, Hispanic, and Cowboy Western artifacts. Daring color schemes, lots of light, and the novel furnishings make for a playful, yet very tasteful, environment. Even the smallest room here, No. 6, has a redeeming asset—a nice bathroom with a Japanese-style tub.

Breakfast, served in your room, in a dining area, or on an upstairs patio, includes oven-fresh pastries, fruit bowls, cereals, juices and coffees. Every evening local wines and hot hors d'oeuvres are served in the inn's living room, which features a large fireplace and hand-glazed adobe walls.

🏨 *427 Water St., Santa Fe, NM 87501, tel. 505/984–1193. 8 double rooms with baths. Cable TV and fireplace in all rooms, voice mail. $90–$155. Continental breakfast, evening wine and snacks. MC, V. No smoking, no children under 7, no pets.*

Taos

Mysterious, spiritual, ageless Taos is an enchanted town of soft lines and delineations. Romantic courtyards, stately elms and cottonwoods, narrow, tangled streets, and a profusion of adobe all add to its timeless appeal.

Taos is 65 miles north of Santa Fe on a rolling mesa at the base of the rugged Sangre de Cristo Mountains, where lofty Wheeler Peak, the state's highest mountain, rises 13,161 feet. Fabulous ski slopes beckon in winter, while summer brings a flood of tourists who just want to soak in the scenery and breathe the good air.

Taos is actually three towns in one. The first is the community itself, which many compare to the Santa Fe of yesterday, before all the glitz and glamour arrived. The second is the Taos Pueblo, 2 miles north of the commercial center of Taos, home of the Taos-Tiwa Indians, whose apartment house-style pueblo dwelling is one of the oldest continually inhabited communities in the United States. Ranchos de Taos, an adobe-house farming and ranching community 4 miles south of town, settled by the Spanish centuries ago and best known for its San Francisco de Asis Church, is the third. These three distinct faces merge at the place where the sky meets the mountains, in a magnificent 6,950-foot-high plateau setting.

With a combined population of some 4,500, Taos, the Taos Pueblo, and Ranchos de Taos offer a unique blend of history and culture. Add to this a remarkable literary and artistic heritage, and the town's appeal is evident. Taos has attracted artists and writers almost forever, but none had a more profound impact on the community than Briton D. H. Lawrence, who has become something of a cottage industry: Places where he, his wife, and his friends stayed are now inns and restaurants.

Like Santa Fe, Taos has received its share of accolades of late. In 1992, the United Nations designated Taos Pueblo a World

Heritage Site—one of only 17 in the United States and the second in New Mexico (the other is Chaco Canyon). The news delights opponents of the long-discussed, hotly disputed plan to build a commercial airport in Taos. Jets landing and taking off in the proximity of the Taos Pueblo would surely rattle its fragile adobe walls into rubble.

Bed-and-breakfasts in Taos, like those in Santa Fe, are for the most part built in the graceful, ground-hugging pueblo style common to both areas. However, because Taos is far less developed than Santa Fe, its B&Bs tend to be more secluded, making the best use possible of the mountain-rimmed, wide-open spaces all around them. Two are National Historic Landmarks: the Taos Hacienda Inn, set in a building that dates back to the 1800s with adobe walls that once formed part of the town's original La Loma Plaza fortification; and the Mabel Dodge Luhan House, a huge, rambling adobe built by the famed art patron.

Places to Go, Sights to See

D. H. Lawrence Ranch and **D. H. Lawrence Shrine** (along NM 522, about 10 mi north of town). When Lawrence and his wife, Frieda, arrived in Taos, heiress and art patron Mabel Dodge Luhan offered them Kiowa Ranch, on 160 acres in the mountains north of Taos, as a place to stay. The property, now owned by the University of New Mexico, became known as the D. H. Lawrence Ranch, although it never actually belonged to the writer. The ranch is closed to the public, but the nearby shrine containing Lawrence's ashes may be visited.

Kit Carson Home and Museum (Kit Carson Rd., tel. 505/758–2036) is the former home of the famous mountain man and scout who left an indelible mark on the history of Taos. Carson purchased the 12-room adobe home in 1843 as a wedding gift for his bride, Josefa Jaramillo, who was 14 at the time. Carson is buried across town, four blocks northeast of the Plaza, in the wooded, 20-acre Kit Carson Park; Mabel Dodge Luhan is buried in the same small graveyard.

La Hacienda de Don Antonio Severino Martínez (4 mi west of Ranchos de Taos, tel. 505/758–0505) is one of the only fully restored Spanish Colonial adobe haciendas open to the public in New Mexico. The fortlike building on the banks of the Rio Pueblo served as the Martínez family's home and a community refuge against Comanche and Apache raids. The restored period rooms illustrate the lifestyle of the Spanish Colonial era, when supplies, other than what could be produced locally, came to Taos by oxcart on the Camino Real. The surrounding landscape, dotted with farms and grazing horses, tall cottonwood trees, and wooden fences, hints strongly of early settlement days.

Millicent Rogers Museum (4 mi northwest of the Plaza, tel. 505/758–2462) is the museum you should visit in Taos if you have time for only one. Representing the core of Standard Oil heiress Millicent Rogers's private collection, it contains more than 5,000 pieces of Native American and Hispanic art.

San Francisco de Asis Church (tel. 505/758–2754). The centerpiece of Ranchos de Taos, this monumental adobe mission church was built in the 18th century as a spiritual and physical refuge from raiding Apaches, Utes, and Comanches; its massive, buttressed adobe walls and graceful twin belfries have inspired generations of painters and photographers, including Georgia O'Keeffe, Paul Strand, and Ansel Adams. In the parish hall nearby, a 15-minute video explains the history and 1979 restoration of the church; the famous mystery painting, *Shadow of the Cross,* may be seen throughout the day.

Taos Plaza, lined with shops, galleries, and restaurants, bears only a hint of the grace, dignity, and stateliness of the Plaza in Santa Fe, although its history is drawn with the same pen. At the center of the Plaza, the U.S. flag flies night and day, as authorized by a special act of Congress in recognition of Kit Carson's heroic stand against Confederate sympathizers during the Civil War. Next to a covered gazebo, donated by Mabel Dodge Luhan, is an antique carousel that delights youngsters during special summer festivals.

Taos Pueblo (tel. 505/758–9593). For nearly 1,000 years, the Taos-Tiwa Indians have lived at or near the present pueblo site, the largest existing multistory pueblo structure in the United States and Taos's No. 1 tourist attraction. The pueblo today, without running water or electricity, appears much as it did when the first Spanish explorers arrived in New Mexico in 1540. Parking fees and camera permits are new, of course.

Restaurants

For a city with a population of fewer than 5,000, Taos has an extraordinary number of fine restaurants. **Casa Cordova** (tel. 505/776–2500), **Brett House** (tel. 505/776–8545), **Doc Martin's** (tel. 505/758–2121), **El Patio de Taos** (tel. 505/758–2121), and the **Trading Post Café** (tel. 505/758–5089) are all upscale, pricey restaurants, serving traditional Northern New Mexican and international dishes; jackets and ties are always recommended but rarely required. A bit more casual in both price and atmosphere are the **Apple Tree** (tel. 505/758–1900), with a stylish, eclectic menu including mango chicken and shrimp quesadillas; **Ogelvie's** (tel. 505/758–8866), which serves prime Angus beef, seafood, and traditional Southwestern dishes in an often rowdy atmosphere; and the current Taos hot spot, the **Double AA Grill** (tel. 505/758–1319), where organic buffalo burgers are the specialty of the house. The low-key **Chile Connection** (tel. 505/776–2005), six minutes north of the Plaza on Ski Valley Road, is also definitely worth a visit.

Tourist Information

New Mexico Department of Tourism (Lamy Bldg., 491 Old Santa Fe Trail, Santa Fe, NM 87503, tel. 505/827–7400). **Taos County Chamber of Commerce** (1139 Paseo del Pueblo Sur, Drawer I, Taos, NM 87571, tel. 505/758–3873 or 800/545–2040).

Reservation Services

Bed and Breakfast of New Mexico (Box 2805, Santa Fe, NM 87504, tel. 505/982–3332). **New Mexico Bed and Breakfast Association** (Box 2925, Santa Fe, NM 87504; write for brochure, and contact participating inns directly). **Taos Bed and Breakfast Association** (Box 2772, Taos, NM 87571, tel. 800/876–7857). **Traditional Taos Inns** (Box 2117, Taos, NM 87571, tel. 505/758–8245 or 800/525–8267).

American Gallery Artists House

The 7-foot-tall, flat, black iron sculpture in front of the American Artists Gallery House isn't Kokopelli, whose flute-bearing image can be seen in every gift shop between San Diego and Santa Fe, but the *God of Bed and Breakfasts*, a special creation of artist Pozzi Franzetti. And it's not for sale—perhaps the only piece among the 500 or so works of art here that doesn't have a price tag. Although almost all B&Bs in northern New Mexico sell works by regional and nationally known artists—"It's a way to get paintings to hang on your walls without paying for them," says one wry innkeeper—this establishment is serious about its artistic endeavors. New owners LeAn and Charles Clamurro, who purchased the B&B in July 1994, have a passion for art, particularly that created by local artists. Charles especially is happy to discuss the array of art found in every room. The B&B frequently hosts art openings for featured artists; at other times, artists are invited to breakfast with the guests.

Another passion of the owners is their fine lodging. Charles is a graduate of the Cornell hotel program, and his experience includes a three-year stint running La Fonda Hotel in Santa Fe; LeAn has a similarly impressive background in hotel management and currently heads the New Mexico Bed & Breakfast Association's marketing committee. The inn is adjacent to a field where the Taos July 4th fireworks and the October Hot Air Balloon Festival take place, providing ringside seats for both.

Its seven rooms are spread throughout the adobe compound: three in the main house, two in an adjacent guest house, and the others in separate garden cottages. The newest of the latter is the relatively secluded Piñon Gallery Suite, or "honeymoon cottage." Like the other rooms, it is decorated and furnished in Southwestern style with an abundance of local art on display. All rooms have kiva fireplaces, colorful Mexican tiles in the bathrooms, Native American rugs covering tile or wooden floors, leather drum tables, and carved furniture.

Breakfast is served promptly at 8 AM around a large table in a glass-enclosed greenhouse-style dining area. One of 10 or so standard breakfast entrées—chili egg frittata, blue corn pancakes with fresh blackberries, pecan-stuffed French toast—is accompanied by fresh fruits, home-baked breads, and fresh-brewed coffee or a variety of teas.

🏠 *132 Frontier Rd., Box 584, Taos, NM 87571, tel. 505/758–4446 or 800/532–2041, fax 505/758–0497. 7 double rooms with baths, 2 minisuites. Kitchens in suites, fax; outdoor hot tub. $75–$105; full breakfast, afternoon beverages and hors d'oeuvres. MC, V. No smoking, no pets.*

Casa Europa

There's a marvelous, ornate, 200-year-old brass bed in the French Room at the Casa Europa that must take an army of maids weeks to keep polished. But gleaming and polished it is, and you'll feel a little like Louis XIV or Catherine the Great as you drift off to sleep with sounds of crickets and field frogs wafting through the partially opened French windows above the courtyard of this 200-year-old adobe farmhouse. Casa Europa is run with care and precision by Marcia and Rudi Zwicker, the owner and chef of the popular Greenbriar Restaurant in Boulder, Colorado, for 16 years.

Current zoning laws prohibit the Zwickers from expanding, but they've purchased the property across the street, so the pastoral and mountain views—horses grazing, massive cottonwoods, wooden fences, and clouds you can almost reach out and touch—will never be obscured. When they restored the inn in 1983, the couple left all its adobe bricks and wood viga ceiling beams intact. Among Casa Europa's many artistic treasures is the oldest door in Taos, discovered years ago in the basement of the Guadalupe Church and now decorating one of the B&B's hallways.

The rooms, whose whitewashed walls are splashed with sunlight, are furnished with an eclectic collection of European antique and traditional Southwestern pieces. Paintings, arranged gallery style, feature Native American and other contemporary artists; there are also three signed etchings by Salvador Dali. Each of the rooms is based on a theme. In the central sitting room of the spacious Southwest Room is a Swedish porcelain woodstove; there's a large white marble bath with a whirlpool and—one of those rarest of creatures in the American Southwest—a bidet.

At breakfast, German-born Chef Rudi pulls out all stops—fluffy popovers, eggs Florentine, quiche, fresh-baked Danish pastries, blue corn pancakes, cheese blintzes, sautéed trout with tomato cups filled with scrambled eggs—but not all at once, of course. The astounding pastry selection includes chocolate mousse cake, truffles, fresh fruit tarts, and Black Forest tortes. Steaming coffee is served in individual decanters.

840 Upper Ranchitos Rd., Los Cardovas Route, HC 68, Box 3F, Taos, NM 87571, tel. 505/758–9798. 6 double rooms with baths. Fireplace in 5 rooms, cable TV in public rooms, Swedish sauna, hot tub. $80–$135; full breakfast, afternoon tea in summer, hors d'oeuvres in ski season. MC, V. No smoking, no pets.

El Rincón

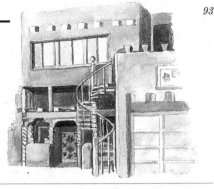

If you're looking for something unique, you've found it here. With its maze of rooms and hallways upstairs and down and its kitchens and courtyards, El Rincón looks like a cross between a set for a melodrama and a Western museum. Up front is the oldest trading post in Taos, still flourishing. Piled high with Western artifacts, feathered Indian headdresses, Navajo rugs, beads, drums, *santos* (saints) carvings, buckles, and pots, it has a one-room museum whose prized possession is a pair of Kit Carson's leather pants.

It's difficult to tell where the store and museum end and the bed-and-breakfast begins. Nina Meyers, daughter of Ralph Meyers, an old-time Taos resident, artist, and trader, has followed in her father's footsteps. Her own work and photographs, paintings, and other art, both contemporary and historic, fill the walls of the B&B.

El Rincón has the look of an organic building that's grown over the century, and now that Taos real estate prices have skyrocketed, the B&B has begun to grow up, instead of out. Paul "Paco" Castillo, who owns the B&B along with his mother, Nina, is currently installing a rooftop deck with hot tub, barbecue, and picnic table above the already luxurious Rainbow Room (it also has a full kitchen, washer and dryer, and dining area). The decor in the Santiago Room evokes images of Old World Spain, and it is only when you open a cabinet to find a TV and VCR or locate the Jacuzzi bathtub that you realize it's better appointed than most any room found in times past. Unit 12 has a canopied bed with a handmade wedding-ring quilt, heavily embellished with Spanish lace; there's a tiled floor-to-ceiling mural of the Garden of Eden in the bath. Unit 8, which has beautiful old corbels, murals, and woodwork created by local artisans, also boasts a kitchenette, hot tub, fireplace, stereo, and TV/VCR. Peek through the lace curtains on the windows and you'll see Kit Carson's house across the street.

The B&B is in the heart of bustling Taos, just a quarter-block from the plaza, and the thick adobe walls provide respite from noise and light. Guests who tire of roaming the plaza or skiing the mountains can retire to the cool depths, choose a movie from an extensive video library, and watch it in their room (all rooms have TVs with VCRs, as well as stereos). They might also wander through the house and get Paco to take a break from his continual building projects and recount a bit about the building's history, such as why there is an old stone well sunk in the floor adjoining the kitchen (it is, of course, grated so you needn't worry if you have intrepid children).

114 Kit Carson Rd., Taos, NM 87571, tel. 505/758–4874. 10 double rooms with baths, 3 suites. Refrigerators, whirlpool tubs, color TVs, VCRs, stereos in all rooms; kitchens and hot tubs in 2 suites, video library. $59–$175; Continental-plus breakfast. AE, MC, V. Pets $5 per night.

Hacienda del Sol

The Hacienda del Sol, which borders 95,000 acres of Pueblo land and overlooks some of the most spectacular scenery in northern New Mexico, was acquired in the 1920s by art patron Mabel Dodge Luhan. She and her fourth husband, Tony Luhan, a Taos Pueblo Indian, lived here while building their main house, Las Palomas de Taos, now the Mabel Dodge Luhan House (*see below*). They kept the Hacienda del Sol as a private retreat and a guest house.

Although it's only about a mile from the Plaza and just off a main roadway, the inn remains secluded. Innkeepers John and Marcine Landon, who bought the property in 1991, make sure everything runs like clockwork. The house, a model of adobe construction built in 1810, has viga ceilings, arched doorways, and large, quiet rooms.

Author Frank Waters was living in the Tony Luhan room when he saw a young Taos Indian being arraigned by three police officials for killing a deer; the incident was the inspiration for his classic novel of Pueblo life, *The Man Who Killed the Deer*. Containing a kiva fireplace, sheepskin rug, and a desk at the window shaded by what's believed to be the oldest cottonwood tree in Taos, the room has undoubtedly changed little. The more contemporary Los Amantes Room adjoins a private room with a double-size black Jacuzzi on a mahogany platform, amid a jungle of potted plants; there's a skylight above, and the attached bathroom is a celebration of decadence with its jet-black sink, tub, shower, and toilet, all with gleaming silver hardware. In the bedroom bookcase are *Edge of Taos Desert, Taos, A Memory*, and *Winter in Taos*, all by Mabel Dodge Luhan, and, of course, *The Man Who Killed the Deer*. Most of the rooms feature kiva fireplaces, Spanish antiques, Southwestern-style handcrafted furniture, and original artwork, much of it for sale. New to the hacienda is an adobe casita with three guest rooms, two baths, and fireplaces, which can be rented as a suite.

Breakfast is served in front of the dining room fireplace or, weather permitting, on the patio. Entrées might include a blintz soufflé or blue corn pancakes with blueberry sauce, complemented by a superb house-blend coffee.

🏠 *109 Mabel Dodge La., Box 177, Taos, NM 87571, tel. 505/758–0287, fax 505/751–0319. 7 double rooms with baths, 2 doubles with separate bath, 1 suite. Cable TV in public room, outdoor hot tub, gift shop. $65–$100, suite $125; full breakfast, afternoon snacks. MC, V. No smoking, no pets.*

Mabel Dodge Luhan House

This classic, rambling, pueblo-style structure, formerly the home of heiress Mabel Dodge Luhan and classified as a National Historic Landmark in 1991, has been a combined B&B and conference center for the past 15 years. Owners George and Susan Otero acquired the property in 1978 from actor Dennis Hopper, who stayed here while editing his film *Easy Rider* and liked it so much that he bought it. There are 10 guest rooms in the main house, parts of which are more than 200 years old; 8 more rooms are in a separate guest house built in the same pueblo style in 1989.

Luhan bought the house in 1915, and she and her husband, Tony Luhan, spent the next seven years enlarging and remodeling it. The three original rooms grew to 17; the main part of the house rose from one story to three. Upon its completion in 1922, Mabel Dodge Luhan took the lead in promoting the Southwest as a utopia, offering her literary and artistic friends an antidote to civilization. Her guests here included D. H. Lawrence, Georgia O'Keeffe, Willa Cather, Mary Austin, and John Marin.

The creative spirit nurtured so lovingly by Luhan, who died in the house in 1962 at the age of 83, still exists today. The inn is frequently used for literary workshops, educational conferences, and cultural seminars.

A living room, sitting room, and separate library are at the center of the main house, joined by a string of bedrooms furnished with turn-of-the-century pieces. The master suite on the second floor still contains Luhan's magnificently carved double bed, as well as a kiva fireplace and entrance from the patio. And in the bathroom is a mural painted on the window glass by D. H. Lawrence, who was shocked that the bathroom had no curtains and anyone could see in when Mabel bathed. In the separate guest house, all the rooms are decorated in Southwestern style, with carved, handpainted furnishings.

If you crave crisp service and linen, designer soaps, and a lot of pampering, don't look for them here. The walls beg for paint, the floors creak, and you have to be part mountain goat to maneuver the loftlike stairs leading to the Solarium bedroom at the top of the house. But if you want to soak up the magic days of the past that made Taos what it is today, this is the place to come.

🏠 *240 Morada La., Box 3400, Taos, NM 87571, tel. 505/758–9456 or 800/846–2235, fax 505/751–0431. 18 double rooms with baths, 2 doubles share bath, 2 suites. Extensive grounds, lunch and dinner available for groups of 10 or more, conference facilities. $75–$200; full breakfast. MC, V. No smoking, no pets.*

Taos Country Inn at Rancho Rio Pueblo

Yolanda Deveaux opened the Taos Country Inn after her children left for college, and in many ways the inn still feels like a family home. Yolanda resembles a hummingbird as she flits through spacious and well-lit rooms ensuring that guests' needs are met and adding thoughtful touches along the way, such as preparing fires in the rooms of guests returning from a day of skiing. In the morning, the aroma of strong coffee and good things cooking wafts through the rooms and hallways of this sprawling Spanish hacienda, parts of it built nearly two centuries ago. Yolanda is from an old-line Taos family that acquired the hacienda 20 years ago. Her father, Dr. Reynaldo Deveaux, "delivered half the people in Taos," she says.

The inn is on 22 acres of pastureland and cultivated orchards and gardens, 1 mile north of town adjoining the Rio Pueblo. Guests can wander about in the fields, marveling at the distant mountain horizons, still snowcapped in the spring; chat with a field hand burning off sections of grass; and photograph the horses and sheep in a neighbor's farmyard.

The house reflects the talents of skilled local craftsmen—doors by Leroy Mondragon and Roberto Lavadi, abstract paintings in huge swatches of shocking red by James Mack, and fireplaces by Carmen Velarde, the Leonardo of fireplace makers. The public rooms, whose large windows bring the outdoors in, are filled with handcrafted furnishings,

couches upholstered in textured desert tones, and glass-topped saguaro or cholla cactus-rib tables.

The guest rooms are spacious and sunny. All have white stuccoed fireplaces, sitting areas, leather sofas, Native American artifacts, Southwestern artwork, and king- or queen-size beds with fluffy down comforters and a mountain of pillows.

At breakfast—served at natural wood tables, one long and formidable, others smaller and more intimate—Yolanda unsuccessfully urges a second plate of Belgian waffles, piled high with whipped cream and strawberries, on a guest who could hardly manage the first. Her entrées might include cream cheese and salmon omelets or *huevos rancheros* or other regional specialties, all accompanied by a buffet of fruit dishes, yogurt, pastries, and breads. A small refrigerator contains juices and other soft drinks to which guests may help themselves at any time.

▥ *Box 2331, Upper Ranchitos and Karavas Rds., Taos, NM 87571, tel. 505/758–4900 or 800/866–6548. 9 suites. Phones and cable TV in rooms, VCR units on request, massage available. $110–$150; full breakfast, afternoon refreshments. MC, V. No smoking indoors, no pets.*

Adobe & Pines

With its 80-foot-long *portale* stretching the entire expanse of the main entryway, this 150-year-old adobe home on 4 acres of pines, fruit trees, and pastures couldn't be more impressive. Set against the backdrop of the Taos Mountains, a stream running through the property—with an old stone bridge inspiring local poets—Adobe & Pines opened in the summer of 1991 after extensive renovation. Owners Chuck and Charil Fulkerson traveled the world before settling on, and in, Taos.

Four guest rooms in the main house have queen-size beds with fluffy goose-down comforters and pillows, Mexican-tile baths, and fireplaces. A separate cottage features a canopy bed, jet whirlpool bath, two fireplaces, and a kitchen, while the Puerta Rosa room contains a sauna, a deep soaking tub, and bathroom fireplace as well as a beautiful wrought-iron bed in the adjoining room. The public area, a living room where hors d'oeuvres and refreshments are served in the afternoon, and the glass-enclosed sunroom and dining area where breakfast is unveiled, are spaciously Western.

▦ *U.S. 68 and Llano Quemado, Box 837, Ranchos de Taos, NM 87557, tel. 505/751–0947 or 800/723–8267, fax 505/ 758–8423. 4 double rooms with baths, 1 cottage. Jet tubs in 2 rooms, fireplaces in all rooms. $95–$145; full breakfast. MC, V. No smoking, no pets.*

The Blue Door

This 100-year-old adobe farmhouse is in the foothills between Taos and Ranchos de Taos, near the famous San Francisco de Asis Church and surrounded by appealing shops. Here you'll find rural Taos at its finest in a picturesque setting amidst orchards, flower gardens, lawns, and patios. In the summer, a tent is set up for kids.

The Blue Door is owned by Bruce Allen, who makes and markets traditional Taos drums, crafted from carved tree trunks and covered with tautly stretched leather. His wares are everywhere to be seen at the B&B—coffee tables, decorative wall displays, end tables, book racks. Each of the two bedrooms is decorated in Southwestern style, with viga ceilings, wood floors, hand-carved beds, and, as you might expect, Indian-drum end tables.

Breakfast here is a treat, with green chili quiche, muffins, blueberry pancakes, bacon, waffles, and homemade jams from the orchard fruit, served in a sunny breakfast nook.

▦ *La Morada Rd., Box 1168, Taos, NM 87571, tel. 505/758–8360 or 800/ 824–3667. 2 double rooms with baths. Cable TV in both rooms. $75; full breakfast, afternoon snacks. MC, V. No smoking, no pets.*

Brooks Street Inn

A rambling house with a circular drive and an adjoining guest house comprise the Brooks Street Inn, designed and built in 1956 by local artist Rose Wodell, who used it as a private gallery. The house, built in the traditional pueblo style, incorporates adobe bricks made on the property, beamed ceilings, polished wood floors, and a large stone fireplace. An elaborately carved corbel arch, the handiwork of Japanese carpenter Yaichikido, spans the entryway, and alongside the house is a shaded, walled garden with a hammock for two.

In the large living room, guests can enjoy any sort of coffee made fresh from the espresso machine—the café mocha is particularly good—while viewing the paintings by local artists that hang on the walls. Southwestern-style guest rooms—three in the main house, three in the guest house—show great attention to detail, with fresh-cut flowers and plump, fluffy pillows. A full breakfast features family recipes, including blue corn pancakes with pineapple sauce, stuffed French toast with apricot glaze, and other home-baked delights. The owners, Carol Frank and Larry Moll, are great conversationalists, and the mood at the Inn is very relaxed, as long as you remember not to smudge the chrome on Larry's Harley Davidson motorcycle.

▦ *119 Brooks St., Box 4954, Taos, NM 87571, tel. 800/758–1489. 6 double rooms with baths. Kiva fireplaces, espresso machine. $75–$100; full breakfast, afternoon snacks. AE, MC, V. No smoking indoors, no pets.*

Casa de las Chimeneas

Casa de las Chimeneas, 2½ blocks from the Plaza and secluded behind thick adobe walls, boasts cool, formal gardens and a stately entryway that wouldn't be out of place in a Loire Valley château. The interior of this Spanish-style hacienda, built in 1912 and renovated a decade ago, shows New Mexican luxury at its most refined, with tiled hearths, lush rugs, carved doors and posts, regional art, and vigas.

Chosen by *Ski* magazine as one of the top rooms in ski country, the Library Suite features a private entrance off the courtyard; a sitting room-library with beamed ceilings, wood floor, kiva fireplace, and bentwood rocker; and a bedroom with another fireplace and white-pine antique furniture. The other three accommodations are also stunners: The Willow has Mexican carved furniture, a pewter chandelier, and a skylight in the bath. A white-washed antique headboard and dresser, two leather chairs, and an ornate hand-crafted tin mirror decorate the Blue Room. The Garden Room has a deep tub, kiva fireplace, and a brilliant view of the garden framed by the boles of two massive cottonwood trees.

▦ *405 Cordoba Rd., Box 5303, Taos, NM 87571, tel. 505/758–4777, fax 505/758–3976. 3 rooms with baths, 1 suite. Cable TV, telephone, bar, minifridge in all rooms, hot tub. $120–$150; full breakfast, afternoon hors d'oeuvres. MC, V. No smoking indoors, no pets.*

Casa de Milagros

A single-story, turn-of-the-century adobe house, ½-mile east of the Taos Plaza, Casa de Milagros (House of Miracles) offers the texture and flavor of the Taos of long ago, with all the conveniences of today. This unique Taos hideaway has everything—ambience, location, a hot tub, cable television, fireplaces, gourmet breakfasts, and a friendly, helpful staff.

Actually two buildings connected by a *portale* (where the hot tub is located), the inn is furnished throughout in a combination of regional styles and talents. Southwestern predominates—viga ceilings, Mexican-tile bathrooms, custom cabinets, and lots of pottery, tapestry, and weavings. Works by Taos Pueblo artist Jonathan Warm Day and other Native American artists hang on the walls. Breakfast can include Häagen-Dazs vanilla French toast, eggs milagros with a chile enchilada sauce, fresh coffee, and homemade granola, aka "Nirvana Crunch."

▦ *321 Kit Carson Rd., Box 2983, Taos, NM 87571, tel. 505/758–8001 or 800/243–9334, fax 505/758–0127. 6 double rooms with baths, 1 2-bedroom suite. Cable TV in all rooms, wood-burning fireplaces in most rooms, kitchenette in one room, full kitchen in suite, hot tub; courtyard garden. $70–$145; full breakfast. MC, V. No smoking, very well-behaved pets only.*

Harrison's Bed and Breakfast

This large pueblo-style bed-and-breakfast, 2½ miles from the Taos

Plaza, is convenient for trips to the Taos Ski Valley. It overlooks a wooded area and the town from the foot of the west mesa, and is dramatically set off by trees and brush. The house, built in 1840 and expanded over the years, is the domain of Bob and Jean Harrison, who have lived in Taos for more than three decades and are happy to act as advisers to area newcomers.

The guest rooms are furnished with handmade, hand-painted desks, tables, and headboards crafted in northern New Mexico, less ornate than their Santa Fe-style counterparts. A full breakfast, tailored when possible to the guest's preference ("Some people just don't like Mexican food," says Mrs. Harrison, incredulously), is served in the rooms or, weather permitting, on the flower-bedecked patio. A warm and friendly stopover, Harrison's is a good buy for travelers on a budget as well as for those who like to get away from the hustle and bustle.

▦ *1134 Millicent Rogers Rd., Box 242, Taos, NM 87571, tel. 505/758–2630. 4 double rooms with baths, 2 doubles share bath. TV and pool table in family room. $20–$70; full breakfast. No credit cards. No smoking, no pets.*

La Posada de Taos

The first B&B in Taos, this opened in 1984. It's a pueblo-style adobe, built circa 1900 with beamed ceilings, a *portale*, and kiva fireplaces, in a quiet, residential area within easy walking distance of the Taos Plaza. Innkeepers Bill and Nancy Brooks-Swan offer a full, hearty breakfast at "the social hour"—from traditional ham and country eggs to a spicy Mexican burrito. Fifty percent of the clientele here are repeats.

Five of the six guest accommodations are in the main house. Decorated with antiques collected from around the world, all have tiled baths, as well as

recently constructed private patios and views of either the mountains or the flowered courtyards. All rooms but the Taos Room have wood-burning stoves or kiva fireplaces, and it compensates for this with a small sitting area, a library, and a window that frames Taos Mountain. The Beutler Room features a chaise longue and a jet whirlpool bath. Across the adobe-walled courtyard, separate La Casa de la Luna de Miel (Honeymoon House) is romantic and cozy, with a skylighted loft bed, sitting room, and kiva fireplace.

▦ *309 Juanita La., Box 1118, Taos, NM 87571, tel. 505/758–8164 or 800/645–4803, fax 505/751–3294. 5 double rooms with baths, 1 cottage. Library, TV in common room. $80–$115; full breakfast. No credit cards. No smoking, no pets.*

Little Tree

On a gentle road outside of Taos stands a little tree silhouetted against the Sangre de Cristo Mountains, welcoming guests to a charming little bed-and-breakfast inn of the same name. Built in 1991 in the traditional Southwestern adobe style, the Little Tree is owned by Kay Giddens and her husband, Charles, a former attorney: "I'd rather clean toilets than be a lawyer," he says, explaining his change in careers. The inn's proximity to the Taos Ski Valley makes it popular with the ski set, and it's also close to the famed Taos Pueblo.

All rooms have viga ceilings and are furnished in Southwestern style, with carved wooden headboards and corn husks on the door. The mud adobe and Saltillo-tile floors are radiant heated. The Piñon and Juniper Rooms have kiva fireplaces and TVs with VCRs, and for families the Juniper and Spruce rooms can be rented together as a two-bath suite.

Breakfast is served in the library, as are refreshments in the late afternoon, when guests are invited to join their hosts for meeting and greeting.

🏠 *226 Honda Seco Rd., Box 960, El Prado, NM 97529, tel. 505/776–8467 or 800/334–8467. 4 double rooms with baths. Clock radio, down comforters, cookies, and fruit in all rooms; TV with VCR in 3 guest rooms, library. $65–$95. Continental-plus breakfast, afternoon refreshments. D, MC, V; checks preferred. No smoking, no pets.*

Old Taos Guesthouse

Nestled in a wooded grove on a rise 2 miles west of Taos and overlooking the town, this restored adobe inn was built as a trapper's cabin in 1860. Expanded considerably over the years, Old Taos Guesthouse is set on 7½ acres of pasture and alfalfa fields. The *portale* in front looks like it could be from the set of "Gunsmoke"; maybe that's why Dennis Weaver often stayed here while building his Taos house. On Christmas Eve, more than 250 *luminarios* (candles in paper bags) light the way to the inn's door.

The guest rooms, each with a private courtyard entrance, have New Mexico-style furnishings, many of them made by owner Tim Reeves, a bartender in the Taos area for more than 15 years. There are Western decorative touches throughout—a bleached cattle skull over a kiva fireplace, local artwork, Mexican pottery, antique farm tools. The Taos Suite features a raised platform bed, fireplace, and kitchen. At breakfast, Leslie Reeves, the lady of the house, serves up an expanded Continental breakfast, including stewed, home-grown apples, home-baked honey bread, and lemon-nut muffins. Tim and Leslie are outdoor enthusiasts, and the Guesthouse draws many from the young, blue-jean crowd.

🏠 *1028 Witt Rd., Box 6552, Taos, NM 87571, tel. 505/758–5448 or 800/758–5448. 6 double rooms with baths, 2 suites. Cable TV in common room, hot tub. $60–$105; Continental-plus breakfast. MC, V. No smoking, no pets.*

Orinda Bed and Breakfast

Orinda is a dramatic adobe estate, built in 1947 and surrounded by towering elm and cottonwood trees. The drive is flanked by pastures where the Pratts keep two llamas, Buck and Moon "Moonie" Shadow. Indoors the B&B is populated by the dogs, Sadie and Kiva, and Grey, the cat. Owners since September 1992, George and Cary Pratt have updated, remodeled, and enlarged the original structure, which is within walking distance of the Taos Plaza.

Under a 30-foot ceiling is the house's spacious common room with a large TV, a video library, and a selection of board games, as well as a fireplace and a huge picture window that frames the Taos Mountains. Orinda's spacious rooms, two of which can be combined into a suite, boast kiva fireplaces, traditional viga ceilings, Mexican-tile baths, and separate entrances. Thick adobe walls ensure peace and quiet.

Breakfast is served in the two-story sun atrium amid a gallery of artwork, all crafted by local artists and all for sale. But don't even think about touching the Navajo blankets!

🏠 *461 Valverde, Box 4451, Taos, NM 87571, tel. 505/758–8581 or 800/847–1837. 3 double rooms with baths. 42-in cable TV in common room, video library, refrigerators, kiva fireplaces. $70–$85, suite $150 for 4 people; full breakfast, afternoon refreshments. D, MC, V. No smoking, no pets.*

The Ruby Slipper

Diane Fichtelbert and Beth Goldman, who consider Taos a mythical land, turned to Oz for the name of their inn; the guest rooms, too, allude to characters who accompanied Dorothy on her voyage. Now in its seventh year, the Ruby Slipper is ecoconscious with spiritualist overtones; only all-natural foods are served and *ochos de Dios* (God's eye) symbols are used for do-not-disturb signs. The inn draws an eclectic clientele and welcomes guests gay and straight.

One of the few adobe structures in Taos with a gabled roof, the central 1930s farmhouse has three guest rooms; two adjoining adobe buildings have two rooms each. All the rooms have private entrances and include either kiva fireplaces or woodburning stoves, Mexican-tile baths, and locally crafted furniture—simple and practical, handmade, and hand painted in the bright colors of the Santa Fe school. The full breakfasts served each morning range from hot apple cheddar omelettes and whole wheat banana pancakes to homemade granola with fresh fruit, and guests can always choose between two options.

🏠 *416 La Lomita Rd., Box 2069, Taos, NM 87571, tel. 505/758–0613. 7 double rooms with baths. Outdoor hot tub with Jacuzzi. $84–$114; full breakfast, in-room coffee and snacks. AE, D, MC, V. No smoking, no pets.*

Salsa del Salto

A combination ski lodge and ranch-style home, Salsa del Salto sits on the mesa at the foothills of the Sangre de Cristo Mountains, in a rural area criss-crossed with ancient *acequias* (irrigation ditches) developed by the Indians and early Spanish settlers to irrigate the fields. Visitors to the famed Taos Ski Valley, only 10 miles east, love this clubby hideaway, designed for owners Mary Hockett and Dadou Mayer by architect Antoine Predock. In the winter, Mayer, a renowned French chef, doubles as a ski instructor; Hockett, a native-born New Mexican, is also an avid skier. Talk about a labor of love.

All of the guest rooms are furnished with hand-crafted New Mexico furniture and have king-size beds with goose-down comforters and tiled baths, as well as spectacular views. The Honeymoon Suite features a fireplace with copper detailing. A full gourmet breakfast, highlighted by jellies, jams, and fresh-baked croissants, is served each morning in the sunny two-story-high common room with a huge fireplace and an antique stove that's used as a buffet counter.

🏠 *Hwy. 150, Box 1468, El Prado, NM 87529, tel. 505/776–2422 or 800/530–3097. 8 double rooms with baths. Outdoor heated pool, hot tub, tennis court. $85–$160; full breakfast. MC, V. No smoking indoors, no pets.*

Taos Hacienda Inn

This new bed-and-breakfast is easily one of Taos's best. A beautifully restored estate with viga and *latilla* (twig) ceilings and thick adobe walls, some dating back to the 1800s, it's only three blocks from the Plaza in a quiet setting of trees, fountains, and mountains. Owners Peggy and Jerry Davis were married in their inn in 1992: She's the mayor of Vail, Colorado, and lives in Taos on weekends; he's a former radio station owner.

The art-filled public areas have fireplaces with built-in alcove seats and overstuffed chairs and couches. A bar serves as a breakfast counter in the morning; an indoor fountain gurgles nearby. The house was formerly owned by artist Carey Moore, whose studio is now the inn's premier suite. Also outstanding is the Happy Trails Room, complete with chaps and spurs, a horse-collar mirror, and an antique wooden rocking horse. All rooms are furnished with hand-crafted pieces, pottery lamps, and Indian rugs.

315 Ranchitos, Box 4159, Taos, NM 87571, tel. 505/758–1717 or 800/530–3040. 5 double rooms with baths, 2 4-person studios. Cable TVs, phones in all rooms, fireplaces, kitchenettes, and hot tubs in studios. $95–$185; full breakfast, afternoon refreshments. AE, MC, V. No smoking.

Albuquerque

*The only major city in northern New Mexico—Santa Fe being
an elaborate set for a scriptwriter's scenario of the Southwest—
Albuquerque wields its fair share of magic nevertheless.
Visitors can ascend a breathtaking 2.7 miles to Sandia Peak on
one of the longest aerial tramways in the world or watch the
sky fill with color each October as 500-plus balloons take to the
clouds in the world's largest hot-air-balloon festival.*

*Time travel is simple here, too. Picturesque Old Town Plaza
hearkens back to 1706, when 15 families petitioned King
Philip of Spain for permission to settle at a bend in the Rio
Grande. Along legendary Route 66, now called Central
Avenue, outbursts of neon celebrate America's mid-century
romance with the automobile. One hour's drive and a thousand
years away, Acoma Pueblo looks much as it did in 1540, when
Spanish conquistadors first sighted the Native American
village atop a towering mesa.*

*With half a million people, or close to one-third of New
Mexico's population, Albuquerque is the largest metropolis in
the state. It's at the intersection of I-25 and I-40, New Mexico's
two most important freeways, and is home to the state's largest
airport, its largest university, many of its major cultural
institutions, and most of its high-tech industry.*

*In many ways, however, Albuquerque still feels like a small
town or, rather; a loosely tied collection of them. Central Avenue
and the railroad tracks divide the city into quadrants—SW, NW,
SE, and NE—which are themselves broken down into smaller
enclaves. New Mexico is typically referred to as a land of three
cultures—Native American, Hispanic, and Anglo—but in fact
a much greater variety of cultures have long spiced the city's
social stew.*

*The terrain of this vast, sprawling city is also diverse. From
an elevation of around 4,800 feet in the north and south Rio
Grande valleys, the land rises slowly in the east until it*

reaches 6,500 feet in the foothills of the Sandias, the dramatic peaks that dominate the city. On the west side, a 1,700-foot-high mesa topped by extinct volcanoes emerges abruptly from the valley floor. Temperatures can vary as much as 10° in Albuquerque, with the sun brightly shining on one side of town and snow falling on the other.

Albuquerque's bed-and-breakfasts are as colorful as the city itself. You'll find everything here, from an ancient adobe farmhouse built on the ruins of a Pueblo Indian village, to a former bordello, to a modern hacienda designed by a stockbroker on the lam. You can stay in the center of Old Town's activities or in a secluded rural setting just 15 minutes away—and pay rates much lower than those in the smaller, more trendy towns to the north. In short, you can generally get exactly the room you want—except during the balloon fiesta (see below), when the town is filled to its vigas with hot-air enthusiasts.

Places to Go, Sights to See

Acoma (40 mi west of Albuquerque, Box 309, Acoma, NM 87034, tel. 505/252–1139). Set atop a 357-foot mesa that rises sharply from the floor of a dry valley, Acoma Pueblo was built more than 1,000 years before the conquistadors discovered it in 1540. It is thought to be among the longest continually inhabited locales in North America. It is a "traditional" pueblo, without electricity or running water. Highlights of a visit, allowed by guided tour only, include the mission church of San Esteban del Rey, built between 1621 and 1641, and the fine, thin-walled pottery of the Acoma Indians.

Albuquerque International Balloon Fiesta (8309 Washington Pl. NE, Albuquerque, NM 87113, tel. 505/821–1000). An estimated 1.1 million folks converge on the city for this nine-day event, held the second weekend of October. Among the highlights are a "rodeo" of specially shaped balloons; parachute jumps; stunt flying; and the sight of hundreds of brightly hued balloons rising at dawn in the clear skies over town.

Indian Pueblo Cultural Center (2401 12th St. NW, tel. 505/843–7270 or 800/766–4405). Boasting the largest collection of Native American arts and crafts in the Southwest, the center's lower-level exhibits trace the history of the Pueblo Indians; upstairs, ceramics, jewelry, rugs, and other authentic items from the various Pueblos are on sale. Ceremonial dances are performed here during the summer and on special holidays.

Old Town. The site of the original Spanish settlement in 1706, this treeshaded, four-block square remains a cultural and commercial hub. Most of the old adobe homes were converted into shops, galleries, and restaurants, but the *San Felipe de Neri Church* (2005 Plaza NW, tel. 505/243–4628), built the year Albuquerque was established, still stands facing the Plaza. Adjacent to Old Town, the *Albuquerque Museum* (2000 Mountain Rd. SW, tel. 505/243–7255) is home to the largest collection of Spanish Colonial artifacts in the nation; it also has a good collection of contemporary New Mexican art. Just across the street, the *New Mexico Museum of Natural History* (1801 Mountain Rd. NW, tel. 505/841–8837) has interactive exhibits that include an active volcano, dinosaurs, and an ice cave, along with a Dynamax theater. Most kids will also love the small *American International Rattlesnake Museum* (202 San Felipe NW, tel. 505/242–6569) in the heart of Old Town, which houses the largest collection of live rattlesnakes in the country. The *Old Town Information Center* (tel. 505/243–3215) is across the street from the San Felipe de Neri Church.

Petroglyph National Monument (6900 Unser Blvd. NW, tel. 505/897–8814), 8 miles west of Albuquerque at the site of five extinct volcanoes, contains nearly 15,000 ancient Native American rock carvings, or petroglyphs. They are believed to have been inscribed on the lava formations of the 17-mile-long West Mesa escarpment between AD 1100 and 1600.

Rio Grand Nature Center State Park (2901 Candeleria Rd. NW, tel. 505/344–7240), on the east bank of the Rio Grande in a cottonwood forest, is home to all manner of birds and migratory fowl. Its unique visitor center is constructed half above and half below ground.

Sandia Peak Ski and Tramway (10 Tramway Loop NE, tel. 505/298–8518 for tram and ski information). A modern Swiss-built tramway lofts visitors to Sandia Crest, the 10,678-foot summit of the Sandia Mountains at the outskirts of Albuquerque. From the sky-top observation deck, you can see as far as Santa Fe to the northeast and Los Alamos to the northwest—a 360° panorama spanning 11,000 square miles. Twenty-five downhill runs, a ski school, and a rental shop operate on the mountain from mid-December through mid-March. From Memorial Day through October, the trails are given over to mountain bikers; call 505/242–9052 for information about facilities and bike and ski rentals. Year-round, the sky-high *High Finance Restaurant* (tel. 505/242–9742) has good food along with great views.

The **University of New Mexico** (east of I-25 on Central Ave., tel. 505/277–0111 for general information) has many outstanding galleries and museums that are open to the public, free of charge. The *Maxwell Museum of Anthropology* (tel. 505/277–4404) chronicles human history in general and the history of the Southwest in particular; a gift shop offers a wide selection of traditional and contemporary crafts. The largest fine art collection in the state, including works by Georgia O'Keeffe and an outstanding photography collection, may be viewed at the *University Art Museum* (tel. 505/277–4001). Lithography is the focus of the *Tamarind Institute* (tel. 505/277–3901), where prints by professionals are displayed alongside those of the school's students. Two blocks south of the campus, the *Ernie Pyle Memorial Library* (900 Girard Blvd. SE, tel. 505/256–2065) is in the memorabilia-filled home of the Pulitzer Prize-winning war correspondent.

Restaurants

Albuquerque's restaurants, as diverse as the city's neighborhoods, tend to be neither very expensive nor very formal. At the upper end are the **Monte Vista Fire Station** (tel. 505/255-2424), serving New American cuisine in a bright, chic setting; the **Artichoke Cafe** (tel. 505/243-0200), with an eclectic Continental menu and a two-level dining room; **Maria Teresa** (tel. 505/242-3900), offering New Mexican specialties in an 1840 Old Town adobe; and, the most formal of them, the **Rancher's Club** (tel. 505/884-2500), a masculine room with white-glove service and fine prime rib and seafood. The three casual and colorful **Garduño's** restaurants (tel. 505/298-5000, 505/821-3030, or 505/898-2772) serve good New Mexican food and margaritas to lively mariachi music. Other moderately priced places include **Scalo** (tel. 505/255-8781), a spirited Northern Italian spot featuring fresh pasta, and **Seagull Street** (tel. 505/821-0020), a seafood restaurant where Cape Cod meets the mesquite grill. Another notable downtown eatery is the **Rio Bravo Brewpub** (tel. 505/242-6800), with a hot mesquite grill and beers—such as the tasty High Desert Pale Ale–created on the premises.

Tourist Information

Albuquerque Convention and Visitors Bureau (121 Tijeras Ave. NE, Albuquerque, NM 87125, tel. 505/243-3696 or 800/284-2282). **Greater Albuquerque Chamber of Commerce** (401 2nd St. NW, Albuquerque, NM 87102, tel. 505/764-3700).

Reservation Services

Albuquerque Bed & Breakfast Association (Box 7262, Albuquerque, NM 87194; write for a pamphlet detailing participating inns). **Destination Southwest** (121 Tijeras Ave. NE, Albuquerque, NM 87125, tel. 800/466-7829).

Adobe and Roses

A blue mailbox marked "1011" is the only indication that you've arrived at Dorothy Morse's place in Albuquerque's North Valley, a rural enclave 15 minutes from downtown; there's literally no sign of a commercial establishment on gravel-lined Ortega Street. And the sense that you're visiting a friend—one who respects your privacy and has unusually attractive guest quarters—lasts throughout a stay at Adobe and Roses.

Dorothy originally rented out an extra suite in her home as a onetime favor to an overbooked innkeeper but later decided, what with her daughters off in college, that running an inn might not be a bad idea. In 1988, she began building a separate two-unit guest cottage, laying the floors and tile herself. After more than three decades on the premises, she has a lovely and comfortable establishment.

The pueblo-style main house and guest cottage are indeed made of adobe, and, yes, there are roses everywhere, but they don't dominate among the wildly colorful blossoms on the two-acre grounds. Most outstanding, maybe, are the rich purple irises that grow along the banks of a tranquil fish pond, so large they look like orchids. At sunset, all colors are transformed as the clouds behind the Sandias, off to the east, turn brilliant shades of pink.

The guest rooms fulfill every Southwest fantasy, with Mexican-tile sinks, terra-cotta pottery, equipale (pigskin) chairs, tinwork mirrors, wood-beam ceilings, Saltillo-tile floors, exposed brick walls, and kiva fireplaces. All are light, airy, and large—the suite in the main house easily fits a baby grand piano in the sitting room and an attached full kitchen—with individual cooling and heating units. Down comforters also help keep things cozy at night, when the 5,000-foot altitude can send the mercury dipping.

You can choose to eat breakfast in the dining room, on the portale, or in your room. Freshly ground coffee, homemade breads, muffins, and coffee cakes are staples; for those who like hot meals, Dorothy will prepare such specialties as a grits, chili, cheese, and asparagus casserole made with eggs laid by the chickens that wander the grounds. Best of all, because you're not *really* at a friend's house, you don't have to offer to do the dishes.

🏠 *1011 Ortega St. NW, Albuquerque, NM 87114, tel. 505/898–0654. 1 double room with bath, 2 suites. Kitchen in cottage units, TV in 1 suite, laundry facilities available; barbecue grill, horse boarding, kiva fireplaces in all rooms, private entrances, outdoor fountains, pets allowed. $50–$79; full breakfast. No credit cards. No smoking; 2-night minimum.*

Bottgër Mansion

This elegant, light blue American Foursquare–style B&B, built in 1912 by German-born Charles Bottgër, was once called "The Pride of Old Town." Under owners Patsy and Vince Garcia, who took control in 1992, it is returning to its former glory. The beauty salon that used to occupy the second floor is now four new double bedrooms, and an upstairs deck overlooking the tree-shaded courtyard has been added. With Old Town right out the door, bus and Sun Tran Trolley stops steps away, the Albuquerque Country Club just a few blocks away, and the downtown area a 15-minute walk, one of the most appealing aspects of this B&B is its location.

Another is the character of the residence. Professional fixer-uppers, the Garcias acquired a real gem in this National Historic Landmark. Many interesting people have passed through its gate, among them Machine Gun Kelly and his cohorts. This and many other stories tumble from the cheerful Patsy, who grew up in the area. Vince's family was one of the 12 families that founded Old Town in 1706, so the Garcias really know this intriguing section of Albuquerque.

The three downstairs suites—each named after a family grandmother—contain wonderful features. The Sofia room has an ornate, delicately imprinted pressed-tin ceiling, a brass bed, and an adjoining sunroom with twin beds, tea table, and view of the courtyard. The Mercedes room has a black marble whirlpool tub, wood shutters, and pink marble floors. Lola has a mural painted by one of the residence's former owners (George Gallegos), a ceiling frieze, a bathtub and shower flanked by marble columns, and a separate sitting room.

The living room has a striking marble fireplace, white pressed-tin ceiling, and antique chairs and couches with ornately worked wood trim. Breakfast burritos smothered in green chili, Russian crepes, stuffed French toast, or whatever's for breakfast is served in your room, outdoors in the courtyard, or in the sunny dining room with white wrought-iron tables and chairs. A refrigerator is well stocked with refreshments, and guests are welcome to it day or night.

▦ *110 San Felipe NW, Albuquerque, NM 87104, tel. 505/243–3639. 4 double rooms with baths, 3 suites. Ceiling fans and radios in all rooms, mobile phone, TV in living room. $69–$129; full breakfast. AE, D, MC, V. No smoking, no pets.*

Casa del Granjero

Casa del Granjero means the "farmer's house," but don't start thinking rustic. It's the rare field hand who hangs his hat in a place that has a glass-enclosed hot tub building and 52-inch stereo TV; business office with copier and fax; and plush white terry guest robes. Some mighty sophisticated folks have stayed here, among them, actor Mickey Rourke.

There *is* a rural quality to the inn's 3-acre North Valley property. But the B&B's Spanish appellation plays on the name of owners Butch and Victoria Farmer, who bought the Territorial-style adobe in 1987. More than 100 years old, the house was in rather sad shape when they acquired it. Butch, a contractor, converted the courtyard to a great room and added three baths, three sitting rooms, a portale, and an outbuilding.

The Farmers hadn't intended to operate a B&B, but when friends began urging them to open up their lovely home to guests, they decided to give it a go. It was such a success that Butch recently added a gazebo, bathhouse, hot tub, waterfall, built-in barbecue, and four more guest rooms in a separate ranch-style home across the street: the Bunk House.

Butch's construction skills can also be seen in many of the touches in the seven guest rooms: Santa Fe-style pine beds, carved wood corbels and beams, bright Mexican tiles inset into the kiva fireplaces. Victoria combs

yard sales and auctions for treasures, coming up with an antique trastero (combination closet and bench) or perhaps one of the colorful kilims or Navajo rugs scattered throughout the house. Even Butch's mother contributes to the cause, stitching pretty quilts for the rooms. Of all the accommodations, the Allegre Suite, with its lace-curtained canopy bed, is the most romantic and spacious.

Victoria cooks up a serious breakfast feast, everything from Italian to New Mexican specialties; one morning you might be served a breakfast burrito with avocado, fresh fruit, and flan. You can indulge, with peer support, at the long dark-wood table in the huge central dining room, or pig out in the privacy of your own patio.

🏠 *414 C de Baca La. NW, Albuquerque, NM 87114, tel. and fax 505/897-4144. 3 double rooms (2 with baths), 4 suites. Desks and kiva fireplaces in all rooms, private entrances onto portale in suites, VCR and video library in common room, washroom. $69-$149; full breakfast. MC, V. No smoking, pets boarded nearby.*

Casas de Sueños

ouses rarely determine their own fate, but that's just one of the many ways in which Casas de Sueños (Houses of Dreams) is exceptional. In 1979, lawyer Robert Hanna commissioned Albuquerque architect Bart Prince to design an office above the entry to his low-slung adobe complex. So many people came by to gape at the result that Hanna spent half his time inviting them in to look around. In 1990 he decided to turn this pleasant but distracting activity into a business—and thus a B&B was born.

The artistic inclinations of this inn, one block from Old Town, aren't limited to its recent addition. Casas de Sueños was designed as an artists' community in the 1930s by painter J. R. Willis; at the perimeter of his house and studio he built a group of rental cottages, which now house guests. Little inspirational paths and niches, some with bubbling streams, abound in the complex, and a profusion of blossoms climbs up walls and spills out onto a lush lawn. There are more than 50 rose bushes and a dozen varieties of grapevines on the acre of grounds.

In addition, the inn's dining room, where a gourmet hot and cold buffet is set out each morning, doubles as a gallery for local artists. With its French doors, lace tablecloths, viga ceilings, and kiva fireplace, the room is warm and cheerful. On nice days, you can head out to the lovely adjoining patio.

The guest rooms, most with private entrances and courtyards, are decorated in different styles, each more attractive than the last. All have fresh flowers and luxurious bedding; many boast kitchens, fireplaces, Oriental rugs, and ornate wood furnishings acquired from the estate of a Spanish nobleman. The La Cascada suite lets out onto its own private waterfall; the Porter features a Willis mural and private patio with outdoor hot tub; and the wonderfully over-the-top Cupid has a skylight, florid gilt mirror, and brass Cupids holding the toilet paper roll.

Oh yes, and Bart Prince's fantastic creation is now used for massages instead of a law practice. Officially named the Dream Space, the loft is a kind of architectural Rorschach test: Locals have dubbed it "the snail," but others have sworn it's anything from a ram's head to an ancient fertility symbol.

🏨 *310 Rio Grande SW, Albuquerque, NM 87104, tel. 505/247-4560 or 800/ 242-8987, fax 505/842-8493. 3 double rooms with baths; 4 1-bedroom suites, 4 2-bedroom suites, 6 casitas. Telephone in most rooms, cable TV in all rooms, kitchens in all casitas, fireplaces in some rooms, library; off-street parking. $85-$250; full breakfast. AE, D, DC, MC, V. No smoking, no pets.*

Casita Chamisa

The first B&B in Albuquerque, Casita Chamisa is also historic in other ways. Originally an adobe farmhouse dating back to 1850, it sits atop the ruins of five successive Pueblo and pre-Pueblo village sites, the oldest dating to around 720 BC! Jack Schaefer, previous owner of the home and author of *Shane*, used to find pottery shards from time to time. The mother lode was hit when current owners Kit and Arnold Sargeant began construction of the B&B's 30-foot pool. Kit, an author and archaeologist, enlisted the help of the University of New Mexico to conduct a thorough excavation. More than 150,000 pottery shards and artifacts were eventually recovered. Some remain on view at the home, along with part of the excavation.

Set in the pastoral North Valley, which was settled in the 1600s by the Spanish colonialists, this B&B has everything you associate with the region. It is shaded by massive river cottonwoods, which keep the place cool on even the hottest days. Chickens, roosters, beehives, herb and vegetable gardens, horses (not for riding), fruit trees, and winding *acequias* (irrigation ditches) retain the former farm's character.

There are only two accommodations, so tranquility is the order of the day. The ivy-covered guest house has a small sitting room with a corner kiva fireplace, a queen bed, a private patio, and a greenhouse where you can sit and read or write. The kitchenette and a separate bedroom with twin beds

covered with French knot bedspreads make this an ideal place for a small family. Animals, a sandbox, swing set, and pool are real attractions for kids. A charming bedroom in the main house is decorated with a Mexican tin mirror, equipale furniture, and a hand-carved Mexican headboard. It also has a kiva fireplace and private entrance onto the covered portale that wraps around two sides of the home.

The home has a great library and a baby grand piano and is filled with wonderful arts and crafts from around the world, including a basket collection, Mexican textiles, and odds and ends gathered by Arnold during his worldwide travels with the U.S. Army.

A country Continental breakfast is served on a plant-filled, enclosed, glass-covered patio, in the dining room before a small fireplace, or out on the portale. It includes fruit, juices, coffee and tea, as well as coffee cakes and muffins, or another slice of history: some of Arnold's fresh sourdough bread, made from a 200-year-old Basque starter.

850 Chamisal Rd. NW, Albuquerque, NM 87107, tel. 505/897-4644. 1 double room with bath, 1 2-bedroom casita. Fireplaces in both rooms, library; enclosed pool, hot tub, greenhouse, gardens, sun-deck. $80–$135. Continental breakfast. AE, D, MC, V. No smoking indoors, pets by prior arrangement.

Elaine's

It might be hard to decide which you like better, Elaine O'Neil or her house, but then the two are inextricably intertwined. One of the nicest building contractors you're ever likely to meet, Elaine supervised the construction of her rough-hewn stone-and-log cabin down to the last interesting detail—for example, the ornate iron braces that anchor the joints of the ceiling beams, which are at once decorative and functional.

A winding dirt road leads up to Elaine's, set in the heart of the Sandia Mountains in Cedar Crest, 15 miles east of Albuquerque on the historic Turquoise Trail to Santa Fe. But the bed-and-breakfast's rustic setting and structure belie its elegant interior. If the Victorians had slalomed, they doubtless would have headed to just such a retreat for après-ski sherries.

Although there are fine antiques all around the house, this is a cheerful, unpretentious place. Light from huge windows in the two-story-high cathedral ceiling streams into an upstairs common area, where an enormous stone fireplace is fronted by comfortable couches. Guests often just flop down on the plush hunter-green carpet and play one of the board games stocked in the rooms, read, or stare into the flames.

One of the second-level rooms has a whirlpool tub, while the third-level room has dramatic views of mountains and plains in three directions. Fresh flowers and soft, downy bedding help make all three accommodations, which mix sturdy wood furnishings and more delicate antiques, very appealing. One disadvantage: Because the romantic top-floor bedroom was built loft style, its occupants can overhear late-night revelers on the lower level—but it is still Elaine's most popular room.

Breakfast here, served in a new airy and plant-filled breakfast room, is simple but hearty; large helpings of fresh fruit, pancakes or waffles, and sausage are standard, but guests can get pretty much what they like. Afterward, many find that the crisp mountain air inspires them to take a long walk. Charlie, a fat golden retriever who likes to laze on "his" front porch bench, will happily accompany guests on a hike through the Cibola National Forest, abutting the inn's 4 acres. Eliot, part wolf, part German shepherd, disdains Charlie's friendly doggie ways but always condescends to come along for the exercise.

🏠 *Box 444, 72 Snowline Estates, Cedar Crest, NM 87008, tel. 505/281–2467 or 800/821–3092. 3 double rooms with baths. Private balcony in 2 rooms, books in rooms, wraparound deck; hiking trails on property, skiing and horseback riding nearby. $77–$85; full breakfast. AE, MC, V. No smoking, no pets.*

Enchanted Vista

Don't be surprised to see a red-tail hawk hunting alongside the dirt road as you pull up to this B&B in the rapidly growing far Northeast Heights of Albuquerque. Inside the Spanish villa B&B, you'll find an equally amazing level of domesticity and warmth in your hosts Tillie and Al Gonzales. Tillie likes to bake her own bread; if you're lucky, she'll pull a lemon-dill or a caraway-seed loaf out of the oven.

The Gonzales's immaculate home, built in 1988, rests just beneath the Sandia Mountains, which rear up almost 4,000 jagged feet in the crystal-clear air. You can wind down from a day of sightseeing on the multi-level redwood deck's swing bench, taking in the great mountain views or perhaps a tremendous sunset. The deck overlooks a rock garden, flower beds, bird-feeders, fountains, and scurrying wild quail.

The next day, you're sure to have Tillie's tasty full breakfast. She will also provide dinner, on special request; another option is to fire up the barbecue and firepit and cook out as the sun slips over the Western skyline and Albuquerque's lights wink on.

🏨 *10700 Del Rey NE, Albuquerque, NM 87122, tel. 505/823–1301. 1 double room (no bath), 2 suites. TVs, refrigerators, coffeemakers, dining table, whirlpool tub in 1 room; basketball court and tetherball. $62–$74. No credit cards. No smoking, no cats.*

Hacienda Vargas

In 1990, when Jule and Pablo Vargas came to tiny Algodones, about 20 miles north of Albuquerque, they bought a sprawling hacienda that had changed a lot in the past 200 years—in a town that had changed very little. Hacienda Vargas, now a repository of New Mexico history and culture, was a group of small adobe units and a stagecoach stop in the late 1700s. In the early 1900s, the house, by then a single structure, was used as an Indian trading post.

The Vargases did a lot of renovating, but the house still retains much of its original flavor, due in no small part to the mature cottonwoods and small Spanish chapel on the 2-acre grounds. The six guest rooms, including the newly added Santa Fe Room, successfully blend antique furnishings with contemporary-Southwest bedspreads and art; the romantic Kiva Room has its own skylit Jacuzzi tub and a separate sitting area. Among the tasty breakfast dishes are "Kika's scramble"—spicy eggs topped with toasted nuts.

🏨 *1431 El Camino Real, Box 307, Algodones, NM 87001, tel. 505/867–9115 or 800/261–0006. 6 double rooms with baths. Kiva fireplaces throughout house; library, art gallery; portale, barbecue, outdoor hot tub; "romance" packages; conferences, catering available. $69–$129; full breakfast. MC, V. No smoking, no pets.*

Old Town Bed & Breakfast

Owner Nancy Hoffman's welcome—a basket of fruit and homemade cookies—is simple but very appealing, and so is her B&B. It's on a tree-shrouded, quiet street just two blocks from charming Old Town, the city's major museums, and an attractive park, and was built in 1940 by Albuquerque architect Leon Watson—a pioneer in the use of adobe in modern home design.

The bright, spacious downstairs suite—with latilla ceiling, kiva fireplace, Saltillo-tile floor, and equipale furniture—is very Southwestern. The adjoining sitting room and library provide additional sleeping space if needed. A beautiful skylit bath with whirlpool tub is adjacent to the suite and shared with the owner. The cheerful, small upstairs room has great views of the mountains and the surrounding flowering trees.

When it's nice out, fresh-squeezed juice, coffee, and homemade breads, muffins, or cobblers are served on the pretty patio; on chilly mornings, a wood stove in the living room warms the adjacent dining area.

🏠 *707 17th St. NW, Albuquerque, NM 87104, tel. 505/764–9144. 1 double room with shower, 1 suite. Off-street parking, drip fountain. $60–$75. No credit cards. No smoking, no pets.*

Sarabande

This tranquil lodging in the quiet Los Ranchos de Albuquerque section of town is a bit formal, in part because the Territorial-style home, built in 1987, still looks brand shiny new. A Japanese garden and fishpond at the side of the house, along with a profusion of well-trimmed flowers and trees surrounding the tiled courtyard fountain and all sides of the home, also add to the sense of orderliness here.

But innkeepers Margaret Magnussen and Betty Vickers, both retired nurses, welcome guests warmly into their lovely home. A common sitting room with contemporary Southwestern art and a kiva fireplace adjoins a country-style kitchen and dining room with a wood-burning stove and huge, old-fashioned butcher block; your favorite hot breakfast is served here. The romantic Rose Room has a raised kiva fireplace, soaking tub, and wall-to-wall carpeting. The Iris Room, with a stained-glass representation of the flower, looks out onto real blooms in the courtyard and onto the B&B's heated, 50-foot lap pool and hot tub.

🏠 *5637 Rio Grande Blvd. NW, Albuquerque, NM 87107, tel. 505/345–4923.*

3 double rooms with baths. Fireplace in sitting room, hot tub; all-terrain bicycles. $75–$110; full breakfast. MC, V. No smoking, no pets.

W. E. Mauger Estate

The residential neighborhoods surrounding Albuquerque's downtown business district have been revitalized in recent years, and the eye-popping restoration of the W. E. Mauger Estate in 1984 helped pioneer this effort. You'd never suspect now that the dignified redbrick Queen Anne, built in 1897 and on the National Register of Historic Places, was once a boarding house.

Victoriana reigns in this antiques-filled B&B, from the dark-blue flowered wallpaper, lace antimacassars, and ancient Victrola in the common room, to various period bureaus, desks, and beds in the guest rooms. All the accommodations are tastefully furnished, but they lack bathtubs. A three-course breakfast, which might include potato pancakes or cheese frittatas, is served on the tiny sunporch or in the indoor dining room.

Its location, smack against downtown, has proven popular with business people, but Martin Sheen and Linda Ronstadt have also stayed here.

🏠 *701 Roma Ave. NW, Albuquerque, NM 87102, tel. 505/242–8755, fax 505/842–8835. 7 double rooms, 1 single, all with baths. Coffeemakers, hair dryers, irons, clock radios, and TVs in all rooms, refrigerators in most rooms, balcony in one room; fireplace, TV in sitting room; sunporch, patio, off-street parking. $75–$115; full breakfast, snacks, evening wine and cheese. AE, MC, V. No smoking, children and pets by prior arrangement.*

Yours Truly

Opened eight years ago by Pat and James Montgomery, this B&B exudes their personal warmth and outgoing nature. Their adventurous side is also evident—from the sunrise hot-air balloon rides they pilot to the commodious hot tub on the large brick patio. Perched on a hillside, it overlooks the Rio Grande Valley, the lazy and charming village of Corrales, and the towering Sandias. It's a great place to watch the mountains turn pink at sunset or to see a moonrise.

The modern adobe's bedrooms are not large, but they are quite comfortable and attractive. One room features a king bed set in an adobe banco; overhead glass brick blocks let in the afternoon light while a gas fireplace illuminates the night. Even the shower in this room's bathroom is fun: Dual heads provide water for two.

Pat pulls out the stops at the breakfast buffet, using her best crystal, sterling, and china to serve tasty, fresh-baked goods—say, praline French toast or jalapeno bread—fruit, and coffee.

🎏 *160 Paseo de Corrales, Box 2263, Corrales, NM 87048, tel. 505/898-7027. 3 double rooms with baths. Guest robes, TVs, and radios in all rooms; kiva fireplaces in 2 rooms, clerestory windows, large music selection, fireplace in living room; hot-air balloon rides ($175 for 2 people). $75; full breakfast, afternoon wine and snacks. AE, MC, V. No smoking in bedrooms.*

Southern New Mexico

Folks who fly into Albuquerque International Airport tend to flock north to chic Santa Fe and Taos—which is all to the advantage of those opting to explore equally beautiful, much less trafficked southern New Mexico. One might almost suspect residents of the region below I-40, casting a wary eye on rocketing real estate rates to the north, of spreading the word that the lower two-thirds of the state is entirely arid and flat.

Nothing could be farther from the truth. In southwestern New Mexico alone, local roads lead to three national forests, a dozen mountain ranges, countless cascading streams, and myriad mineral hot springs. On NM 90 west from Silver City, for example, the road rises from the foothills of the Pinos Altos Mountains and winds up through the thick pines of Gila National Forest to Emory Pass, where, from a vantage point of 8,228 feet, the breathtaking Black Range Mountain valley spreads out as far as the eye can see.

The landscape of south-central New Mexico is equally dramatic. Between the towns of Las Cruces and Socorro, the Rio Grande widens out into Elephant Butte Lake and into the Bosque del Apache, a wintertime sanctuary for the endangered whooping crane. East of Las Cruces, the shifting gypsum sands of White Sands National Monument predict the snowy peaks of the Sacramento Mountains, set against the lush green of Lincoln National Forest. The more northerly route to Lincoln forest and the White Mountains from Socorro arrows past Valley of Fires State Park, 44 miles of gray-and-pink volcanic rock formed by one of the nation's best-preserved lava flows.

If the southeastern region seems to conform most to the stereotype of desert desolation, it provides a geological lesson in the value of looking below surfaces. Beneath miles of flat, scrubby terrain lies one of the most wondrous natural spectacles of all—Carlsbad Caverns National Monument—its huge, subterranean chambers a showcase for massive stalactites and stalagmites and delicate aragonite crystal sculptures.

The history of the West is painted in broad strokes on this richly textured natural canvas. Ancient pottery and dwellings of the Mimbres, Pueblo, and Gila peoples bear witness to some of the complex civilizations that existed here before Spanish conquistadors and priests put their mark on the area in the 17th century, while vast, open pits and abandoned cities such as Hillsboro and Kingston attest to the gold-, silver-, and copper-mining madness that literally had its impact 200 years later. On the heels of the rush for mineral riches rode Billy the Kid, whose legends were made and played out in such boomtowns as Silver City and Mesilla. Rough-and-tumble as those times may have been, it was all minor mayhem compared to the act that gave the region its sobering global significance: On July 16, 1945, the world's first atomic bomb was detonated at Trinity Site, in the Tularosa basin northwest of Alamogordo.

Outdoor activities abound in the area, too—fishing in Caballo Lake, say, or skiing in Cloudcroft or Ruidoso, where a worldclass horse track also draws those whose idea of exercise is filling out a racing form. Indeed, the region's surprising array of attractions tends to inspire many to stay longer than planned—which is not a problem. Laid-back southern New Mexico may not have the abundance of upscale accommodations that the north enjoys, but friendly, scenic, and often sophisticated inns are here for the finding, almost all at reasonable rates.

Places to Go, Sights to See

Carlsbad Caverns National Park (3225 National Parks Highway, Carlsbad, NM 88220, tel. 505/785–2232), at the southeastern end of the state, is one of the largest and most impressive cave systems in the world. Touring it on the longer Natural Entrance Route, on foot, offers a truer experience of the cavern's depth, but the Big Room Route, which takes visitors down via high-speed elevator, is an easier way to view all the major formations. If you visit between late May and mid-October, be sure to come back at sunset to see tens of thousands of bats fly en masse out of the cavern.

Gila Cliff Dwellings National Monument (NM 15, 44 mi north of Silver City, Route 11, Box 100, Silver City, NM 88061, tel. and fax 505/536–9461) is at the edge of the Gila Wilderness, surrounded by the Gila National Forest. A 1-mile loop trail leads to and through seven natural caves that hold 40 well-preserved rooms constructed of stone and mud mortar by the Pueblo Indians in the 13th century. Near the visitor center are the remains of a pit house used by the Mogollón Indians somewhere between AD 100 and AD 400.

Las Cruces and Mesilla. At the junction of two major highways, I-10 and I-25, Las Cruces and the adjacent town of Mesilla have long been transportation hubs: El Camino Real, the old Spanish trade route, ran through Las Cruces, and Mesilla was a major stop for the Butterfield Trail Overland stagecoach. Now the largest city in southern New Mexico and home to New Mexico State University, Las Cruces hosts a number of small museums and galleries; information on these and a self-guided walking tour of two historic districts are available at the convention and visitors bureau (*see* Tourist Information, *below*). The lovely plaza and surrounding buildings in the restored 19th-century town of La Mesilla, where the Gadsen Purchase was signed and Billy the Kid was tried and sentenced to death, are now a state monument and house small shops and businesses. Mementos of the adobe fort set up on the Rio Grande in 1865 to protect residents of Mesilla Valley from Apache attack may be viewed at *Fort Selden State Monument* (15 mi north of Las Cruces, tel. 505/526–8911).

Lincoln. Tiny Lincoln was most notoriously the site of the 1878 Lincoln County War, in which two opposing factions clashed over lucrative government contracts for one year. Billy the Kid, who took part in a number of the gun battles, spent the last four years of his life here. Today, the town is a National Historic Landmark, its only street (Hwy. 380) lined with buildings dating from its tumultuous past, including the *Tunstall Store Museum* (tel. 505/653–4372) and the *Lincoln County Courthouse Museum* (tel. 505/653–4372). The *Historical Center* (tel. 505/653–4025) runs a 15-minute slide show introducing Lincoln's attractions.

Ruidoso. On the eastern slopes of the pine-covered Sacramento Mountains, Ruidoso is a sophisticated year-round resort that retains its rustic smalltown charm. Each summer the town becomes the epicenter of American quarter horse racing, thanks to *Ruidoso Downs* (Hwy. 70, tel. 505/378–4431), a state-of-the-art track. Down the road, the 40,000-square-foot *Museum of the Horse* (Hwy. 70, tel. 505/378–4142) has more than 10,000 equine items, including paintings, drawings, and bronzes. Bordering Ruidoso to the west is the *Mescalero Apache Indian Reservation*, which has a general store, a trading post, and a small museum. The real attractions here, however, are the Apache-owned and -operated *Inn of the Mountain Gods* (Carrizon Canyon Rd., Box 269, Mescalero, NM 88340, tel. 505/ 257–5141), a resort with a minicasino, and the *Ski Apache* area (Hwy. 70, tel. 505/ 336–4357) on the nearby 11,400-foot Sierra Blanca, which has fine-powder skiing from Thanksgiving until mid-April.

Silver City. One of many mining towns that mushroomed in the southwestern corner of the state in the latter half of the 19th century, Silver City, unlike others, survived the crash of the silver market in 1893. A number of self-guided walking tours are available from the chamber of commerce (*see* Tourist Information, *below*): One leads to the well-preserved Victorian downtown area, while another allows you to explore various landmarks in the life of the town's most infamous son, Billy the Kid, who spent most of his teenage years here. The *New Mexico University Museum* (Fleming Hall, tel. 505/538–6386) houses the largest display in the United States of prehistoric pottery by the Mimbres Indians, and the *Silver City Museum* (312 W. Broadway, tel. 505/538–5921), in an 1881 mansion, exhibits mining tools and household effects of early town inhabitants. Two open-pit copper mines close by display a harsh beauty: the *Phelps-Dodge mine,* at the end of town south on NM 90, and the *Santa Rita/Chino mine,* 15 miles east on NM 152.

Socorro. About 75 miles south of Albuquerque in the Rio Grande valley, this small city dates back to 1615, when Spanish Franciscan priests built Nuestra Senora del Socorro (Our Lady of Help) mission on what was then the land of the Pueblo peoples. Its rowdy heyday, however, was in the 1880s, when the advent of the railroad transformed this mining town into a major shipping center. A self-guided walking-tour brochure of the town's historic buildings, including the *San Miguel Mission,* built on the site of the original mission between 1819 and 1821, is available at the Socorro Chamber of Commerce (*see* Tourist Information, *below*). Also of interest is the *Mineral Museum* at the New Mexico Institute of Mining and Technology (Workman Center, tel. 505/835–5420), with samples of more than 10,000 minerals from around the world. In the winter, the 57,000-acre *Bosque del Apache National Wildlife Refuge* (18 mi south of Socorro, tel. 505/835–1828) is a must-see: From late November through early February, tens of thousands of Arctic-bred snow geese and ducks, along with sandhill cranes, bald eagles, and red-tailed hawks, rest here on their migratory route south.

Truth or Consequences. This slow-paced western town doesn't seem to have changed much since 1950, when it changed its name from Hot Springs as part of a promotion for the 10th anniversary of a popular radio quiz show. A health resort at the turn of the century, T or C (as it's known locally) still retains a number of the mineral bathhouses that drew people in droves. *Geronimo Springs Museum* (211 Main St., tel. 505/894–6600), which explores the history of the area, devotes a wing to Ralph Edwards, host of the "Truth or Consequences" radio show (the town also holds an annual festival in his honor). Fishing and water sports are popular at nearby *Elephant Butte Lake State Park* (7 mi to the north, tel. 505/744–5421) and *Caballo Lake State Park* (14 mi south, tel. 505/743–3942).

White Sands National Monument (15 mi southwest of Alamogordo, Box 1086, Holloman Air Force Base, NM 88330, tel. 505/479–6124). A scene out of *Lawrence of Arabia,* with shifting sand dunes 60 feet high, White Sands encompasses 145,344 acres, the largest deposit of gypsum sand in the world; it's one of the few landforms recognizable from space. There's a 16-mile loop trail from the visitor center for those who want to explore the monument in a vehicle, and a mile-long, self-guided nature trail for walkers.

Restaurants

Tiny Capitán, near Ruidoso, is home to **Hotel Chango** (tel. 505/354–4213), an excellent restaurant with a surprisingly sophisticated Continental menu. In Cloudcroft, **Rebecca's** at The Lodge (*see* review, *below*) serves fine Southwestern-inspired dishes in a stunning mountain setting. Visitors to Hillsboro's **Sweetwood**

BBQ (tel. 505/895–5642) can enjoy tender brisket of beef smoked with sweet applewood; seating is outside in an apple orchard or in a rough-cut cedar barn; keep in mind that this closes at nightfall. In Mesilla, the informal **La Posta** (tel. 505/524–3524) dishes up good Mexican fare in a 200-year-old building where the Butterfield stagecoach used to stop; **Mesón de Mesilla** (*see* review, *below*), with its fine Continental fare, is the more upscale dining choice in town. **La Lorraine** (tel. 505/257–2954), in Ruidoso, serves classic French cuisine in cozy country-French surroundings. At Silver City's low-key, family-run **Jalisco Restaurant** (tel. 505/388–2060), you can't go wrong ordering anything with green chili in it. In Socorro, the casual-clubby **Val Verde Steak House** (203 Manzanitas St., tel. 505/835–3880) is great for ribs and sirloin, and the stuffed sopaipillas at **Frank & Lupe's El Sombrero** (210 Mesquite, tel. 505/835–3945), a colorful, down-home eatery, can't be beat. In Silver City, **The Black Cactus** (107 W. Yankie St., 505/388–5430) offers a fine selection of wines and Italian fare, as well as a patio where summer guests can dine while listening to live jazz, flamenco, or folk music.

Tourist Information

Las Cruces Convention and Visitors Bureau (311 N. Downtown Mall, Las Cruces, NM 88001, tel. 505/524–1422 or 800/343–7827). **Lincoln Hospitality Group** (Box 27, Lincoln, NM 88338, tel. 505/653–4676). **Ruidoso Valley Convention and Visitors Bureau** (720 Sudderth Dr., Box 698, Ruidoso, NM 88345, tel. 505/257–7395 or 800/253–2255). **Silver City Chamber of Commerce** (1103 N. Hudson St., Silver City, NM 88061, tel. 505/538–3785 or 800/548–9378). **Socorro Chamber of Commerce** (Box 743, Socorro, NM 87801, tel. 505/835–0424). **Truth or Consequences Chamber of Commerce** (Drawer 31, Truth or Consequences, NM 87901, tel. 505/894–3536 or 800/831–9487).

Reservation Services

Bed & Breakfast of New Mexico (Box 2805, Santa Fe, NM 87504, tel. 505/982–3332). **New Mexico Bed and Breakfast Association** (Box 2925, Santa Fe, NM 87504; write for a list of member inns).

Eaton House

Unlike other adventurers who headed west to seek their fortune but built homes in familiar East Coast-style when they arrived, Colonel E. W. Eaton—Civil War hero, founder of a smelter, and, later, mayor of Socorro—constructed a thick-walled Territorial adobe for his young New Mexican bride in 1881. This is not to suggest the wealthy Eatons did not indulge in "civilized" Eastern touches: lead-glass windows and a built-in classical-revival colonnade bookcase grace their elegant home, which remained in family hands for nearly 100 years.

Innkeepers Anna Appleby and Tom Harper have retained the original blend of New Mexican and Victorian styles in their upscale B&B. Their five guest rooms—all offering private entrances from a shaded brick portale—are decorated with impeccable taste. The Vigilante Room features a Santa Fe-style bed and trastero (combination closet and bench) crafted by a local artisan, as well as a colorful Mexican-tile sink. Matching carved wooden beds built for twin girls 80 years ago are set in Daughters' Room, which also boasts a fluted-glass light fixture original to the house. The Colonel Eaton Room has a queen-size pencil-post bed so high you need a stool to climb in, flowered imported Dutch tile in the bath, and delicate English lace curtains. The Marcellina Chavez Casita, named for the wife of Colonel Eaton, is a spacious new suite in spite of the king-size bed, and features a Pueblo-style fireplace and massive vigas that cross the ceiling;

also new is the Bosque Casita, similarly roomy, with a Mexican-tile full bath. All rooms have luxurious European-goose-down blankets.

The B&B is an extremely popular spot for bird-watchers, largely because it's near the Bosque del Apache, a wildlife refuge on the banks of the Rio Grande. The Sevilleta National Wildlife Refuge and Cibola National Forest are also nearby. Both Tom and Anna are avid bird-watchers, and Anna will prepare a light "Early Birder" breakfast basket for guests who want to set off first thing in the morning. They can return to a full gourmet breakfast in the high-ceiling dining room. Main dishes are sinful—soufflés topped with chopped bananas, banana cream liqueur, whipped cream, and homemade pomegranate sauce, for example—but all the fruits used are organic, and the meats are made without nitrates or preservatives.

🏠 *403 Eaton Ave., Socorro, NM 87801, tel. 505/835–1067. 1 single room with bath, 4 double rooms with baths. Ceiling fans in rooms; library, fireplace; binoculars and field guides available. $75–$120; full breakfast, afternoon tea. No credit cards. No smoking indoors, no pets, no children under 14.*

The Ellis Store & Co. Bed and Breakfast

This lodging's history dates back to 1850, when it was a modest, two-room adobe in territory where the Mescalero Indians still posed a threat to settlers. During the Lincoln County War, the building's thick walls provided refuge for members of the McSween faction, and Billy the Kid was kept here pending his trial. Today, the house looks out on a peaceful lawn where deer graze in the evening.

In 1993 David and Jinny Vigil ended their 10-year search for a B&B with this one. David, a former engineer whose family has been in New Mexico for nearly 300 years, has done a lot of work on the building, adding bathrooms and meticulously restoring the front portale to include its historic sag. Guests sit under it in the quiet of the morning while enjoying Jinny's gourmet cooking. In the evenings, her culinary skills draw people from as far away as Carlsbad. They come to enjoy such delicacies as veal Madeira as part of a six-course meal served in the spacious depths of a dining room glowing with light from the fireplace.

Three of the guest rooms in the main house have wood-burning stoves; the fourth, Nancy's Room, has a fireplace. Each is named for a former resident of the house (though Billy the Kid only needed to stay a few days to get one named after him) and is decorated with antiques. The accommodations are interesting but not necessarily private, as many rooms have adjoining doors, and a pair share a bath. Behind the building sits the Mill House, which contains four rooms sharing a bath and a large family den.

However, it would be hard to imagine a guest staying indoors when there is so much to see in the surrounding area. David leases 6,400 acres nearby and offers horseback hunting trips for ruggedly inclined guests, and there is fishing in the creek that runs through the property. Guests also have the option of hiking or taking a historical tour of Lincoln.

🏨 *Hwy. 380, mile marker 98, Box 15, Lincoln, NM 88338, tel. 505/653-4609 or 800/653-5460, fax 505/653-4610. 2 double rooms with baths, 2 doubles share bath, 4 doubles share bath in Mill House. Woodburning stove or fireplace in 4 rooms, 6-course dinners served by reservation; fishing, hunting, hiking. $60, Continental breakfast; $69–$79, full gourmet breakfast. D, MC, V. No smoking indoors, no pets.*

The Lodge

Cloudcroft's Lodge embodies the yin and yang of late-Victorian design in a singularly appealing fashion. Built in 1899 by the Alamogordo and Sacramento Mountain railway to house its workers, this ornate but imposing structure has a lobby where any hunter would be proud to rest a gun: A stuffed bear stands snarling in the corner, and a long-horned eland stares down from over the copper fireplace at deep-maroon leather couches and chairs. But pink-floral carpets lead down the hallway to individually decorated rooms with chenille bedspreads, period antiques, pastel-flocked wallpaper, ceiling fans, and, in many cases, four-poster beds.

Some of the accommodations are rather small, but they're accordingly less expensive. And if you get one with a view, it'll open up the space immeasurably. If you don't, you can always climb up to the hotel's copper-covered bell tower, which Judy Garland visited with Clark Gable. On a clear day, you can see White Sands National Monument in the distance. Those who really want to hide away with friends can rent the Retreat, a four-bedroom cottage with a kitchenette, located just across the front parking lot from the main building.

The pool on the lush back lawn is inviting in warm weather, but winter is as delightful as summer in this mountain retreat. A gently sloping, pine-shrouded golf course on the grounds becomes a playground for cross-country skiers; downhill runs at the Cloudcroft Ski Area are only 2 miles away; and snowmobiling and horse-drawn-sleigh rides can be arranged through the front desk.

Any time of year, it's a treat to visit Rebecca's, the Lodge's elegant American-Southwestern dining room, named after the putative resident ghost. A Continental breakfast at Rebecca's is included in room rates for those who stay at the Pavilion: A Bed and Breakfast, about ½ mile to the south of the main building, but also part of the Lodge. This single-level structure is rustic in style—rooms have beamed ceilings, knotty-pine walls, and, in some cases, enormous stone fireplaces.

⊞ *1 Corona Pl., Box 497, Cloudcroft, NM 88317, tel. 505/682–2566 or 800/ 395–6343, fax 505/682–2715. 10 single rooms with baths, 30 doubles with baths, 7 suites in hotel; 11 doubles with baths in B&B; 1 4-bedroom cottage. Telephone and cable TV in all rooms, sauna, spa, bar, 2 gift shops, conference facilities. $49–$169, the Retreat cottage $269; breakfast not included for Lodge or Retreat guests, Continental breakfast for B&B guests. AE, D, DC, MC, V. No pets.*

Lundeen Inn
of the Arts

You'll think you've died and gone to Santa Fe when you wake up at this arty, upscale bed-and-breakfast, but you'll be paying Las Cruces prices for the experience. Owned and designed by architect Gerald Lundeen and his wife, Linda, whose art gallery is on the premises, the inn is designed to nurture aesthetic impulses in its visitors.

Gerald seamlessly joined two 1895 adobe houses, one Mexican Colonial and the other Pueblo style, in order to create the B&B; what was once the patio between them became the 18-foot-high Marienda Room, where most of the inn's activity takes place. Guests attend art classes, conferences, and performances in this unusual space, which is decorated in an eclectic (and ecumenical) fashion: The ornate wood balustrade is from a synagogue in El Paso and the pressed-tin ceiling frieze is from a Methodist church in Lordsburg. Huge Palladian windows let in lots of light at breakfast, when guests enjoy elaborate meals here—at least one hot entrée as well as a tempting variety of baked goods.

Reading niches and comfortable sitting areas abound in both wings of the house. Guest rooms are named for Western artists such as Georgia O'Keeffe and Frederic Remington. The one dedicated to Native American painter R. C. Gorman has a kiva fireplace, viga beams, and a curved seating nook with built-in bookcases. The connection between artist and decor is occasionally mysterious—one wonders, for example, how cowboy painter Gordon Snidow might feel about being represented by a room with a bidet in it—but never mind: All the accommodations are beautifully furnished with a whimsical mix of antiques and newer, handcrafted pieces. And, naturally, the walls are decked with art prints and reproductions. A newly restored adobe in the back of the Inn adds three casitas with full baths to the rooms available. In fact, the Lundeen Inn offers long-term residence if you find you just can't separate yourself from Las Cruces.

The Inn offers courses in silver-smithing, ceramics, coil pottery, and architecture, all of which are taught monthly. Most of the classes last a week, and people sign up months ahead for them, but guests can sign up for single classes. There is also a course on breadmaking, and to this end the Lundeens have installed an indian *horno*, a lumpy adobe oven that can bake up to 18 loaves at a time.

🏠 *618 S. Alameda Blvd., Las Cruces, NM 88005, tel. 505/526–3327, fax 505/526–3355. 20 double rooms with baths, 6 suites. Telephones, TV, fireplaces, balconies, kitchenettes in some rooms; off-street parking, $61, suites $75–$105; full breakfast. AE, D, DC, MC, V. No smoking, children and pets by advance arrangement.*

Bear Mountain Guest Ranch

Myra McCormick, the crusty proprietor of the Bear Mountain Guest Ranch, has a firm house rule: Her guests must introduce themselves at dinner. (Three fresh-cooked, low-fat meals are included in the room rates.) She also urges visitors to enjoy the outdoors; bird-watching is especially encouraged. If it all feels a bit like summer camp for grown-ups, it's hard to resist the lovely setting, the camaraderie, or Myra herself, who's been running the place since 1959 and clearly has her guests' best interests at heart.

The two-story, white Territorial-style ranch house was built in 1928, and Myra runs it as you would a lodge in that era. As she says, "This isn't a wine and cheese place" (although guests may bring their own). The ranch sits on 160 acres abutting the Gila National Forest on the outskirts of Silver City and is an ideal base for hiking and bird-watching. Nights are often chilly, but guests can warm themselves at one of the two stone fireplaces in the high-ceiling, wood-beamed main room. Accommodations are spartan, with what looks to be 1950s- or '60s-era furnishings.

🏠 *Box 1163, Silver City, NM 88062, tel. 505/538–2538. 11 double rooms with baths, 2 3-room suites, 1 2-person cottage, 1 4-person cottage. Electric blankets, kitchenettes in 2 cottages; outdoor ramada, sunporch, nature classes available. $95–$105 (includes meals); weekly and "lodge & learn" rates available. No credit cards. No smoking in indoor common rooms.*

The Black Range Lodge

If you've taken the mountain road from Silver City to Kingston (population 30, down from 7,000 in 1880), nestled in the Gila National Forest, chances are you're not looking to drive anywhere else very soon. And the Black Range Lodge, a rustic three-story brick, stone, and straw-bale building, will only strengthen your urge to stay put. Parts of it date from when Kingston was booming. When silver prices fell, much of the stone in the lodge was taken from the defunct casino and dance hall.

Los Angeles filmmaker Catherine Wanek and Pete Fust (who holds a Guinness World Record for frisbee throwing) have created a fun, relaxed environment. The first floor of the lodge has a wall of free video games, Foosball, and a pool table, and the surrounding area offers extensive hiking, mountain biking, and bird-watching. Expect to do a fair amount of cooking in the spacious, sun-filled kitchen, as the nearest restaurant is in neighboring Hillsboro and isn't open for dinner. Guest rooms are furnished in an eclectic but pleasing blend of Victorian and Southwestern styles, antiques and Oriental rugs counterpointing terra-cotta and turquoise doors, wood floors, and, in some cases, wagon-wheel chandeliers.

🏠 *Star Rte. 2, Box 119, Kingston, NM 88042, tel. 505/895–5652, fax 505/895–3326. 4 double rooms with baths, 3 suites. 2 rooms have private balcony; patio, greenhouse, piano, ping-pong, Foosball, pool, TV/VCR room, video library. $60 first night, $45 each additional night (except holidays); full Continental breakfast. D, MC, V. Smoking outside or on balconies only.*

The Carter House

The lovely Colonial Revival-style Carter House, set on a rise next to Silver City's old county courthouse, was built in 1906 by the owner of the nearby Tyrone Copper Mine. In 1989, Lucy Dilworth restored the residence, which was a medical clinic in the 1930s. A B&B occupies most of the building; the former X-ray rooms in the basement are now an immaculate youth hostel (B&Bers can use the facility's washer/dryer and kitchen).

The five first-floor guest rooms are not overly large, but all are light-filled and decorated in a cheerful Southwestern and country-French combination of earth-tone floral bedspreads, pine or wicker headboards, light-wood furniture, and tasteful art prints. In the evening, you'll make the morning's breakfast selections on a form; a copious cold spread supplements the hot dishes, cooked when you arrive at the table.

🏠 *101 N. Cooper St., Silver City, NM 88061, tel. 505/388–5485. 4 double rooms with baths, 1 suite. Clock radios, ceiling fans in all rooms; newspaper, free local calls, library, TV room; off-street parking; arrangements made for bird-watching, horseback riding, massage. $58–$69; full breakfast. MC, V. No smoking, no pets.*

Casa de Patrón

Billy the Kid stayed here against his will in 1879, when the Territorial-style adobe house belonged to Lincoln County clerk Juan Patrón. These days folks come voluntarily to enjoy the warm hospitality and attention to detail—handmade soaps and nightlights in the baths, for example—by hosts Jeremy and Cleis Jordan. Many visitors are history buffs, and conversations in the viga-beamed sitting room of this spotless B&B can go on into the wee hours. The talk often continues over breakfast, a hearty country-style repast that might include citrus-pecan waffles.

In the three guest rooms, you'll find wood floors with area rugs and a mix of contemporary Western-style pieces and antiques; lace curtains set a genteel tone. Two spacious guest casitas a few minutes' walk from the main house are decorated in a similar style; one has a loft bedroom.

🏠 *Box 27, Lincoln, NM 88338, tel. 505/653–4676, fax 505/653–4671. 3 double rooms with baths (1 adjoining), 1 1-bedroom casita, 1 2-bedroom casita.*

Kitchenette in 1 casita, coffeemaker and refrigerator in other, clocks in rooms, fireplace, pipe organ, and piano in common areas; patio, portale, off-street parking. $79–$97; full breakfast in rooms, Continental breakfast in casitas. D, MC, V. No smoking indoors, no pets.

The Enchanted Villa

This white Territorial-style adobe, built on the main street of tiny Hillsboro in 1941, once served as a mountain retreat for a British nobleman, Sir Victor Sassoon. It was designed by the great-aunt of the current innkeeper, Maree Westland, who returned from Alaska to buy the home she'd played in as a child.

Family pictures line the staircase walls of this airy, light-filled lodging, which has the welcoming, casual warmth of a family home. This is not a showcase for period antiques or Southwestern artifacts: Furnishings tend toward the contemporary and nondescript. And the turquoises and pinks of the guest rooms—all of which have king-size beds, dressing rooms with sinks, and recently remodeled bathrooms—may be a bit bright for some tastes. But the two outdoor patios are lovely, and Maree is a knowledgeable, genial hostess. She'll send you off to explore historic Hillsboro with a full, delicious morning meal: fancy egg dishes, soufflés, or casseroles with fruit, home-baked muffins, coffee cake, or biscuits, and juice and fresh-ground coffee.

🏠 *Box 456, Hillsboro, NM 88042, tel. 505/895–5686. 5 double rooms with baths. Fireplace, TV/VCR room, video library; dog run. $50; full breakfast. No credit cards. No smoking in guest rooms.*

Mesón de Mesilla

It'd be worth staying at this 1983 pueblo-style inn, 10 minutes from historic Mesilla Plaza, for its restaurant alone. Folks drive here from all over southern New Mexico to enjoy such well-prepared Continental dishes as seared sturgeon in pesto or chateaubriand for two. For inn guests only, a full gourmet breakfast is served in a lovely glass-enclosed atrium. If you're planning to explore the area and return for lunch or dinner, keep in mind that the restaurant's popularity makes parking tricky during peak hours.

The view from the inn's back patio and from the second-floor balcony is also a lure; it's easy to forget you're near Las Cruces, the second-largest city in the state, when you look out across rows of well-tended cotton fields to the towering Organ Mountains. Rooms are decorated in attractive Southwestern colors with light-wood furniture and a few antiques; all have TVs, clock radios, and ceiling fans. Lower-priced singles are a nice option for students or traveling businesspeople.

🏠 *1803 Avenida de Mesilla, Box 1212, Mesilla, NM 88046, tel. 505/525–9212 or 800/732–6025. 3 single rooms and 6 double rooms with baths, 4 suites. In-room phones available; suites have kiva fireplaces, 1 has private balcony; pool, free Las Cruces airport pickup, off-street parking, picnic baskets available, banquet room. $45–$82; full breakfast. D, DC, MC, V.*

Sierra Mesa Lodge

This sprawling, blue, country French-style house, with a gray stone chimney and white trim, stands in colorful contrast to the deep-green pines of the Lincoln National Forest that surround it. After they decided to open an inn, graphic designer Larry Goodman and his wife, Lila, an accountant, spent 12 years researching the perfect place and architectural design for it. In 1987, they came up with a winner on both counts about 10 minutes from downtown Ruidoso.

Above all, the lodge is geared toward romance. The five lovely theme rooms have ceiling fans, queen-size beds with fluffy down comforters and pillows, built-in window seats, and delicate porcelain dolls. The Victorian room is pretty in pink, with a satin settee, claw-foot tub, fringed lamp, and marble tables, while the Oriental is a stunning Japanese-inspired study in black and red. An elaborate breakfast— green chili soufflés, say, or croissant French toast—is presented on fine china. And, oh, the soothing hot tub, set in its own redwood room looking out into the woods, which are lighted with strings of tiny bulbs after dark.

🏠 *Fort Stanton Rd., Box 463, Alto, NM 88312, tel. 505/336–4515. 5 double rooms with baths. Clocks, kimonos in rooms, TV available, hot tub, hiking trails. $90; full breakfast, afternoon tea. D, MC, V. No smoking indoors, no children under 14, no pets.*

Texas

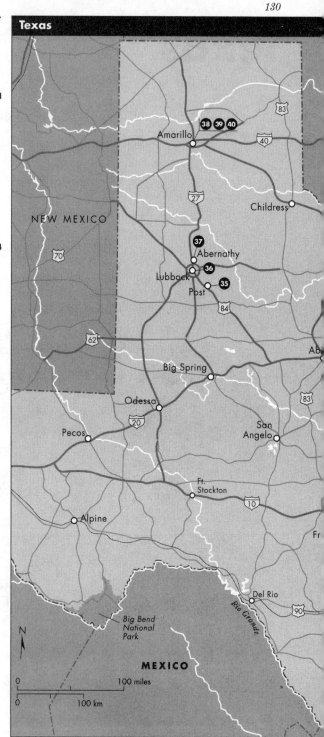

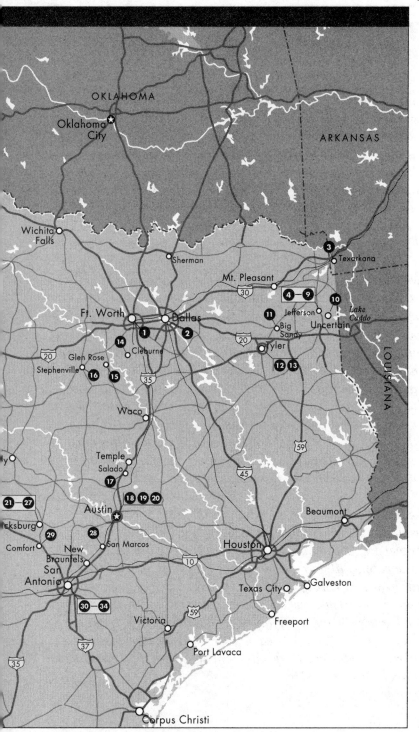

East Texas
Including Dallas and Fort Worth

*Bordered on the north by Ross Perot's hometown of
Texarkana; on the east by Texas's only natural lake, Caddo
Lake; to the west by onetime rollicking Fort Worth; and to the
south by historic Waxahachie and the first rumblings of the
Hill Country, east Texas is a land of piney woods, antiques
shops, hallowed century-old neighborhoods, and traditional
stone-faced Baptists proud of their roots and their property.*

*When railroad baron Jay Gould offered to run track through
the east Texas port town of Jefferson and was rebuffed more
than a century ago, local folklore has it that Gould angrily
scrawled in the register of the Excelsior House Hotel the
words, "The End of Jefferson." And indeed, Jefferson was soon
a port town no longer. The natural log dam on the Red River
broke, draining water from Cypress Bayou and bringing an
end to the city's steamboat commerce forever. The city's
population dwindled from 35,000 to 3,000. Ironically, however,
the historic town has returned to prominence in recent years,
not despite—but precisely because of—its refusal to change
with the times. The Excelsior House still stands after about
140 years of continuous operation and is surrounded by scores
of well-preserved Greek Revival and Victorian homes.*

*The preservation of things past is a theme that extends
throughout much of east Texas. As you travel west from
Shreveport, Louisiana, to Dallas on I-20, detour to Jefferson,
Gladewater, Pittsburg, and Mount Pleasant; you'll discover
that the woods lining the highway drape an antiques shopper's
paradise. Marshall, where potters have been mining clay from
east Texas's rolling hills for more than a century, turns out
more than a million pots each year. In Rusk, the Texas State
Railroad Historical Park's ancient steamers take visitors on a
19th-century train ride.*

The region's identity changes abruptly, however, as the shiny, sharply angled skyscrapers of Dallas come into view. Dallas is defined by the progress of "bidness"—the forward march of bankers, high-techsters, and oilmen—and the tearing down of the old and the building of the new. Its critics say Dallas is a city obsessed with appearances. And indeed, this metropolis offers a beautiful skyline, a thriving nightlife inhabited by bright young émigrés from parts north, a Super Bowl champion football team, and a splashy, $157-million symphony hall.

Yet, for all these attractions, visitors from around the world still mostly come to Dallas to view the totems that recall the city's greatest shame—the Texas School Book Depository, the grassy knoll, the site on Commerce Street downtown where President John F. Kennedy was fatally shot.

About 30 miles west of Dallas, the city of Fort Worth manages to retain the flavor of its Wild West past while burgeoning as a modern city. The former rip-roaring cowboy town, known for its gunfights and cattle drives, has preserved its roots both institutionally, through the maintenance of the historic Stockyards, and culturally, through the down-to-earth approach to life that still permeates the city. But Fort Worth is no backwater; its cultural establishment is the envy of many larger cities, including Dallas. Some may sneeringly dismiss it as "Cowtown," but in many respects the city provides the best of what both tradition and progress have to offer.

Jefferson's first bed-and-breakfast opened in 1983 as a response to the lengthening waiting list for lodging at the fabled Excelsior House. Since then, Jefferson has gone B&B crazy, with about 60 such establishments in operation. Fort Worth, by comparison, has only a handful of inns, largely because of zoning laws, and Dallas's offerings tend toward the unadorned host home, better suited for the business traveler than the tourist. A number of charming hideaways do exist, however, on the outskirts of the two major cities.

Places to Go, Sights to See

Antiques. The main thoroughfare of tiny Gladewater, the region's self-styled "antiques capital," is lined by a seemingly endless parade of retailers peddling collectibles. But the town has become such a popular stop among travelers that it's difficult to find real bargains here. One might have better luck in other east Texas towns, from Pittsburg to Marshall, where antiques shops can be found in abundance. Jefferson, in particular, has nearly 40 such stores. The largest antiques event in the area, a flea market with as many as 5,000 vendors known as Trade Days, is held the Friday, Saturday, and Sunday preceding the first Monday of each month, in Canton.

Arlington. Largely because of its location between the population centers of Dallas and Fort Worth, this overgrown suburb of 284,000 has evolved into a kind of municipal amusement park. Arlington's many diversions include *Six Flags over Texas* (tel. 817/640–8900), *Wet 'n' Wild* (tel. 817/265–3356) water park, and *Texas Rangers baseball at The Ballpark in Arlington* (tel. 817/273–5222, ballpark information; tel. 817/273–5100, ticket office).

Caddo Lake. Hung with Spanish moss and edged with bald cypresses, Caddo Lake is a fishing mecca straddling the Texas-Louisiana border. At various times it has been home to the beleaguered Caddo Indians, to bootleggers hiding out in its dense shore growth, to the great singer of spirituals Leadbelly (reared at Swanson's Landing), to thriving steamboat traffic from New Orleans, and to all manner of legend. *Caddo Lake State Park* (Rte. 43, tel. 903/679–3351), on the southern shore of the lake near Karnack, offers camping, cabins, fishing, swimming, and boating.

Glen Rose. A popular day trip for Dallas-Fort Worth urbanites, this beautiful town in the countryside 80 miles southwest of Dallas was once aptly known as "Glen of Roses." Its attractions include the *Fossil Rim Wildlife Center* (turnoff on U.S. 67, 3 mi southwest of town, tel. 817/897–9453), where visitors can see a wide variety of rare endangered species; *Dinosaur Valley State Park* (4 mi north of town on Park Rd. 59, tel. 817/897–4588), which displays fossil prints of prehistoric reptiles; the leisurely Paluxy River; and one of Texas's premier golf courses, *Squaw Valley* (on U.S. 67, ½ mi east of town, tel. 817/897–7956).

Jefferson. This town of 2,200 offers more than its share of quiet pleasures, particularly for those who love architecture and history. Museums include the *Texas Heritage Archives & Library* (202 Market St., tel. 903/665–1101), housing one of the finest collections of Texas historical material, including first-edition books by Davy Crockett. For information on horse-drawn-carriage and trolley tours of the town's *historic homes*, contact Tour Headquarters, tel. 903/665–1665. A fun time to visit Jefferson is during *Pilgrimage Weekend*, the first weekend in May, when residents dress in period garb, private historic homes open up for public tours, and a historic drama is performed at the Jefferson Playhouse.

The **Stockyards Historic District.** This area near downtown Fort Worth recalls the prosperous days of 1902, when two major Chicago meatpackers, Armour and Swift, set up plants to ship meat across the country in refrigerator cars—an innovation. In the Livestock Exchange Building where cattle agents kept their offices, you'll find the *Stockyards Museum* (131 E. Exchange Ave., tel. 817/625–5087). Nearby, *Cowtown Coliseum* (121 E. Exchange Ave., tel. 817/625–1025) is the site of Saturday night rodeos. Also here are what's left of a complex of cattle, goat, and sheep pens; horse and mule barns; and, of course, *Billy Bob's Texas* (2520 Rodeo Plaza, tel. 817/624–7117), billed as the "world's largest honky-tonk." *Exchange Avenue* is lined with restaurants, clubs, western-wear stores, and famous spots like the White Elephant Saloon and the Stockyards Hotel. The *Tarantula Excursion Train* (2318 8th Ave., tel. 817/763–8297) offers tours from its south-of-downtown base to the stockyards.

The **West End Historic District.** A gathering of brick warehouses built between 1900 and 1930, this corner of downtown Dallas had deteriorated badly before it was resurrected as an entertainment district in 1976. Now filled with restaurants, shops, and nightclubs, it is one of the city's biggest tourist draws. It is anchored by the *West End MarketPlace* (1701 N. Market St., tel. 214/748–4801), once a candy and cracker factory and now a lively, five-story shopping and dining center built around an atrium. The West End is located around the corner from a considerably more somber Dallas tourist stop: The former *Texas School Book Depository*, from which Lee Harvey Oswald fired the shots that killed President Kennedy houses the *Sixth Floor Exhibit* (tel. 214/653–6666)—displays on Kennedy's fateful 1963 Dallas visit.

Restaurants

In Jefferson, the chef-owned **Stillwater Inn** (tel. 903/665–8415) offers Continental cuisine, ranging from roast Cornish hen to tasty pork tenderloin, in a charming converted home (*see* review, *below*). For more casual dining, **Auntie Skinner's Riverboat Club** (tel. 903/665–7121) serves up homestyle cooking and the restaurant's own bottled hot sauce. Zydeco and Cajun bands entertain on Saturday evenings.

For those who like their seafood with a Mexican accent, **La Calle Doce** (tel. 214/941–4304), in a remodeled home, offers the most mouthwatering *mariscos* (shellfish) in Dallas. Also moderately priced, **Jennivine** (tel. 214/528–6010) looks like an English pub and features a Continental menu that includes fine fish dishes and specialty salads; the sherry trifle alone is worth the trip. For real Texas-style barbecue, you can't top **Sonny Bryan's Smokehouse** (tel. 214/357–7120; 5 locations, call for addresses), whose inexpensive menu includes thick-sliced smoked brisket, tasty sausage, and chicken.

In Fort Worth, **Joe T. Garcia's** (tel. 817/626–4356) serves up family-style Tex-Mex dinners, either indoors or in a sprawling open-air garden. Another moderately priced downtown restaurant, **Rodeo Steakhouse** (tel. 817/332–1288) has an Old West theme, hearty steaks, and a good salad bar.

Tourist Information

Arlington Convention and Visitors Bureau (Box A, Arlington, TX 76004, tel. 817/640–0252 or 800/342–4305). **Dallas Convention and Visitors Bureau** (1201 Elm St., Suite 2000, Dallas, TX 75270, tel. 214/746–6677). **Fort Worth Convention and Visitors Bureau** (415 Throckmorton, Fort Worth, TX 76103, tel. 817/336–8791 or 800/433–5747). **Marion County Chamber of Commerce** (116 W. Austin St., Jefferson, TX 75657, tel. 903/665–2672). **Marshall Convention and Visitors Bureau** (213 W. Austin St., Box 520, Marshall, TX 75671, tel. 903/935–7868 or 800/953–7868). **Texarkana Chamber of Commerce** (Box 1468, Texarkana, TX 75504, tel. 903/792–7191). **Tyler Area Convention and Visitors Bureau** (407 N. Broadway, Box 390, Tyler, TX 75710, tel. 903/592–1661 or 800/235–5712).

Reservation Services

A & L Reservations (603 E. Elizabeth St., Jefferson, TX 75657, tel. 903/665–1017 or 903/665–1019). **Bed and Breakfast Texas Style** (4224 W. Red Bird Lane, Dallas, TX 75237, tel. 214/298–8586 or 800/899–4538). **Book-A-Bed-Ahead** (Box 723, Jefferson, TX 75657, tel. 903/665–3956 or 800/468–2627). **Jefferson Reservation Service** (124 W. Austin, Jefferson, TX 75657, tel. 903/665–2592 or 800/833–6758).

Annie's Bed & Breakfast

Annie's is more than the only bed-and-breakfast in Big Sandy; Annie's is an industry—and, for most people, the only reason to come to Big Sandy.

"Annie" is Annie Potter, whose multi-million-dollar mail-order needlecraft and pattern business, Annie's Attic, Inc., got started with a $100 investment in 1973. When mailorder customers began to trickle into Big Sandy (population 1,200), Annie would serve them tea but had no real means of entertaining them. So, about a decade ago, she began assembling the Victorian Village, a cluster of three brightly painted, converted Victorian homes. In addition to the B&B, the complex now includes a restaurant and tearoom and a needlecraft gallery and gift shop.

The bed-and-breakfast is a large, gray-and-white, seven-gabled house, which had only one story when it was constructed in 1901 for the former mayor and postmaster G. A. Tohill. Potter had a second floor and attic added and filled virtually every corner of every room with antique Victorian furnishings. They are often draped with quilts or other craft works, including many crocheted by Potter. Antique sewing machines are also on display throughout.

The 12 guest rooms are designed for two people, but many can sleep more because they include sitting areas with sofa beds. The best of them all, the Queen Anne Room, offers a queen bed, a sofa bed, and a spiral staircase that leads to twin beds in a loft. And, like the Garret and Balcony rooms, it has a private balcony.

Needlecraft festivals, crochet seminars, and other events are often held on the village grounds. Annie's guests receive a complimentary breakfast in the tearoom; choices range from New York strip steak and eggs to several low-fat gourmet entrées. Saturday breakfast is served in the home.

Innkeepers Clifton and Kathy Shaw will organize a barbecue for your group, chat with you on the front porch—or leave you alone if you crave privacy. For those not interested in crochet and needlepoint, there are precious few attractions in Big Sandy itself. This is especially true on Saturday, when the town pretty much shuts down in deference to the Sabbath of the Worldwide Church of God, headquartered in the area. Still, given the quality of rooms and service, Annie's is one of the B&B bargains in the region.

🏨 *Hwy. 155 N., Box 928, Big Sandy, TX 75755, tel. 903/636–4355 or 800/BB–ANNIE, fax 903/636–4744. 7 double rooms with baths, 5 doubles share 3 baths. Telephones and minifridges in all rooms, TV in some rooms. $50–$115; full breakfast. AE, D, MC, V. No smoking, no pets.*

Charnwood Hill

I n the city that hosts the famed Texas Rose Festival, you can pay no greater compliment to a residence than to say that a Rose Queen lived there and that the Queen's Tea was held on the lawn. Tyler's Charnwood Hill, converted to a B&B in 1993, has housed not one but two queens. Margaret Hunt, daughter of the late oilman H. L. Hunt, was crowned in 1935; Jo Anne Miller received the honor in 1954.

As much as the yellow rose of Texas, the name Hunt is the stuff of Lone Star legend. And the Charnwood Hill estate, where the Hunt family lived before moving to Dallas in 1938, does not disappoint. Built in the 1860s by the headmaster of a school for girls, the three-story structure housed both a college and a hospital during the 19th century. The elegant, Greek Revival-influenced residence was bricked in 1901 by J. B. Mayfield, who raised a family here before selling the home to Hunt.

Hunt added his own touch to the home: a third-floor Art Deco suite constructed for daughters Margaret and Caroline. The suite's stark whites, barely-there pastels, and indirect lighting combine to stamp an indelible air of *Great Gatsby*-era privilege on the accommodation, and they contrast sharply with the frilly, floral guest bedrooms that dominate the first and second floors.

Male business travelers tend to favor the sprawling Millers' Trophy Room, named for H. C. Miller, who bought the house from Hunt. The blue-and-burgundy room has a full bar, gun cabinet, and bed that can be folded into the wall to make room for a small conference area.

Throughout the high-ceiling home, the furnishings are extravagant. The Walker family purchased the residence from the Millers in 1978, and in a four-year restoration, they have spared no expense to create a regal atmosphere, with crystal chandeliers, 100-year-old Oriental rugs, and antique pieces.

Common areas include a library and TV room, two second-floor balconies, and a screened swing porch. Guests enjoy a breakfast that might feature eggs Benedict or French toast in the formal dining room. And, more than 50 years after it served as the setting for Hunt's Queen's Tea, the west garden is as lovely as ever.

🏠 *223 E. Charnwood Rd., Tyler, TX 75701, tel. 903/597–3980, fax 903/592–2369. 5 double rooms with baths, 1 suite. Phones in rooms, TV/VCR in most rooms, gift shop and art studio; free airport transfers. $95–$175, suite $270; full breakfast, complimentary beverages. D, MC, V. No smoking indoors, children over 12 by prior arrangement, no pets.*

The Excelsior House

The Excelsior House is the remarkably restored centerpiece of Jefferson, a town sometimes called the "Williamsburg of Texas." Built in the 1850s by riverboat captain William Perry, the historic hotel has remained in continuous operation since then, although by the middle of this century, the brick-and-timber structure had slowly deteriorated and was largely forgotten.

Its rebirth began in 1954, when Estella Fonville Peters purchased the inn and undertook its renovation. Opening the building to public tours, filling the drawing room with the music of noted orchestras, and hosting elaborate balls, she revived interest in the hotel—and, in the process, sowed the seeds of Jefferson's commercial future. The Jessie Allen Wise Garden Club bought the hotel when Peters died in 1961 and has maintained and operated the facility with care ever since. The club has also made significant improvements, such as adding bathrooms and tearing down walls between the tiny rooms once consigned to traveling salesmen.

With iron columns and a lacy ironwork gallery that lend flourish to the simple rectangular edifice, the Excelsior House looks like it came to the Wild West by way of New Orleans. The ballroom features a French chandelier, Oriental rugs, antique marble mantles, and a pair of period pianos. The dining room includes a glassed-in patio, where guests can enjoy a Plantation Breakfast of orange blossom muffins, country ham, scrambled eggs, and biscuits.

Each of the inn's 13 guest rooms and suites has a story to tell. Past guests have included William Vanderbilt and Oscar Wilde; both Ulysses S. Grant and Rutherford B. Hayes slept in what is now the Presidential Suite. Lady Bird Johnson was a frequent visitor and donated a good deal of the furniture in the room that bears her name. All the rooms are furnished with antiques, including marble-topped dressers, spool beds, and mahogany, cherry, and maple pieces.

Spurned railroad tycoon Jay Gould had predicted doom for Jefferson in the Excelsior House lobby in the 1870s, so it's fitting revenge that one of the hotel's most popular rooms is named after him. Across the street from the hotel, "Atalanta," Gould's decadently ornate private railroad car, is open to public tours.

211 W. Austin St., Jefferson, TX 75657, tel. 903/665–2513. 11 double rooms with baths, 2 suites. TV, air-conditioning in all rooms. $45–$90; breakfast not included. No credit cards. No smoking, no pets.

The Hotel St. Germain

In a city known for glitziness, the Hotel St. Germain is perhaps the definitive lodging. Nestled amid some of Dallas's most exclusive restaurants and shops, the boutique hotel, opened in 1991, offers visitors the chance to indulge in the high life of a different time and place: 19th-century France.

A Victorian prairie mansion built in 1906 for a prominent Dallas financier and home for many decades to a variety of commercial ventures, the inn was purchased in 1989 by Claire Heymann. She set out to reclaim the structure's noble origins while paying tribute to her own French-Creole roots. From the moment the hotel's front doors are opened, revealing the large entry hall embellished with crackle-back moldings and crystal chandeliers, the visitor is swept into a lavish, self-contained universe.

Heymann's secret is painstaking authenticity. A New Orleans native whose mother was an antiques dealer, she has been assembling French collectibles almost since her childhood. Her acquisitions are complemented by her knowledge of French design, developed through frequent trips abroad and study at the University of Paris.

The entry hall gives way to a pair of sitting rooms, a parlor, and a library, each housing its own treasures—such as the library's grand piano, bedecked with ancient, marbled candelabras. The dining room, which looks out onto a New Orleans-style walled courtyard with a fountain, is perhaps the most evocative of Gaul: The long table, draped in a burgundy damask tapestry, is topped by a rose-filled centerpiece that rests on a silver Alsatian platter; a mid-19th-century French basket chandelier hangs from the room's ceiling. Breakfast—which typically includes fresh fruit compote, croissants, quiche, and café au lait—is served on a rare, century-old set of Limoges china. Dinner, which could be lamb tenderloin or game hen, is served Friday and Saturday nights.

Upstairs, the seven spacious guest suites feature plush, canopied feather beds. All have wood-burning fireplaces, sitting rooms, and baths with soaking tubs or Jacuzzis. Although rates are prohibitive, and the hotel has a reputation for boarding the glitterati, Heymann promotes her inn as a place where common folk can come for that once-in-a-lifetime splurge.

2516 Maple Ave., Dallas, TX 75201, tel. 214/871–2516, fax 214/871–0740. 7 suites. Cable TV, robes in all rooms, VCRs available, room service, Crabtree and Evelyn soaps, concierge, valet parking, nightly turndown service; privileges at nearby fitness club, limited restaurant. $225–$600; full breakfast. AE, DC, MC, V. No smoking, no pets.

McKay House

In 1877, when Jefferson was a worldly river port, it was rocked by the brief visit of "Diamond Bessie"—the stage name of Annie Stone Moore Rothchild, a popular entertainer. While in town with her husband, a wealthy Cincinnati gambler named Abe Rothchild, the pair walked alone into a field. A gunshot was heard, and Abe returned alone, claiming his wife had shot herself by accident. After three trials over seven years, Rothchild was a free man, but the people of Jefferson never accepted the "not guilty" verdict.

One of the attorneys who successfully defended Rothchild was Hector McKay, the first of two generations of McKays that lived in this 1851 Greek Revival. In the early 1980s, the McKay House was purchased by Dallasites Tom and Peggy Taylor, who, through extensive renovations, transformed it into the city's most luxurious B&B.

The inn is furnished almost entirely with antiques, mostly Eastlake, many of them quite valuable. But this place is anything but stuffy. Innkeepers Joseph and Alma Anne Parker know how to help folks break the ice, from the funny period hats distributed for visitors to wear at breakfast, to Victorian gowns and nightshirts provided in the rooms, and, in one room, his-and-hers clawfoot tubs that offer an opportunity for simultaneous scrub-downs. An ancient Packard pump organ is played to call guests to the hearty "Gentleman's Breakfast," which is served in period dress and may consist of honey-cured ham, cheese biscuits, and homemade pineapple zucchini bread and strawberry preserves. Afterward, guests can relax on the wide front porch, outfitted with a swing and white wicker chairs.

The guest rooms are individual in personality but uniform in elegance; each offers such furnishings as a canopy bed and antique armoire. The two downstairs rooms have coal-burning fireplaces; the two upstairs suites feature a balcony, skylight, and his-and-hers tubs; and a downstairs suite includes two bedrooms, each with its own fireplace. But perhaps the most memorable rooms are the two set off from a central, dog-trot hall in the tin-roofed Victorian garden cottage located behind the main house. The Keeping Room, in particular, is amusingly authentic: a claw-foot tub sits exposed in a bay window, next to a transplanted outdoor privy, fully equipped with a lantern and a Sears Roebuck catalogue.

🏨 *306 Delta St., Jefferson, TX 75657, tel. 903/665-7322. 4 double rooms with baths, 3 suites. Phones in rooms, cable TV on request. $85–$95, suites $125–$145; full breakfast. MC, V. No smoking, no pets; 2-night minimum on holiday weekends.*

Miss Molly's Bed & Breakfast

As the drovers on the street below brought in herd after herd of longhorns, hitting every saloon and dance hall on the way to the stockyards, the guests in the second-floor walk-up gazed down, primly elevated from the fray. In the early 1900s, the eight rooms that now make up Fort Worth's best bed-and-breakfast housed the guests of Miss Sylvia Marquis's Furnished Rooms, an oh-so-proper hotel.

By the 1930s, however, the wild ways of the stockyard district had had their influence; the hotel had become an infamous brothel named for its madam, Miss Josie. When Mark and Susan Hancock renovated and reopened the abandoned space as Miss Molly's in 1989, they decided to name adjacent rooms after Miss Josie and Miss Sylvia—provoking the guest to wonder whether either, or both, of the former proprietors might be turning in their graves.

Located over the Star Cafe steak house in the Fort Worth Stockyards Historic District, Miss Molly's may be the most mythically Texan of Texas's bed-and-breakfasts. The rooms, which form a circle around the registration desk at the top of the stairs, are chock-full of saddles, stirrups, cowboy hats, buckskin, and other Western paraphernalia. What keeps the whole thing from being hokey is that the artifacts are authentic: The rope that dangles from the wall mirror in one room, for example, is the actual one used to win the Fort Worth rodeo in 1928.

The rooms have been furnished to appear as they did in the 1920s: iron beds draped with colorful quilts; ceiling fans; a washstand with a bowl and pitcher. With the exception of Miss Josie's room, none of the rooms have private baths. Three bathrooms with pedestal sinks, claw-foot tubs, and pull-chain toilets stand side by side in one corner of the establishment.

The Hancocks encourage folks to mingle; they say they measure success by the number of friends they and their visitors have made here. Guests are given custom-made blue-and-white ticking robes to wear to the copious Continental breakfast buffet, which typically features coffee cakes, muffins, strawberry bread, and a fruit cup.

🏨 *109½ W. Exchange Ave., Fort Worth, TX 76106, tel. 817/626–1522 or 800/996–6559, fax 817/625–2723. 1 double room with bath, 7 doubles share 3 baths. Fans in all rooms, air-conditioning. $85–150; Continental breakfast. AE, D, DC, MC, V. No smoking, no pets.*

Caddo Cottage

Retirees Pete and Dorothy Grant went into the lodging business by accident. They moved to the cottage they owned on Taylor Island in moss-draped Caddo Lake for the peace and quiet, but the run-down place next door was such an eyesore that they were spurred to buy it and spruce it up. The result is Caddo Cottage, a homey, comfortable spot for those who want to enjoy a day or a weekend casting their lines into the best and biggest fishing hole in East Texas. Shoppers from nearby Jefferson also frequent the cottage, as do gamblers headed to the casino riverboats in Louisiana, 45 minutes away.

The Grants know that the lake, and its pleasures, are the main reason folks visit tiny Uncertain, and they have fashioned a bed-and-breakfast well suited to that purpose. Their functional two-story cottage includes a fully equipped kitchen, a laundry room, and a covered patio with a gas grill. The furniture is contemporary and comfortable—guests don't have to worry about breaking expensive antiques. The property also has a private pier with a deck and boathouse. A Continental breakfast might include pastries and croissants, fresh juice, and just-ground coffee.

🏠 *Rte. 2, Box 66, Uncertain, TX 75661, tel. 903/789–3988 or 903/789–3297, fax 903/789–3916. 1 2-bedroom cabin. TV, air-conditioning, full kitchen. $85; Continental breakfast. No credit cards. No pets; 2-night minimum on weekends.*

Cleburne House

Built in 1886, the Cleburne House was owned by a railroad inspector; its later incarnations included a domino parlor. And current owners Steve and Drew Griffin were embarrassed to discover that their inn had been a house of prostitution: Numbers were scrawled over each of the rooms, as well as over the closets, to direct customers to the alotted place.

Completely overhauled by the Griffins, the squeaky-clean Queen Anne residence is now all frills, ruffles, and lace. Rooms are adorned with cat-shaped pillows and other cutesy collectibles, and they all have tubs. Breakfast is served on fine china and often includes dishes made with strawberries, herbs, and other edibles that flourish on the grounds.

There's not much to do in Cleburne, an old railroad town, save walk around the picturesque downtown area or perhaps visit nearby Venus, where *A Trip to Bountiful* was filmed.

🏠 *201 N. Anglin St., Cleburne, TX 76031, tel. 817/641–0085. 2 double rooms with baths, 2 doubles share bath. Whirlpool bath in 1 room, 2 rooms share balcony sitting area, TV in rooms. $55–$85; full breakfast. No credit cards. Smoking on balcony only, no children under 12, no pets.*

House of the Seasons

One of East Texas's most intriguing architectural specimens, this 1872 house exemplifies the transitional period between Greek Revival and Victorian styles, with Italianate touches all its own. The most dazzling feature is the large dome that juts from the roof; the cupola's interior walls feature sunlit frescoes representing the four seasons, which can be viewed from the first floor.

The guest rooms are in a re-created carriage house on the estate, but visitors are welcome in the main house, where owners Kirby and Cindy Childress live. Breakfast is served in the antique-laden dining room. The public pays for tours of the house, but the Childresses enjoy taking their B&B guests around at night and allowing them to climb into the cupola.

The exquisite 1870s period suites in the Carriage House are dominated by huge beds stacked with soft linens; all have baths with stained-glass windows. Personalized touches include a spinning wheel in one room and an antique pump organ in another.

🏠 *Box 686, 409 S. Alley St., Jefferson, TX 75657, tel. 903/665–1218. 3 suites. Jacuzzis, cable TV in suites. $125; full breakfast. MC, V. No smoking indoors, no pets.*

Inn on the River

Originally part of a popular spa and sanatorium run by Dr. George P. Snyder, a self-proclaimed "magnetic healer," the Inn on the River remains a soothing resting place for the world-weary traveler. Nestled among 200-year-old trees on the banks of the Paluxy River, this is one of the largest country inns in Texas and is run as professionally as a fine hotel.

This B&B, located 80 miles from Dallas, offers a "Complete Meeting Package" for small corporate groups, with single-occupancy accommodations, three meals, refreshment breaks, and use of the inn's top-notch conference center starting at $175 per person per day. Individual travelers are accepted on weekends only. Four-course gourmet dinners are also served on weekends for $30 per person.

Most rooms include queen beds and a combination of antiques and reproductions. An extraordinary breakfast may include hot berry cobbler in winter or a cold banana bisque in the summertime.

🏠 *205 S. Barnard St., Glen Rose, TX 76043, tel. 214/424–7119, fax 214/424–9766. 19 double rooms with baths; 3 suites. Climate control in each room; heated outdoor pool. $115–$165; full breakfast. AE, D, DC, MC, V. No smoking indoors, no children under 18, no pets.*

Maison-Bayou

On moss-draped Big Cypress Bayou, just past downtown, lies Jefferson's most ambitious B&B. Jan and Pete Hochenedel's Maison-Bayou is set on 55 wooded acres and is patterned after an 1850s Louisiana antebellum plantation in Pete's family.

The main house is an authentic reproduction of a plantation overseer's home. Here the Hochenedels serve a full breakfast on weekends, with Southern entrées such as "swamp eggs," an oven-baked omelet filled with spinach, and brandied peaches.

But the most unique aspect of this B&B is the guest accommodations. Three cabins, modeled after slave quarters, offer primitive-style furnishings (but with the luxuries of full baths and central air and heat). Even the smallest details evoke authenticity: Mosquito netting hangs over one bed, sugar cane grows in front of the quarters, burlap curtains provide privacy. One dogtrot cabin features an open porch separating two accommodations. All the cabins overlook Beaver Pond, an oxbow lake that's popular with anglers. If you don't bring your fishing gear, the Hochenedels will supply cane poles.

🏠 *300 Bayou St., Box 175, Jefferson, TX 75657, tel. 903/665–7600, fax 903/665–7383. 4 double rooms with baths. Air-conditioning and heating, games in rooms; flatbottom boat with one cabin, canoe for rent, fishing, horseback riding. $85–$125; full breakfast. MC, V. No smoking indoors.*

Mansion on Main

Tom and Peggy Taylor, who own Jefferson's McKay House (*see above*), chose a good spot to open their second B&B: Texarkana received lots of attention as the hometown of Ross Perot. Down the street from the Taylors' mansion, in fact, is the Perot Theatre, a performing arts center renovated with the billionaire's help.

The wood-frame, neoclassical Mansion on Main was built for the widow of a Confederate veteran in 1895; the structure's most striking external features—14 two-story cypress columns—were added later. The residence has been well preserved, retaining its original oak, walnut, and mahogany parquet floors, and a glamorous winding staircase. The Taylors added four bathrooms.

This inn follows the McKay House's strategy of blending elegance and fun, down to many of the same distinctive details such as the period hats, gowns, and nightshirts distributed to guests. All densely adorned with antiques, the guest rooms vary from the modest Butler's Garret to the elegant, two-chambered Governor's Suite.

🏠 *802 Main St., Texarkana, TX 75501, tel. 903/792–1835 or 214/348–1929. 5 double rooms with baths; 1 suite. Telephones and cable TV in rooms. $60–$99; full breakfast. AE, MC, V. Smoking on balconies and veranda only, children by prior arrangement, no pets.*

Oxford House

The Oxford House of tiny Stephenville, just a few miles from Glen Rose, is one of the more squeaky clean, professionally run B&Bs in Texas. It's also distinguished by the fact that it's been owned by the same family since 1898. It was built by Judge W. J. Oxford and is now in the hands of his grandson, Bill, and Bill's wife, Paula.

Guests are offered complimentary beverages when they arrive at the Oxfords' well-preserved Victorian home, painted pale blue with dark-blue-and-burgundy trim. Perhaps the home's most prized antique is the pump organ brought to Texas on covered wagon from Ten-

nessee by Bill's great-grandparents. An 1890s sleigh bed, beveled-glass mirrors, antique armoires, marble-top dressers, and claw-foot tubs are among the home's other treasures.

Breakfast may include baked French toast with hot fruit topping, sausage biscuits, or German cinnamon rolls. The dining room can accommodate up to 40 guests for catered luncheons, birthday dinners, bridal showers, or business meetings.

🏠 *563 N. Graham St., Stephenville, TX 76401, tel. 817/965–6885 or 817/968–8171, fax 817/965–7555. 4 double rooms with baths. Climate control in each room; tearoom-gift shop. $65–$75; full breakfast, afternoon tea. MC, V. No smoking, no children under 6, no pets.*

Pride House

The Pride House has the distinction of being the first B&B in Jefferson and, according to the owner, the oldest in Texas. A gabled mansion built from a mail-order blueprint in 1888, the house had been badly damaged by fire when Sandy and Ray Spalding purchased it in 1978. They meticulously restored the old home, and then—inspired by the spillover of customers at the Excelsior House—opened it to lodgers the next year. The Spaldings have since moved to Oregon, leaving managers Carol Abernathy and Christel Frederick to run the place. In addition to being personable, the innkeepers whip up a mean egg casserole.

The stick-style Victorian home (named after the Spaldings' son, Pride) is caramel colored with white gingerbread trim and stained-glass windows. The antiques found throughout come in a variety of styles, including Eastlake and country primitive. Behind the lodging's main house, which has six guest rooms, an expanded former servants' cottage offers four additional bedrooms, all with English country decor. Guests eat breakfast at comfortable tables in the main house.

🏠 *409 E. Broadway, Jefferson, TX 75657, tel. 903/665–2675. 10 double rooms with baths. Ceiling fans, climate control, stained-glass windows in all rooms, some TVs available. $65–$100; full breakfast. MC, V. No smoking, no pets; 2-night minimum on Saturday.*

The Seasons

Regardless of the season, the living is easy at The Seasons, an elegant 1911 home that invites guests to enjoy a romantic getaway. Lumberman Sam Littlejohn, the original owner, imbued his estate with the finest woods, from the tiger oak floors to the curly pine woodwork that frames doorways and the parlor fireplace.

Nestled between Tyler's historic and azalea districts, this home is the neighbor of the larger Charnwood Hill B&B (*see above*) and shares the same opulent atmosphere. After a recent renovation, The Seasons was converted into a B&B by Jim Brown, a petroleum engineer working in banking, and his wife, Myra, an artist who specializes in wallscapes. Myra has transformed each of the four guest rooms into a representation of a season. The Summer Room comes alive with geraniums; the Fall Room is crisp with rag rolled walls done in an autumnal shade; and the Winter Room re-creates a Victorian ice-skating park, complete with small park benches and white sheepskin rugs in front of a fireplace, with a painted backdrop of skaters on an outdoor pond.

Cheeriest is the Spring Room. Sunny with corner windows, the room has a picket fence bed, a painted arbor on the walls, light green carpet, and furnishings that carry on the Secret Garden theme. The rooms also contain memorabilia from Jim's family, such as photos and hatboxes.

🏠 *313 E. Charnwood, Tyler, TX 75701, tel. 903/533–0803. 4 double rooms with baths. Air-conditioning, ceiling fans in all rooms. $95–$125; full breakfast. AE, D, MC, V. No smoking, no children under 13, no pets.*

Stillwater Inn

The Stillwater Inn is Jefferson's best restaurant, and atop that restaurant is the town's most unusual B&B. Wishing to take advantage of the bed-and-breakfast craze in Jefferson but short on space, owners Bill and Sharon Stewart ingeniously built three guest rooms into the structure's gables. With their dramatically pitched ceilings, stained-glass windows, and sunny skylights, the rooms are bright and cheerful and well complemented by the simple, stripped-pine furnishings throughout.

Among the pines and magnolias on the Stewarts' estate, a private cottage behind the Stillwater Inn is also available to guests. It is adorned simply, with pine floors, vaulted ceilings, and wicker furnishings. Another outbuilding houses conference and party facilities for up to 48 guests.

All overnight guests enjoy a free breakfast at the inn's restaurant. You might notice something different about the black coffee table in the living area of the restaurant's adjoining parlor: It is actually an enormous, 8-foot-long bellows, once used for industrial purposes but not recommended for stoking the parlor's own fireplace.

🏠 *203 E. Broadway, Jefferson, TX 75657, tel. 903/665–8415, fax 903/665–8416. 4 double rooms with baths. Air-conditioning, cable TV, and phone in all rooms, refrigerator in common area. $85–$90; full breakfast. AE, MC, V. No smoking, no pets; 2-night minimum on weekends.*

San Antonio, Austin, and the Hill Country

The heart of Texas is a place of hills and valleys, of rivers and dust.

San Antonio is the home of the Alamo, where the famous defeat ultimately inspired the United States to annex Texas at Mexico's expense—and, ironically, to create the nation's most Mexican-American-powered metropolis.

Austin is the home of both the state capitol, where the legislature is known for its cowboy-hatted, hang-'em-high politicos, and the city's most laid-back liberal enclave, the University of Texas, whose tie-dyed student population inspired the 1992 cult film Slacker.

Hill Country is the home of hundreds of bed-and-breakfast establishments. Many of these are in Fredericksburg, a Teutonic town of fewer than 7,000 people, with a reputation for peace and quiet that has turned it into a busy tourist mecca.

All in all, San Antonio, Austin, and the Hill Country form Texas's most intriguing triangle, in terms the area's geography and its diverse mix of cultures and attractions. German settlers left a thick accent on Comfort and Fredericksburg and New Braunfels, where the würstfests are as common as the pink granite hills, blanketed with cedars and live oaks, that define the region. Native American, Mexican, and Polish cultures have melded in Bandera, the state's dude ranch capital. A politician who started out along the Pedernales River and ended up in the White House left a mark on the Hill Country, too—in the town of Johnson City.

You should find a cure for whatever ails you somewhere in these parts. Choose from the gently rolling hills and friendly little towns of Hill Country; the cheering hubbub of San Antonio's River Walk or the beer gardens of Fredericksburg;

*the soothing natural springs in San Marcos and Austin; or
rivers ripe for water sports, among them the Guadalupe,
Medina, Blanco, Pedernales, and Llano.*

*In the past few years, as demand among visitors has grown,
bed-and-breakfasts have blossomed like the wildflowers found
throughout the region. The styles range from Southern
plantation houses to German* fachwerk *(log-and-stone cabin)
homes, with nearly everything in-between. Most of the bed-and-
breakfasts in Fredericksburg are* gästehauses, *or unattended
guest houses; the morning meal is in the home's refrigerator
when visitors arrive. Recently, upscale establishments, such as
San Antonio's Ogé House, have emerged on the scene, setting
new standards of quality and professionalism for bed-and-
breakfasts throughout the region.*

Places to Go, Sights to See

The Alamo (Alamo Plaza, San Antonio, tel. 210/225–1391). At the heart of San
Antonio, the Alamo stands as a repository of Texas history, a monument to the
189 volunteers who died here in 1836 during a 13-day siege by the Mexican
dictator General Santa Anna. When the Alamo was finally breached, at a terrible
cost to the Mexican Army, the slaughter that followed would be remembered as
the catalyst of the Texas Revolution. Today, the Alamo is filled with guns and
other paraphernalia belonging to William Travis, David Crockett, James Bowie,
and the other martyrs. Nearby, at the 1859 Menger Hotel in Alamo Plaza, you can
sample the mango ice cream so cherished by President Bill Clinton that he had
hundreds of gallons shipped in for his inauguration.

Aquarena Springs Resort (1 Aquarena Springs Dr., San Marcos, tel. 512/396–
8900 or 800/999–9767). Famous for its glass-bottom boats that tour the crystal-
clear waters of Spring Lake, the Aquarena Springs Resort is built around the
natural springs that have risen for millions of years from the limestone strata of
the Balcones Fault. Both children and adults can enjoy the theme park here: For
kids, there's the Alpine Sky Ride, Submarine Theatre, a bird show, and Ralph the
Swimming Pig, who takes an invigorating plunge into the spring daily. Adults can
admire the more than 100 varieties of aquatic life that inhabit Spring Lake.

Bandera County. This Hill Country county, once a staging ground for the
thrilling cattle drives of yesteryear, has earned its reputation as the "Cowboy
Capital of the World" in more recent times by cornering the Texas dude ranch
market: When ranching fell on hard times in the 1930s, an enterprising rancher
began charging city slickers to show them the ropes. Today, dude ranches dot the
county, and rodeos, trick-roping exhibitions, and country-and-western dances are
the county's bread and butter. The *Lost Maples State Natural Area* (Vanderpool,

tel. 210/966–3413), which preserves the rare and majestic Big Tooth Maple; the *Hill Country State Natural Area* (10 mi southwest of Bandera, tel. 210/796–4413), the largest state park in Texas open to equestrians; and the canoe-friendly Medina River round out the county's attractions. Kayaks, canoes, and tubes can be rented at Fred Collins Workshop (Hwy. 16, ½ mi north of Bandera, tel. 210/796–3553).

Barton Springs. Austin's natural, rock-bottom swimming hole is on Barton Creek about half a mile from its junction with the Colorado River; like Spring Lake in San Marcos, its waters rise from the ancient Balcones Fault. Located amid the picnic areas, soccer fields, and other recreation options of 400-acre *Zilker Park* (2201 Barton Springs Rd., tel. 512/476–9044), the 68° springs bubble to the surface at a rate of 32 million gallons daily and attract about 200,000 visitors a year.

Fredericksburg. This little town (population 7,000) swells with visitors who have discovered its quaint German ancestry and picturesque setting atop Edwards Plateau in the heart of Hill Country. Founded in 1846 by German immigrants and now the seat of Gillespie County, the town has a mile-long Main Street populated by a mix of century-old limestone houses and storefronts and newer structures born of the tourist trade. These include a number of lively restaurants, most notably the *Altdorf Biergarten* (301 W. Main St., tel. 210/997–7865). The *Admiral Nimitz Museum and Historical Center* (340 E. Main St., tel. 210/997–4379), in the restored steamboat-shaped Nimitz Hotel and extending into the outdoor Japanese Garden of Peace, chronicles the Pacific War and the life of Fleet Admiral Chester Nimitz, commander in chief of the United States' Pacific troops during World War II. The *Pioneer Museum* (309 W. Main St., tel. 210/997–2835), a converted home and general store built in 1846, houses items of all kinds from the city's earliest German settlers.

King William Historic Area. San Antonio's leading German merchants built their Victorian mansions here in the late 19th century, and it's still a quiet, leafy neighborhood. Madison and Guenther streets are particularly pretty for a stroll or drive. A few houses, like the 1876 Steves Homestead (509 King William St., tel. 210/225–5924), offer daily tours; you can pick up a brochure there for a self-guided walking tour of the neighborhood.

River Walk. Several miles of scenic stone pathways on both banks of the San Antonio River downtown are built a full story below street level, accessible by stairway. In some places the River Walk, or Paseo del Rio, is peaceful and quiet; in others, you'll find a mad conglomeration of restaurants, bars, hotels, and strolling mariachi bands, all of which can be seen from river taxis. In January, when parts of the river are drained to clean the bottom of debris, locals revel in the River Bottom Festival and Mud Parade. San Antonio's most beautiful attraction at all times, the River Walk is best at night.

Restaurants

In Fredericksburg, the Teutonic soul of the Hill Country, you can feast on eight types of schnitzel and gravy-soaked potato dumplings at **Friedhelm's Bavarian Inn** (tel. 210/997–6300), moderately priced and low-key. About 9 miles north of Fredericksburg on U.S. 87, the **Hill Top Cafe** (tel. 210/997–8922) is one of the region's most famous and reasonably priced restaurants. The owner, a former member of the country-and-western band Asleep at the Wheel, often entertains guests at the piano while his cooks serve up top-quality Cajun and Greek fare.

Threadgill's (tel. 512/459–3855) home-cookin' restaurant dishes up the best chicken-fried steak in Austin—and, arguably, all of Texas—but also offers creative vegetable dishes, including a mean vegetable jambalaya. A more expensive Austin favorite, but not as stuffy as it sounds, **Jean-Pierre's Upstairs** (tel. 512/454–4811) eschews the expected haute French cuisine in favor of creations with a Texas twist: grilled quail with pecan honey sauce, say, or salmon poached in corn husks.

Decorated with photographs of the Alamo City, San Antonio's **Alamo Cafe** (tel. 210/341–4526) offers an authentic Tex-Mex dining experience, with moderately priced specialties such as tortilla soup and chicken fajitas. Just one flight up from the River Walk, the upscale **Stetson Restaurant** (tel. 210/222–1400) in the Hilton Palacio del Rio Hotel combines a fabulous view of the river with a fine American menu that includes good steak and fresh seafood with a Southwestern flair. **Zuni Grill** (tel. 210/227–0864), also on the River Walk, serves hip and delicious Southwestern food and potent Cactus Margaritas.

Tourist Information

Austin Convention and Visitors Bureau (201 E. 2nd St., Box 1088, Austin, TX 78701, tel. 512/474–5171 or 800/926–2282). **Bandera Convention and Visitors Bureau** (1808 Hwy. 16 S, Bandera, TX 78003, tel. 210/796–3045 or 800/364–3833). **Fredericksburg Convention and Visitors Bureau** (106 N. Adams Rd., Fredericksburg, TX 78624, tel. 210/997–6523). **Salado Chamber of Commerce** (Box 81, Salado, TX 76571, tel. 817/947–5040). **San Antonio Convention and Visitors Bureau** (Box 2277, 121 Alamo Plaza, San Antonio, TX 78298, tel. 210/270–8700 or 800/447–3372). **San Marcos Convention and Visitors Bureau** (Box 2310, San Marcos, TX 78667, tel. 512/396–2495 or 800/782–7653, ext. 177).

Reservation Services

Bed and Breakfast Hosts of San Antonio (1777 N.E. Loop 410, Ste. 600, San Antonio, TX 78217, tel. 210/824–8036). **Be My Guest Travel Services** (402 W. Main St., Fredericksburg, TX 78624, tel. 210/997–7227). **Gastehaus Schmidt Reservation Service** (231 W. Main St., Fredericksburg, TX 78624, tel. 210/997–5612).

Austin Street Retreat

Tucked only a block from Main Street and minutes from Fredericksburg's shopping district, this B&B is actually a compound of five historic homes. Owned by a Chicago couple and managed by a local reservation service, these stylish retreats have created a new standard for area properties. The luxurious whirlpool tub for two found in each structure is your tip-off that hedonistic luxuries are emphasized here.

From the outside, you might wonder how Annie's Cabin could be one of the top guest houses in Fredericksburg, requiring reservations months in advance. The answer comes as soon as you walk in the room: over-the-top decadence, handcrafted for honeymooners. With smoky-rose-colored walls in the bedroom, the cabin is dominated by a king-size bed made from a fence reconfigured by a craftsman Cupid to resemble hearts and arrows; it's covered with a thick layer of linens, a tapestry duvet, and a sumptuous pile of pillows.

In Kristen's Cabin, a king-size iron bed overlooks a fireplace in the front bedroom. An Italian tapestry sofa and chair complete the look, and a painting of the owner's grandmother in her wedding dress lends a romantic air. Connected to the bedroom by a Saltillo-tiled hallway is the bath, its focal point a whirlpool on a limestone pedestal. The bars on the windows are there because the room served as a cell in 1885 when the town jail burned. Outside, a private flagstone courtyard with a three-tiered fountain offers a quiet, private retreat.

Eli's Cabin is less frilly, starting with the cast iron mantle saved from a Philadelphia mansion. A pencil-post bed, Mexican tin mirror, and a staghorn chandelier add a Southwestern touch. This cabin also has a private courtyard with a double hammock.

The oldest structure of the five is Maria's Cabin, a log cabin built in 1867. Its two bedrooms preserve its historic flavor with plank floors, twig furniture, chinked log walls, and historic paintings, but pamper visitors with extras the pioneers never enjoyed: two queen-size beds with down comforters and a whirlpool bath.

But none of the other getaways shares the aged elegance of El Jefe (The Boss). Decorated in 1900s Southwestern style, this two-story cottage has beamed ceilings and appointments that range from frayed sombreros to well-worn leather chairs to antique suitcases. Upstairs, the whirlpool bath overlooks the complex through French doors.

🏠 *231 W. Main St., Fredericksburg, TX 78624, tel. 210/997–5612, fax 210/ 997–8282. 4 1-bedroom guest houses, 1 2-bedroom guest house. Central heat and air-conditioning, whirlpools, fireplaces in 4 homes, cable TV in 2 homes, CD players in 2 homes, phone, coffee bar with microwave. $95–100; Continental breakfast. D, MC, V. No smoking, no pets.*

Crystal River Inn

rystal River Inn hosts Mike and Cathy Dillon might have been content to rely on their proximity to the rivers San Marcos, Blanco, and Guadalupe to attract visitors to San Marcos, a small city 51 miles north of San Antonio. But the Dillons are more creative than that: They offer guests murder mystery weekends, "ladies' escape" weekends, gourmet picnics, and other diversions to make a visit to their inn a special experience.

Mike, a manager of high-rise office buildings in Houston, and Cathy, a nurse, were shopping for a peaceful place to live when they fell in love with this 1883 mansion. It was built by Judge William Wood, a rancher, banker, and co-founder of San Marcos's Southwest Texas State University, and mixes Greek columns with Victorian gables and a double-decker porch. In order to justify its purchase and costly renovation, they decided to turn it into a B&B. That was 1984; more than a decade later, the Dillons's business includes two other buildings: the Young House, a restored 1885 Victorian home across the street, and the Rock Cottage, also a former residence.

The houses are decorated, as the Dillons put it, "with furniture we like"; the emphasis is not on antiques but on casual elegance. The guest rooms—each named for a Texas river—have themes that range from Victorian to Southwestern. The four suites are luxurious: The Blanco, which overlooks the main house's second-floor veranda,

has 12-foot ceilings and unusual fabric-upholstered walls; the San Marcos, in the Rock Cottage, features a marble garden tub with 24-carat gold fixtures, fireplace, and skylight.

As part of the popular murder mystery weekend, where the foul deed that costumed guests work to unearth is based on people and events in San Marcos history, guests enjoy a welcoming party and dessert buffet on Friday and a sunset cruise at Aquarena Springs and a multicourse dinner on Saturday. During the summer, a tubing trip down the San Marcos River is also included. Year-round, the owners put together packages including treats as diverse as massages, European facials, and carriage rides.

🏠 *326 W. Hopkins St., San Marcos, TX 78666, tel. 512/396–3739, fax 512/ 353–3248. 7 double rooms with baths, 4 2-bedroom suites. TV in most rooms, private phone in some rooms, mini-fridge and microwave in cottage; $55– $110; full breakfast. AE, D, DC, MC, V. No smoking, children by prior arrangement, no pets; 2-day minimum most weekends.*

Inn on the Creek

Suzi Epps is a picky one. Ask her about most any bed-and-breakfast in Texas and she's been there—and found it lacking. That kind of perfectionism, along with Epps's experience as a professional architect, has helped turn the Inn on the Creek into a reason to stop in Salado, a little town 45 miles north of Austin known mostly for its well-preserved 19th-century Main Street.

Inn on the Creek is a collection of five houses, three of which were salvaged from condemnation and brought to a shady spot on Salado Creek from elsewhere in Texas; all were painstakingly restored by Suzi, along with parents, Bob and Sue Whistler, and husband, Lynn. The oldest of the houses, an 1892 woodframe Victorian imported from Cameron, is connected to another house by a covered wooden walkway to form the inn's main complex. The second building, a two-story, wood frame, includes a large dining room that on weekends opens for dinner as a full-service restaurant. The breakfasts served here tend toward the exotic, ranging from German puff pancakes to Italian frittatas.

The furnishings throughout the main complex are anything but exotic; they run toward the simpler, more understated pieces of the Victorian age. The rooms exude a quiet elegance, each furnished with Victorian antiques, family photographs, and antique dresser sets. White wrought iron and wicker fill the Tyler Room. In the Rose Room, a Victorian walnut bed is covered with a collection of antique pillowcases. The most impressive is the spacious, third-floor McKie Room, which has a king-size bed as well as a library nook with a daybed that overlooks the creek—the perfect spot for a lazy weekend afternoon.

Directly across the street is the Holland House, built circa 1880, and up the block the Reue House, a Civil War–era farmhouse with four guest rooms. Its highlight is the Kiowa Room, which has a bed made from a 300-year-old loom. Sally's Cottage, a tiny one-bedroom hideaway with an adjoining living room, rounds out the inn's facilities.

All the guest rooms at Inn on the Creek have private baths—some with a pair of vintage bloomers hanging from the wall. Evenings at the inn, and throughout Salado, are quiet. Most guests just sit on the back porch and listen to the cicadas sing on a warm summer evening.

🏨 *Box 858, Salado, TX 76571, tel. 817/947–5554, fax 817/947–9198. 16 double rooms with baths; 1 cottage suite. Cable TV, phone, ceiling fan in all rooms, small refrigerators in some rooms, limited restaurant; golf privileges. $70–$115; full breakfast. MC, V. No smoking, children by prior arrangement, no pets.*

The Ogé House on the Riverwalk

Aclassic plantation house built during the Greek Revival craze that spread across the South in the years before the Civil War, the Ogé (pronounced *OH-jhay*) House is the crowning glory of San Antonio's historic King William neighborhood. Owners Patrick and Sharrie Magatagan have created an understated tribute to the antebellum South, complete with a veranda from which one can look out over the pecan-shaded estate. But it has all the modern amenities: From the registration desk to the in-room premium cable TV and the state-of-the art telephone system, their inn has the ambience of a luxury hotel.

Built in 1857 by pioneer Texas ranger and cattle rancher Louis Ogé, the three-story manse sits on 1.5 acres of landscaped lawns and gardens overlooking the Paseo del Rio. It had been a boardinghouse before the Magatagans purchased it in 1991 and set out to transform it into San Antonio's brightest B&B. Kitchenettes were turned into lovely vanities; walls were painted in creamy whites; bathrooms were overhauled; and pine floors were polished and draped with fine Oriental rugs.

Patrick, who had lived with San Antonio native Sharrie in Connecticut for eight years before returning to the Alamo City, fell in love with antiques while living in the Northeast, and—ironically, in this antebellum Southern mansion—purchased many of the furnishings for the inn there. Even one of the home's tributes to things Texan—a

bullhorn sofa in an upstairs lounging area—was purchased "up nawth." Texas-theme furnishings are also found in the Bluebonnet Room, complete with a rolling-pin bed and a West Texas judge's desk. Otherwise, early American Victorian furniture dominates the guest rooms and suites.

The house's second floor is the main floor, with an entryway, sitting room, library, kitchen, dining room, and two guest rooms. The first floor is an English basement, which houses a guest room and suite as well as the Magatagans' living quarters. The three third-floor suites are the most impressive: Each has access to the wide veranda or, in one case, a small private balcony.

Sharrie prepares the Continental breakfast, which may consist of scones, croissants, sweet rolls, popovers and hot and cold cereals. It's served in the formal dining room or on the front veranda.

🏠 *209 Washington St., San Antonio, TX 78204, tel. 210/223–2353 or 800/242–2770, fax 210/226–5812. 5 double rooms with baths, 4 suites. Air-conditioning, cable TV, telephone, refrigerator in all accommodations; fireplace in 2 rooms, all suites. $135, suites $165–$195; Continental breakfast. AE, D, DC, MC, V. No smoking indoors, no children under 16, no pets; 2-night minimum on weekends.*

Settlers Crossing

Ever wondered what it was like for German settlers on the American frontier in the 19th century? You and your clan can spend the weekend in your own "Little Haus on the Prairie" at Settlers Crossing, a 35-acre tract located in the rolling countryside between Luckenbach and Fredericksburg. Dotted by log cabins, mesquite trees, and friendly farm animals, this is easily the best family-oriented B&B in the Hill Country.

Of course, the German settlers didn't have access to a Jacuzzi—a feature of the luxurious Von Heinrich Home, one of four guest houses on the estate of hosts David and Judy Bland. The structures are close enough to one another to be convenient for groups or family reunions, but far enough apart to allow for private getaways.

The Pioneer Homestead, a stone-and-log cabin original to the property, was constructed in the 1850s by the Kusenberger family, German immigrants who were among Fredericksburg's first settlers. The modern appliances in the full kitchen of the two-bedroom house are skillfully tucked away to preserve a feeling of authenticity. The most striking feature is a robin's-egg-blue stenciled ceiling, painted when the house was built. Also original to the grounds, the Baag Farm House was built in the 1920s as a wedding gift for a Kusenberger descendant. The simple, blue wood-frame house has a wood-burning stove and antique dining room table that seats eight.

Outside the Indiana House, you may well encounter bleating sheep, grazing goats, and braying donkeys, who like to approach the split-rail fence surrounding the house. The log cabin was built in the Hoosier state in 1849 and transported to Settlers Common by the Blands. The mood of the living room is set by an antique camelback sofa; the high-ceiling master bedroom features a queen-size, four-poster bed with acorn finials. The hosts live in a nearby three-story house imported from Kentucky.

But the most remarkable guest home on the property is the Von Heinrich Home, a two-story German *fachwerk* cottage built in Pennsylvania in 1787. Inside is an outstanding collection of 19th-century folk art, including an antique horse sculpture and an old hooked rug over the fireplace.

🏠 *231 W. Main St., Fredericksburg, TX 78624, tel. 210/997–5612, fax 210/ 997–8282. 3 2-bedroom guest houses, 1 3-bedroom guest house. Central heat, air-conditioning, TV, VCR, phones, fireplaces or wood-burning stoves in all houses; full kitchen in 3 homes; Jacuzzi in 1 home. $79–$110; Continental breakfast. D, MC, V. No smoking, no pets.*

Ziller House

The premier host home in Texas's capital city is the perfect antidote for those weary of formal, frilly Victorian B&Bs. Ziller House owners Sam Kindred and Wendy Sandberg offer a unique brand of contemporary sophistication that has drawn such famed visitors as Dennis Quaid, Meg Ryan, and Linda Ellerbee. Sam and Wendy nonetheless remain prime examples of the unaffected Austin spirit; they love to sit around the living room with their guests and shoot the breeze.

A gated, secluded estate on the cliff above the south bank of Town Lake, the 1938 Italian-style mansion is at the very center of Austin, a stone's skip from the Texas capitol. The entryway leads to an eclectic living room with Eastern accents, including a Chinese lacquered screen and artificial bonsai trees. The room, which has contemporary furnishings, is dominated by a stone fireplace that was cut from a fossil bed.

The four guest rooms, three of which are upstairs, have their own personalities. The Library Room, for example, is lined with bookshelves and offers a pretty view of the lake. The balcony that gives the Balcony Room its name is surrounded on all sides by live oaks; the room's bathroom, with its dynamic black-and-saffron-yellow color scheme, is also striking. The Sun Suite has a canopy bed and a separate sitting area with a sleeper sofa.

There are plenty of places to relax on the grounds, from the stone patio, to the cliffside gazebo, to the spa. A masseur lives on the property, and guests can schedule a massage any time. Visitors with children are welcome; those who want to get away from the kids for an evening can leave them with the hosts' baby-sitter, who also takes care of Sam and Wendy's two children. And Sam, a wine dealer and gourmet chef, knows all the best restaurants in Austin.

Sam—who will prepare dinner for guests on request—usually cooks breakfast in the afternoon on an enormous Wolf stove in the kitchen. Arriving visitors find the meal—usually an egg dish, breakfast meat, pastry, and fresh fruit—tucked away in the small refrigerator that is in each room's service cabinet, along with a microwave oven. The self-contained quality of the guest rooms (each also has a cordless cellular phone) is especially appealing to business travelers, who are welcome to use the hosts' 18-chair dining room table for meetings.

🏨 *800 Edgecliff Terr., Austin, TX 78704, tel. 512/462–0100 or 800/949–5446, fax 512/462–9166. 3 double rooms with baths, 1 suite. Cable TV and VCR in each room, CD player in living room, 2,000 video library; outside dog run, Jacuzzi hot tub. $110; full breakfast. AE, MC, V. No smoking indoors, pets in runs only; 2-night minimum on weekends.*

The Beckmann Inn And Carriage House

Betty Jo and Don Schwartz, Illinois natives, fell in love with San Antonio as a result of many trips to visit their children in college. During those excursions, the couple liked to drive through the King William District to a home they dreamed of owning. Built for a daughter of the Guenther flour mill family and later owned by noted architect O'Neil Ford, the 1886 Greek Revival–style home features an original cypress picket fence and a wraparound porch.

Five years after first admiring the historic structure, they found it was for sale. They bought it and turned it into an elegant B&B. Today guest rooms are filled with Victorian furnishings, public areas have such touches as a wood mosaic floor imported from Paris and arched pocket doors, and there are wide porches to sit on and enjoy the quiet neighborhood. The most private rooms are in the adjacent Carriage House, and they have more modern decor, carpeting, and a shady brick courtyard.

All guests enjoy a full breakfast that might include cinnamon-stuffed French toast with apricot glaze or Canadian bacon, and, in keeping with the area's German heritage, a breakfast dessert.

▦ *222 E. Guenther St., San Antonio, TX 78204, tel. 210/229–1449 or 800/945–1449. 5 double rooms with baths. Cable TV in all rooms, turndown service, refrigerator in home for guests' use, minifridges in carriage house rooms; trolley stop. $80–$130; full breakfast. AE, D, DC, MC, V. No smoking indoors, children over 12 only, no pets; 2-night minimum on weekends.*

The Bonner Garden

The Bonner Garden was built in 1910 in what is now San Antonio's historic Monte Vista area. Louisiana aristocrat Mary Bonner's four previous residences all burnt to the ground, so she wanted a structure guaranteed to be fireproof. Atlee Ayers, the architect commissioned for the project, responded with a concrete house, reinforced with steel, cast in iron, and coated with stucco.

Bonner, who spent much of the time in Paris, became known for her etchings and prints. Current owners, the Stenoien family, decorated the interior of the 4,000-square-foot Palladian-style villa in keeping with the house's artistic heritage. Bonner's work is displayed throughout. Detached from the main residence, the artist's former studio is now a guest cottage. With a Saltillo-tile floor, stone walls, and Santa Fe furniture, it is the most private room on the property. The villa's architectural embellishments, including hand-painted porcelain fireplaces and tile floors original to the house, are splendid, and Battenburg lace and antique armoires fill the bedrooms. A rooftop garden affords a 360° view of the city.

▦ *145 E. Agarita St., San Antonio, TX 78212, tel. 210/733–4222 or 800/396–4222, fax 210/733–6129. 5 double rooms with baths. TV, VCR, and phone in all rooms; CD player in sitting room; videotape library; outdoor pool. $75–$95; Continental breakfast. AE, D, DC, MC, V. No smoking, children by prior arrangement, no pets; 2-night minimum on weekends.*

The Bullis House Inn

The Bullis House was built in 1906 for John Lapham Bullis, the commander of the Seminole Indian scouts used by the U.S. cavalry in the late 1800s to track the enemy Comanches and Apaches during the Indian wars. The neoclassical-style main house offers bed-and-breakfast facilities to visitors, and the former carriage house serves as an international youth hostel.

Bed-and-breakfast guests are treated to large rooms, most equipped with TVs; however, only two have private baths. One is the Harvey Page Room, featuring a king-size four-poster bed, a sitting area with a large round oak table, and a fireplace. In the morning, guests can enjoy a Continental breakfast while innkeeper Mike Tease cranks up classical music on a state-of-the-art player piano. Three nights a week, the Bullis House shows movies (with popcorn) in the main house, bringing hostelers from Germany, England, Australia, and other nations into contact with the B&Bers.

🏠 *621 Pierce St., Box 8059, San Antonio, TX 78208, tel. 210/223–9426, fax 210/299–1479. 2 double rooms with baths; 5 doubles share 4 baths. Individual climate control in rooms, phone in 1 room; outdoor pool. $49–$69; Continental breakfast. AE, D, MC, V. Smoking in guest rooms only, no pets; 2-night minimum on weekends.*

Carrington's Bluff

Look out from the 35-foot front porch of Carrington's Bluff, where the woodsy yard takes a sharp drop to meet rippling Shoal Creek, and it's not difficult to imagine what it was like to live on this estate 115 years ago. Then, this Texas farmhouse was on the edge of no-man's-land—the line between the settlement of Austin and Indian country. There's still the hint of wilderness about this place, though it is only seven blocks from the University of Texas and nine from the state capitol.

There's also more than a hint of civilized hospitality here. Before hosts David and Gwen Fullbrook opened Carrington's Bluff, they owned another Austin B&B and were assistant innkeepers at the 30-room Village Country Inn in Manchester, Vermont. David is a native Englishman, with an undiluted accent, and the decor here is country English, complete with Laura Ashley prints in

the guest rooms. In addition to the main house, where teas and coffees, including the inn's own grind, are available the hosts also book visitors in the Writers Cottage, a creamy stucco home across the street. Its three guest rooms are named for local scribes who have stayed at the inn.

🏠 *1900 David St., Austin, TX 78705, tel. 512/479–0638. 6 double rooms with baths, 2 doubles share bath. TV in some rooms, phones in all rooms. $60–$89; full breakfast, tea. AE, MC, V. No smoking indoors, no children under 10, no pets.*

The Comfort Common

They don't tear down many buildings in Comfort. Since the late-19th century, when the business district was erected, only the livery stable has been razed, making the downtown area of this Hill Country city the best preserved in the state. At the heart of the business district is the Comfort Common, called the Ingenhuett-Faust Hotel when it was built in 1880.

The two-story limestone structure, its wide porch and balcony stretching across the building and fronted by wood posts, was designed as an eight-room facility; eight more rooms were added before the turn of the century. The hotel had been in decline for several decades when it was purchased in 1985 by Bob and Diane Potter, who used the property as an antiques shop. Current owners and hosts Jim Lord and Bobby Dent converted the complex to a B&B and oversee the 13 antiques shops on the premises, maintaining the place with enthusiasm. Each of the six guest rooms, along with the small cottage behind the hotel, is decorated with authentic antiques, in themes ranging from handcrafted Early American to lacy Victorian to cowboy kitsch.

🏠 *717 High St., Box 539, Comfort, TX 78013, tel. 210/995–3030, fax 210/ 995–3455. 4 double rooms with baths, 3 suites. TVs and fireplaces in some rooms. $55–$90; full breakfast. AE, D, MC, V. No smoking, no children under 12, no pets; 2-night minimum on holiday and special-event weekends.*

Das Kleine Nest

In a fitting testament to this "Little Nest's" charm as a honeymoon retreat, owners Pat and Toni Keating constructed a chapel on the premises. But there's a certain irony to this act: The limestone cottage was built in 1875 by a bachelor for his betrothed—just before their nuptials were called off.

As the German name suggests, Das Kleine Nest is a tiny place, a two-room cabin with a spiral staircase that leads to a bedroom loft. The loft has barely enough room for the queen-size bed it supports; below, the doll-house-size kitchen spills into the living room. But for those who don't mind their surroundings cozy—or who prefer them that way—this snugly fits the bill. The house mixes antiques and contemporary furnishings, including colorful Mexican-tile floors and hand-loomed rugs. An enclosed patio at the back door and a larger patio area in the yard are fine for lounging with a good book.

🏠 *231 W. Main St., Fredericksburg, TX 78624, tel. 210/997–5612, fax 210/997–8282. 1 double room with bath. Cable TV, central heat and air-conditioning, ceiling fans, phone, coffeemaker, small refrigerator, stove, microwave. $65; breakfast not included. D, MC, V. No pets.*

Delforge Place

One of the few traditional host homes remaining in Fredericksburg, where self-contained guest houses are the norm, Delforge Place is the lair of Betsy Delforge, the great-granddaughter of a sea captain. With help from her hus-band, George, Betsy has turned her 1898 Victorian house into a veritable walking tour of American history, with an emphasis on things nautical.

The Map Room features an original oil painting of her ancestor Captain B. Jones, sailing into the port of Hong Kong in 1860. The room's other heirlooms include a trunk that Jones took to sea and an 1854 atlas presented to him aboard his ship in Singapore. The Quebec and American rooms each have their own sitting area and are furnished with antiques from the American Revolution and Civil War eras. An exterior staircase leads to a wooden platform shaped like a ship's bow, where the Upper Deck room, with porthole windows, resembles a captain's quarters. Betsy, a retired home economist, serves a breakfast that usually includes her famous sour cream twists, along with homemade crepes and a cold fruit soup. The Delforges recently began operating a restored 1926 guest house next door.

🏠 *231 W. Main St., Fredericksburg, TX 78624, tel. 210/997–5612, fax 210/ 997–8282. 3 double rooms with baths; 1 suite. Cable TV and refrigerator in each room. $50–$83; full breakfast. D, MC, V. No smoking, no children under 6 unless family rents entire house, no pets.*

Fredericksburg Bed and Brew

The sign says ROOMS FOR RENT UPSTAIRS, and downstairs are a restaurant, beer garden, and meeting hall. More unusual is how rooms are furnished, but this new B&B is in the book because the second "B" is for beer, not necessarily breakfast: Included in the room rate is a sampler of the Fredericksburg Brewing Co.'s four current beers. The food there is also quite good.

A stay here fits in well with a weekend shopping trip—why not try out the furniture you're considering buying? Each room is done by a different store, with themes ranging from kinky (Red Stallion) to Mexican (El Nicho) to rustic (Happy Trails), and everything is for sale. Some guests switch rooms nightly. Because the B&B is right on Main Street, it's convenient for shopping and local sightseeing.

🏠 *245 E. Main St., Fredericksburg, TX 78624, tel. 210/997–1646, fax 210/ 997–8026. 12 rooms with baths. $79– $89; beer sampler. AE, MC, V. No smoking, no children, no pets.*

The Herb Haus

For lovers of herbs, gardening, or just originality, the Herb Haus offers one of the more unusual B&B experiences in Texas. The 1940s frame guest house is on the Fredericksburg Herb Farm, a 4-acre plot of organic herb and flower gardens just six blocks off Main Street. Guests can sample the farm's homemade herb teas and breads in the tearoom. In the chemist's shop, owners William and Sylvia Varney sell items from their national mail-order business, including oils, potpourris, and fragrances.

A botanical theme fittingly dominates the two-bedroom guest house, once the home of the town's midwife. Dried flowers and herbs hang from the ceiling; one of the bed frames is fashioned out of grapevines. Herbal toiletries are provided in the bath, and the breakfast of choice is "Continental herbal cuisine," including herb breads, spiced butter, fresh fruit, and even juice garnished with edible flowers. The gardens that surround the guest house are creatively landscaped, and the Varneys' faith is echoed in flowers arranged to resemble various Christian symbols.

🏠 *Drawer 927, 402 Whitney St., Fredericksburg, TX 78624, tel. 210/*

997–8615 or 800/259–4372. 1 2-bedroom guest house. Cable TV, phone, ceiling fans, air-conditioning, kitchen. $95; Continental breakfast. AE, D, DC, MC, V. No smoking, no children under 12, no pets.

The Nagel House

In 1907, this two-story house was built by 14 men in 11 days. When its current owners, retired minister Charlie Tatum and his wife, Joan, restored the deteriorating homestead in 1986, the process was considerably more time-consuming. The effort paid off, however; the Nagel House is one of the prettier Victorian guest homes in Fredericksburg.

Smooth pastels and lace curtains lend a soft touch to the period light fixtures and antiques in each room. The downstairs guest room is formal and elegant; its bathroom includes an etched-glass window, claw-foot tub, and pedestal sink. The two upstairs bedrooms have an English country flavor.

The kitchen is stocked with food for guests to prepare, including sausage rolls, ham, and muffins. Depending on your mood, breakfast can be a dressy affair in the dining room, complete with fine china and crystal, or a casual nosh in the breakfast area, with its country decor and brightly colored stoneware.

🏠 *231 W. Main St., Fredericksburg, TX 78624, tel. 210/997–5612, fax 210/ 997–8282. 1 3-bedroom cottage. Cable TV, phone, microwave, refrigerator, and stove. $85; Continental breakfast. D, MC, V. No smoking, no children under 10 except infants, no pets.*

Schmidt Barn

Charles and Loretta Schmidt, both German speakers who trace their families to Fredericksburg's founders, can claim much of the credit for the transformation of their sleepy town into Texas's B&B capital. After they restored an

1860s farmhouse as their own residence, they turned their attention to the roofless remains of a century-old barn in the backyard. By 1983, the Schmidts had transformed it into one of the city's first guest houses and launched the Gastehaus Schmidt Reservation Service, which now books the great majority of the city's more than 90 such establishments.

The downstairs living area of the tastefully furnished barn features a comfortable sleeper sofa and a rustic kitchen and bath, both accented with blue-and-white terrazzo tile; a sunken tile tub is the bathroom's highlight. The bedroom is in an upstairs loft. The Schmidts are happy to furnish firewood for the antique wood-burning stove; they also stock the house's refrigerator with a German-style breakfast of meats, cheese, and pastries.

▦ *231 W. Main St., Fredericksburg, TX 78624, tel. 210/997–5612, fax 210/ 997–8282. 1 1-bedroom guest house (sleeps 4). Phone, central heat and air-conditioning, ceiling fan, CD and tape player, microwave, coffeemaker. $77; full breakfast left in guest house. D, MC, V. Pets by special permission only.*

Woodburn House

Herb and Sandra Dickson run the only B&B in Hyde Park, Austin's oldest residential suburb. About a mile north of downtown, the turn-of-the-century neighborhood hosts a collection of Victorian homes, Texas frame farmhouses, and craftsman-style bungalows. Sandra can provide a brochure detailing a walking tour of this historic area, pointing out the Elisabet Ney Museum and moonlight towers that once illuminated the neighborhood.

Built in 1909, the Woodburn House is named for former owner Bettie Hamilton Woodburn, the daughter of a provisional governor of Texas. Its rooms are simply and functionally decorated, with rocking chairs and firm mattresses. The two rooms upstairs have access to a wide balcony, from which you can watch squirrels darting up the pecan and elm trees. This is the kind of place where you can feel comfortable lounging on the living room couch, shoes off, watching a ball game on TV. Breakfast may include eggs, waffles, or any number of treats; Herb boasts that a guest can stay 10 days and never be served the same thing twice.

▦ *4401 Ave. D, Austin, TX 78751, tel. 512/458–4335. 4 double rooms with baths. Desks, phones in all rooms, TV and VCR in living room, exchange library. $75–$85; full breakfast. No credit cards. Smoking on porches only, no children under 10, no pets.*

A Yellow Rose

Who says you can never go home again? Clifford and Jennifer Tice, former controller and Wall Street banker, respectively, have done it. They're so glad to be back in San Antonio that they've given their B&B a Lone Star State moniker. "We're dyed-in-the-wool Texans, and we wanted a name that was Texan," explains Clifford. The Yellow Rose of Texas was the nickname of Emily Morgan, a slave who, as mistress to Santa Anna during the Texas Revolution, gave secrets to the Texan defenders and helped win independence for Texas.

Nestled in the King William Historic District, A Yellow Rose is an 1878 Texas Victorian structure. After a major renovation in 1982, the Tices have produced a home that's dressy but not stuffy, filled with Victorian antiques. Personal service, from champagne and flowers for anniversary and honeymoon guests to a cup of coffee in the afternoons, is typical. And, for those vacationers looking for a real escape, the Tices work hard to remain unobtrusive, offering conversation when it is wanted and privacy when it's desired.

Guests have use of a parlor, living room, and dining room furnished with period antiques and also wide porches where they can spend the evenings unwinding after a day downtown.

🏨 *229 Madison St., San Antonio, TX 78204, tel. 210/229–9903 or 800/950–9903. 5 double rooms with baths. Cable TV in all rooms, Caswell and Massey products in baths, trolley stop one block away. $75–$110; full breakfast. AE, D, MC, V. Smoking on porches only, no children under 9, no pets; 2-night minimum on weekends.*

West Texas

When Francisco Coronado and his explorers arrived in West Texas more than 400 years ago, they found the grass high and the terrain devoid of landmarks. Resembling Hansel and Gretel on horseback, the Spaniards drove stakes in the soil to blaze a path across the region they called Llano Estacado, or staked plain.

Today, interstates carve the vast, high plains of West Texas into manageable chunks and connect the widely scattered cities. This is the Texas that many picture with a mention of "the Lone Star State," a land of leathery-faced cowboys, rolling tumbleweeds, lonesome windmills, and pumping oil derricks. Roads stretch straight to the horizon, and distances are measured not in miles but in hours. Locals consider an 80-mile haul "right around the corner."

Country singer Mac Davis once sang "happiness is Lubbock, Texas, in my rearview mirror," but for many this plains community is an oasis. With more than 20,000 students at Texas Tech University, the city has many cultural events. Lubbock is also the heart of Texas's burgeoning wine business, and its award-winning operations recall the tradition of the staked plain, albeit for grapevines these days.

About 120 miles north, Amarillo is the cultural and commercial capital of the Texas Panhandle. From a humble beginning as a staging area for the Fort Worth and Denver City Railroad in the 1880s, the city became a center for cattle ranching, wheat and cotton farming, and oil production. Today, Amarillo is a city of 170,000, home of Amarillo College, Amarillo Symphony Orchestra, and the Lone Star Ballet.

Amarillo is also the gateway to the nation's second largest canyon: Palo Duro. Here, majestic cliffs create a backdrop for the Lone Star State's most popular outdoor drama, the summer production of TEXAS.

The few B&B establishments in West Texas operate as pioneers, functioning without centralized reservation services. Most do not share the opulent atmosphere found in the long-running B&B capitals of East and Central Texas, but they do provide plenty of West Texas hospitality and a chance to look at the most rugged portion of the Lone Star State.

Places to Go, Sights to See

Antiques. Route 66, one of the nation's most famous highways, slices through downtown Amarillo as Sixth Street. This historic strip is lined with more than 200 antiques and specialty shops. South of Lubbock, Post is home to Old Mill Trade Days, an antiques show and flea market, on the Friday, Saturday, and Sunday before the first Monday of each month. The sale draws as many as 500 vendors.

Cadillac Ranch. What do you get when you cross 10 old Cadillacs, one eccentric Texan, and a large pasture? The Cadillac Ranch—a collection of junkers representing the golden age of Route 66—west of Amarillo. Buried nose down at the same angle as Cheops's pyramid, the cars are dotted with graffiti and are likely to be surrounded by grazing cattle.

Palo Duro Canyon State Park. Truly a Texas-size attraction, this natural wonder stretches 120 miles and drops 1,200 feet, making it the nation's second-largest canyon. Visitors to *Palo Duro State Park* (tel. 806/488–2227) can tackle the park on foot along miles of hiking trails, on horseback, or on the *Sad Monkey Railroad* (tel. 806/488–2222), a miniature train that offers a 2-mile narrated tour. Summer guests can enjoy *TEXAS*, (tel. 806/655–2181), an outdoor production that brings to life the struggles of the area's pioneers and native residents. The drama, featuring everything from blizzards to sandstorms, resonates within the canyon walls.

Wineries. The rich soil and temperate weather of this region has drawn wineries and international acclaim to Lubbock. *Llano Estacado* (tel. 806/745–2258) is probably the most celebrated. *Cap*Rock Winery* (tel. 806/863–2704), housed in a European-style chalet, is the state's second largest. Both offer tours and tastings.

Restaurants

In Lubbock, the Warehouse District is home to many of the city's best eateries and nightspots. **Stubb's Bar-B-Q** (tel. 806/747–4777) serves up brisket and ribs with live music on the side. Nearby, the **Depot Restaurant and Bar** (tel. 806/747–1646) has a diverse menu ranging from chicken fried steak to chili relleno to fillet of sole bearnaise.

The **Big Texan Steak House** (tel. 806/372–2000) is Amarillo's most famous restaurant and also a tourist attraction—there's a free 72-ounce steak for anyone who can eat it in one hour. Along with good ol' Texas beef, there are more exotic dishes such as rattlesnake and buffalo.

Tourist Information

Amarillo Convention and Visitors Council (1000 Polk St., Amarillo, TX 79101, tel. 806/374–1497 or 800/692–1338). **Lubbock Convention and Visitors Bureau** (Box 561, Lubbock, TX 79408, tel. 806/747–5232 or 800/692–4035). **Post Chamber of Commerce** (One Post Santa Fe Plaza, Post, TX 79356, tel. 806/495–3461).

Galbraith House

Galbraith House might make guests feel like breaking out in song—and with good reason. Besides being Amarillo's most elegant bed-and-breakfast, it is owned by Emmy Award–winning opera singer Mary Jane Johnson and her husband, David. Posters of the singer's career with the Santa Fe Opera and autographed photos of Mary Jane with her co-stars fill the home. Her Emmy for *La Boheme* with Pavarotti and the Philadelphia Opera Company hangs in a second-floor sitting room.

But the real star at the Galbraith House is the home, wrapped in lavish woods and filled with comfortable but elegant antiques. Visitors are welcome to make a snack in the country kitchen, decorated with Royal Copenhagen china that once belonged to Mary Jane's grandmother, or to play a tune on the living room piano. Closets invite inspection; games and books are tucked inside for visitors to enjoy.

The Craftsman-style home was constructed in 1912 for H.W. Galbraith, co-owner of the Foxworth-Galbraith Lumber Company, a business that served three states. Being a lumber magnate, the owner used numerous woods in the home, in such forms as three-inch-thick sliding panel doors made of Philippine mahogany and a parquet floor in the solarium that boasts over a half dozen varieties.

In 1977 the Johnsons restored the structure, which had been boarded up for 10 years, and then moved to another home in Amarillo. Today the Galbraith House operates as a guest house without a resident manager. A full breakfast, which may include egg-and-sausage casserole, fresh granola, or homemade bread, is served by the innkeeper in the large dining room. During the afternoons, many visitors enjoy a glass of tea or cup of coffee and snacks on the front porch swing or the wicker furniture on the second-floor balcony.

Guests have full run of the kitchen, as well as two sitting rooms, a living room with gas fireplace, and a lavishly paneled library filled with volumes displayed behind leaded glass doors.

Each of the guest rooms reflects the taste of the Johnsons, who selected the antique quilts for every bed. The two largest rooms, although not suites, do include comfortable chairs to create a reading area. The Christmas Room, named for its red ceiling and green-and-red decor, is cheery and overlooks the front lawn. The corner Blue Room, with its star quilt and antique trunk, is also slightly larger than the others.

🏨 *1710 S. Polk, Amarillo, TX 79102, tel. 806/374–0237 or 800/687–7655, fax 806/374–0237. 5 doubles with baths. Air-conditioning, cable TV in two sitting areas, use of full kitchen. $85; full breakfast and snacks. AE, D, DC, MC, V. Smoking on balconies only, no pets.*

Hotel Garza

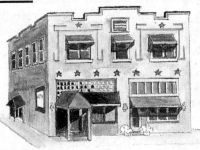

Innkeepers Janice and Jim Plummer are a busy pair. They left their respective jobs as legal secretary and radio executive in Lubbock to be self employed and work together. The result is a completely restored historic property that is the only B&B in town.

Located 45 miles southwest of Lubbock, Post was founded as a utopian community by Charles Post, of Post Toasties fame. The cereal king had visions of a city where saloons were prohibited and residents were required to have three references before moving to town. The Hotel Garza, built in 1915 (after Post's death), had lesser ambitions. Post's version of a red-light district, the hotel was the kind of place that locals crossed the street to avoid.

But in 1992 the Plummers saw that the hotel, vacant beneath a heavy coat of West Texas dust, had potential. Post had recently undergone transformation as a federally designated "Main Street City," and the Plummers began their own renovation. Room by room, they refinished floors, repainted, and added baths to produce a two-story inn with still more rooms planned. Today's B&B combines elegant dining with clean, simple accommodations that reflect the mood of an earlier time.

The expansive lobby, with over a dozen antique tables and a corner sitting area, greets guests. Its wood floors were protected through the years by layers of linoleum and now gleam with a new finish. Above, the original pressed-tin ceil-

ing has fresh white paint. Ceiling fans hum on warm afternoons, and chandeliers illuminate the room.

Like a Western hotel in the area's earliest days, its guest rooms are off long hallways, now lined with antique benches. In the small, spartan rooms, many of the furnishings are original to the hotel. Most have an iron bed, antique dressers, and area rugs. Guests are free to enjoy the mezzanine-level library filled with a collection of first editions, along with popular titles, games, and a TV. Wainscoting and a stained glass window recall the hotel's early days.

Early risers can head to the kitchen to brew a pot of coffee or wait for a plate of Janice's egg casserole, sausage, and homemade breads. On Friday and Saturday, the Plummers serve lunch to the public. On evenings when the neighboring Garza Theater hosts a production, the Hotel Garza also serves dinner.

302 E. Main St., Post, TX 79356, tel. 806/495-3962. 6 double rooms with baths, 4 doubles share 2 baths, 1 suite. Air-conditioning, TV in library, limited restaurant, theater packages. $45–$65 for doubles, $35–$55 for singles; full breakfast on weekends, Continental breakfast on weekdays. MC, V. No smoking, no pets.

The Abernathy Inn

Medical transcriber Freida Johnson and husband Clint, a pharmaceutical employee, have found the prescription for happiness: a two-story hotel in tiny Abernathy. Although there's little to do in town, visitors are just a short drive from Lubbock along I-27.

This structure was built just after the turn of the century, operating as a pharmacy, a telephone exchange, and, since the 1930s, a hotel. A few years ago the Johnsons purchased the property and set about returning the stucco building to its early glory—with a few special touches. Extensive travels in England have given the couple a love for the English country style. Freida displays her English china on the dining room's sea foam–colored walls and uses lace curtains from the British Isles throughout the home. She also planted an English rose garden, a rare treasure in the harsh West Texas climate.

The guest rooms, however, reflect various facets of West Texas life, from the blue-and-white checkered linens of the Farm Room to the blackboard and 1958 state map in the School Room. Each is decorated with antiques, including quilt coverlets and 1930s radios in working condition.

🏠 *Box 283, Abernathy, TX 79311, tel. 806/298-2956. 7 double rooms with baths. TV in living room, access to full kitchen, air-conditioning; free use of tandem bicycle. $45–$50; full breakfast. MC, V. No smoking, no pets.*

Broadway Manor

Just down the street from Texas Tech University, the Broadway Manor exudes the style of an aged professor—dignified, traditional, and a wee bit world-weary.

Built in 1923 by a prominent Lubbock banker, this home was once a fraternity house. With a complete restoration, it was converted to a B&B and is also a popular site for social functions and business meetings because of a large game room and its proximity to campus. There are several common areas: a formal living room with a gas fireplace and Oriental rug; a large game room with TV and VCR; and a burgundy-walled dining room sprinkled with tables where the resident manager serves Continental breakfast and fresh juice.

Each guest room features antique furnishings, such as the Music Room's lamp styled from a clarinet found in the attic that belonged to the original owner's son. Most unique is The Lodge, the basement-turned-guest quarters, which has a separate outdoor entrance. Caramel-colored pine walls, antlers above a rock fireplace, antique sewing tables, and a buffalo-plaid comforter give the room a woodsy feel.

🏠 *1811 Broadway, Lubbock, TX 79401, tel. 806/749-4707 or 800/749-4707. 2 double rooms with baths, 2 doubles share bath with resident manager. Phone hook-ups in rooms, TV with VCR in game room, air-conditioning. $65–$85; Continental breakfast. MC, V. No smoking, no pets.*

Harrison House

Two of Amarillo's homes share more than just their roles as bed-and-breakfasts: they were built at the same address. In the 1920s, Parkview House (*see below*) was located on South Harrison Street. After it was hauled to Jefferson Street, today's Harrison House rose on the lot.

Now owned by David and Michele Horsley, a writer and attorney, respectively, this classical-revival home has one guest room downstairs. The Horsleys had enjoyed B&Bs on their travels, and in 1994 their home became Amarillo's newest accommodation.

Visitors enjoy a sunny bedroom with antique furnishings and a large bathroom. Guests also have full use of the downstairs—they can converse with David while he prepares his special whole wheat pancakes in the country kitchen, watch a movie with the family's two children in the TV room, or play the piano in one of two living areas.

David has a special interest in old homes, and he's happy to point out the features of his, from its coved ceilings to the montage of items he recovered from the home's duct work. Mounted and displayed in the kitchen, the collection includes everything from Victrola needles to hair pins to a brass cartridge found in the attic, which the original owners used as a shooting gallery on rainy days.

🏠 *1710 S. Harrison St., Amarillo, TX 79102, tel. 806/374–1710. 1 double room with bath. TV with VCR in TV room, use of full kitchen. $75; full breakfast. MC, V. Smoking on porches only; pets outside, in garage, or in yard only.*

Parkview House

A collector's dream, or a minimalist's nightmare, the Parkview House is packed to the rafters with items Carol and Nabil Dia have gathered from antiques shops and garage sales. Filling display cases, covering kitchen walls, and spilling into the guest rooms, Carol's collectibles are conversation starters for visitors, many of whom come to shop in Amarillo's famed antiques shopping area.

But more than the colonial hats or cutwork glass, it's the personalities of the owners that bring guests to this B&B. Carol, from upstate New York, and Nabil, from Jordan, bring to their establishment a love of after-dinner conversation. Together, they personify "Texas-friendly." Their home, too, has a history of welcoming guests: In the 1920s it operated as Amarillo's Waldorf Hotel, and in the next decade it served as a railroad hotel.

Room styles vary from colonial to country, but romantics should request the Victorian Rose Suite, with its own sitting area and reading niche with a fur rug. The Kindernook has a sleigh bed tucked beneath the eaves and is filled with memories of childhood: toys, books, and some child-size furniture.

🏠 *1311 S. Jefferson, Amarillo, TX 79101, tel. 806/373–9464. 3 double rooms with baths, 2 doubles share bath. Cable TV in living room and kitchen, phone hookups in rooms, hot tub; bicycles. $65–$85; Continental breakfast. AE, MC, V. No smoking, children by prior arrangement, no pets.*

Utah

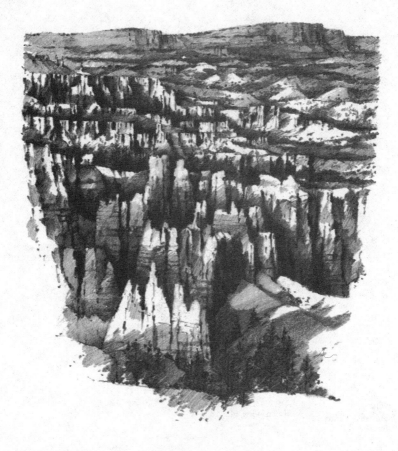

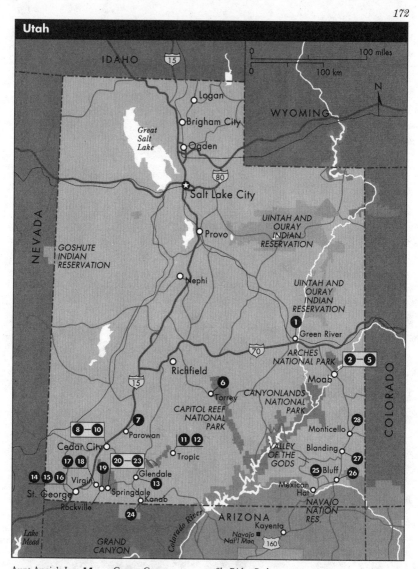

Aunt Annie's Inn, **14**

Bankurz Hatt, **1**

The Bard's Inn, **8**

The Blue House, **19**

Bluff Bed and Breakfast, **26**

Bryce Point Bed and Breakfast, **12**

Castle Valley Inn, **2**

The Desert Chalet, **3**

Francisco's, **11**

Grandma Bess' Cottage, **7**

Grayson Country Inn, **27**

Greene Gate Village, **15**

The Grist Mill Inn, **28**

Harvest House, **20**

Morning Glory Inn, **21**

Nine Gables Inn, **24**

O'Toole's Under the Eaves, **22**

Pack Creek Ranch, **4**

Paxman's Summer House, **9**

Seven Wives Inn, **16**

SkyRidge Bed and Breakfast, **6**

Smith Hotel, **13**

Snow Family Guest Ranch, **17**

Sunflower Hill, **5**

The Theater Bed & Breakfast, **10**

Valley of the Gods Bed and Breakfast, **25**

Zion House, **23**

Zion's Blue Star, **18**

Southwestern Utah

Dubbed "Color Country" by Utah boosters, the southwestern part of the state is a region of exceptional beauty, encompassing both alpine and desert climate zones at vastly differing elevations. The area has forests, lakes, and farmlands, but punctuating it all is ancient red rock that has been buffeted by wind and sand, carved by rivers, and thrust up and apart by geologic forces deep within the earth.

These days millions of travelers arrive each year from all over the world to marvel at the scenery of Zion and Bryce Canyon national parks, but the area's early Anglo settlers did not come for the views. They were Mormon pioneers in the mid-1800s who, after enduring arduous journeys across the United States, were asked by their church leaders to leave the growing towns of northern Utah and colonize the southern reaches of the territory.

All across southwestern Utah, the homes that these Mormon pioneers built, whether simple or elegant, have been preserved with an uncommon devotion. Most of the area's towns have historic districts where yards bright with carefully tended flower beds hearken back to the days when the pioneers were striving to meet the challenge issued by their leader, Brigham Young, to "make the desert blossom as a rose."

Southwestern Utah thrives for most of the year on a healthy tourist trade. Although summer remains the busiest time, each season brings a different face to the land. Spring dots the meadows and riversides with wildflowers and provides excellent hiking, biking, and golf weather before the hotter days of summer. Savvy travelers plan to visit the region before Memorial Day or in the fall when autumn leaves add extra fire to the ruddy sandstone found everywhere.

In winter, the climate of southwestern Utah remains more moderate than that of the state's northern half. However, because of the area's vast differences in elevation, snow ranges

*from a dusting at Zion National Park to more than 400 inches
a season at Brian Head Ski Resort. There's almost always
enough to ensure satisfying cross-country skiing around the
rim of Bryce Canyon. The contrast of dazzling white snow set
on warm-toned red rock is a sight not soon forgotten by winter
visitors.*

*Throughout the region, bed-and-breakfast establishments
range from simple homestays to elegant inns in grand pioneer
homes and newer houses decorated with flair. B&Bs here are
generally better established and more sophisticated than those
in the southeastern part of the state. Prices are accordingly
slightly higher, but B&B room rates here are still roughly
equivalent to those of area motels.*

Places to Go, Sights to See

Bryce Canyon National Park (Rte. 12, Bryce Canyon, UT 84717, tel. 801/834–
5322). A Paiute legend has it that the formations of Bryce Canyon National Park
were once exotic animals and birds who were turned to stone for angering the god
Coyote. Today, visitors to the park enjoy hiking and horseback riding through
thousands of delicate spires and pillars and mazes walled with quilted drapes of
stone in variegated tones of orange, pink, and cream. A 37-mile round-trip drive
visits several viewpoints overlooking these huge natural amphitheaters.

Capitol Reef National Park (Rte. 24, Torrey, UT 84775, tel. 801/425–3791).
Named for a formation resembling the U.S. Capitol, Capitol Reef is an inviting
mixture of wild desert and stone canyons and domes carved out of the Waterpocket
Fold, a 100-mile bulge and uplift of the earth's crust. The Fremont River, which
flows through the park, has encouraged settlement of the area—from the ancient
Fremont Native American culture to hardy Mormon pioneers. Visitors can view
1,000-year-old petroglyph panels, hike through canyons and gorges, or explore the
backcountry in four-wheel-drive vehicles. Verdant orchards planted in the 1800s
border the campground at the settlement of Fruita, inviting grazing deer on
summer evenings. A 25-mile scenic drive is also popular.

Cedar Breaks National Monument (82 N. 100 East, Cedar City, UT 84720, tel.
801/586–0787) is similar to Bryce in that it, too, is a natural amphitheater filled
with jutting columns of multicolored sandstone. However, Cedar Breaks is much
smaller than Bryce, and its west slope location and 10,000-foot elevation have
encouraged the growth of forests and grassy meadows around its rim. Hiking
trails pass through ancient bristlecone pines to a variety of scenic overlooks.

Cedar City. When Mormon settlers arrived in late 1851, they named the town for
its abundance of cedar trees; it turned out they were junipers, but the name stuck.

Cedar City is a quiet place with wide, tree-lined streets and well-maintained homes, but from June to September, the *Utah Shakespearean Festival* (tel. 801/586–7878) transforms this university town into an Elizabethan village; featured plays rotate nightly in two indoor theaters and an outdoor replica of Shakespeare's Globe Theatre. About 12 miles from Cedar City on S.R. 14, the *Zion Overlook* offers a sweeping vista and an interpretive chart detailing the formations of distant Zion National Park.

Coral Pink Sand Dunes State Park (12 mi off Hwy. 89, near Kanab, tel. 801/874–2408) has undulating piles of coral-color sand. Although it's popular with off-highway vehicle users, it can also be a very introspective spot with the sunshine playing up the vibrancy of the sand.

Scenic Rte. 9. Picturesque and quiet *Rockville* is one of several tiny towns sprinkled along S.R. 9 between I-15, north of St. George, and Zion National Park. Just off S.R. 9, across an old bridge, a dirt road leads to the ghost town of *Grafton*—the setting for the famous bicycle scene in the film *Butch Cassidy and the Sundance Kid*—and its mournful desert cemetery.

Skiing. *Brian Head Ski Resort* (S.R. 143, Brian Head, UT 84719, tel. 801/677–2035), 12 miles southeast of tiny Parowan, gets at least as much snow as the more famous resorts in northern Utah. In summer, the seven chairlifts become high-speed transportation for mountain bikers, ascending to a height of 10,850 feet for the ultimate downhill ride. Low-key *Elk Meadows Resort* (Box 511, Beaver, UT 84713, tel. 801/438–5433), 17 miles east of Beaver on S.R. 153, has an excellent children's ski school, making it a particular favorite with families. Cross-country enthusiasts enjoy the miles and miles of trails, both groomed and pristine, offered in *Cedar Canyon*, about 10 miles east of Cedar City on S.R. 14. *Ruby's Inn* (Box 1, S.R. 63, Bryce Canyon, UT 84764, tel. 801/834–5341), near Bryce Canyon National Park, grooms canyon-rim trails and provides ski rentals; many ungroomed trails within Bryce Canyon are also popular.

St. George. Named for George Albert Smith, a beloved counselor to Brigham Young, St. George was the site of the *first Mormon temple in Utah* (200 E. 400 South); although the stately white structure is not open to visitors, the grounds and visitor center are open daily. A self-guided walking tour of the many homes and buildings of the town's *historic district* is available from the Washington County Travel and Convention Bureau (*see* Tourist Information, *below*). At the bureau you can also pick up a listing of the town's seven public golf courses, which attract enthusiasts year-round.

Snow Canyon State Park (11 mi northwest of St. George, tel. 801/628–2255) is one of the most photogenic spots in southwestern Utah, its red Navajo sandstone contrasted by an overlay of harder black lava rock and soft beige sandstone layers. Several trails lead to hidden formations and secluded spots. A paved road, particularly popular with bicyclists, runs through the wide canyon to the town of Santa Clara.

Zion National Park (Rte. 9, Springdale, UT 84767, tel. 801/772–3256). Towering monuments with awestruck names such as The Great White Throne and Angel's

Landing dominate the views at Zion, where the Virgin River has carved a deep canyon whose ruddy walls are stained with carbon residue (a.k.a. "desert varnish"). This is Utah's most popular national park; each summer the 6-mile scenic drive from the mouth of Zion Canyon to the Zion Narrows Trail begins to resemble a parking lot. After exploring Zion Canyon, continue east on S.R. 9, which climbs high above the canyon floor and passes through two tunnels carved out of solid rock. Overlooks and trails on this side of the park are generally less crowded. The surprisingly easy Canyon Overlook Trail, just east of the tunnels, is a 1-mile round-trip route that leads to unmatched views of the Zion Canyon formations.

Restaurants

Although 3.2% beer and wine coolers are widely available in grocery and convenience stores throughout southern Utah, restaurants in some smaller towns may not have liquor licenses. When in doubt, call ahead or ask your server, who is frequently able to serve (but not offer) alcohol to customers.

The **Capitol Reef Cafe** in Torrey (tel. 801/425–3271) serves everything from peanut butter, honey, and banana sandwiches to shrimp-stuffed mushrooms and flaky, smoked rainbow trout caught locally.

In Cedar Canyon, east of Cedar City, **Milt's Stage Stop** (tel. 801/586–9344) is *the* place for tender steaks and all the trimmings, served in a rustic western environment. **New Garden Cafe** (tel. 801/635–9825) in Hurricane is decidedly casual and a little New Age, featuring vegetarian and ethnic specialties and the only espresso machine for miles. In St. George, **Basila's Cafe** (tel. 801/673–7671) serves both Greek and Italian entrées in a small cobalt-blue-and-white room; salads here are delicious and have lovely edible embellishments. Also in St. George, the **Pizza Factory** (tel. 801/628–1234) in Ancestor Square offers a lengthy pizza-topping list and standard pasta and sauces; dessert means scoops of chocolate chip cookie dough (served baked as well). The **Bit and Spur Saloon** (tel. 801/772–3498) in Springdale has out-of-the-ordinary Southwestern-style Mexican food in a dining room lined with the works of local artists. Visitors to Bryce Canyon enjoy the Continental cuisine at the **Bryce Lodge** (tel. 801/834–5361), recently renovated to its original 1920s rustic charm with exposed beams and massive native stone fireplaces.

Tourist Information

Color Country Travel Region (906 N. 1400 West, Box 1550, St. George, UT 84771, tel. 801/628–4171 or 800/233–8824). **Iron County Tourism and Convention Bureau** (Box 220, Cedar City, UT 84720, tel. 801/586–5124). **Kane County Travel Council** (Box 728, Kanab, UT 84741, tel. 801/644–5033). **Washington County Travel and Convention Bureau** (425 S. 700 East, St. George, UT 84770, tel. 801/634–5747 or 800/869–6635).

Reservation Services. There are no bed-and-breakfast reservation services in southwestern Utah. **Bed and Breakfast Inns of Utah, Inc.** (Box 3066, Park City, UT 84060) and the **Utah Travel Council** (Council Hall/Capitol Hill, Salt Lake City, UT 84114, tel. 801/538–1030 or 800/200–1160) both publish free directories.

The Bard's Inn

Now pillars of the Utah Shakespearean Festival Guild in Cedar City, Jack and Audrey Whipple got hooked on the bard during their first visit to town. Their 1900s-era golden shingle-and-brick bungalow reflects their passion for the playwright, from dolls in Elizabethan costumes to guest rooms named after the characters in Shakespeare's plays.

The well-traveled Whipples have acquired scores of unique antiques and decorations for their inn. Audrey designed and created the stained-glass panels—some reassembled from discarded church windows—seen throughout the house. A salvaged oak banister follows the slow curl of the stairway from an enclosed porch to the three upstairs guest rooms.

It is the unexpected touches—creamy crocheted gloves lying across a dropleaf desk in the upstairs sitting room, a Chinese checker board in a bathroom—that make this such a fascinating place to stay. Everything in the house seems to have a story; ask Audrey to tell you how she rescued the claw-foot stool from a sheep pasture in northern Idaho.

The Katharina Room has a turn-of-the-century high-back walnut bed with spring-colored linens, and a big braided runner on the floor; its small alcove hosts a twin walnut sleigh bed. Across the hall, the Olivia Room features cranberry carpeting, antique oak furnishings, and a collection of ceramic figures on an intricately carved wall

shelf. A strawberry border trails around the ceiling of the Titania Room, and stained-glass circles are suspended in two windows. On the main floor is the sophisticated Mistress Ford suite, with a sunny private library. The Beatrice Suite, in the basement, is fitted with matching twin oak beds and a double bed. Thoughtful items in all the rooms include night lights and plump pincushions bristling with needles and thread.

The inn has a refrigerator and sink for guest use and a small dining area with a festive collection of marbles centered on the table. Audrey's healthy but delicious breakfasts might include her home-baked Boston raisin bread, poppyseed rolls, almond cherry zucchini bread, and Jack's personal favorite, made from an old recipe passed down verbally—dainty, frosted *colachis* filled with apricots.

🏠 *150 S. 100 West, Cedar City, UT 84720, tel. 801/586–6612. 3 double rooms with baths, 2 suites, 1 duplex cottage. Kitchen in cottage and 1 suite; off-street parking. $65–$80; full breakfast. MC, V. No smoking indoors, no pets; open June–Sept. only (other dates by prior arrangement).*

Greene Gate Village

Located diagonally across from the historic adobe Mormon Tabernacle, Greene Gate Village looks like a tiny pioneer settlement, and, in a way, it is. This unusual complex brings together seven pioneer-era structures—among them adobe homes, a rock granary, and spruced-up wooden cabins—moved from sites scattered across the St. George Valley. In most cases, an entire house can be rented, making this an excellent place to stay with family or a group of friends. The spacious interior yard is a perfect group common area, with its flower beds, tidy lawns, and postcard-pretty swimming pool.

Built in the mid-1800s and the only village structure original to this site, the tan stucco Orson Pratt House sports a gingerbread-trimmed porch. The first-floor Shanna suite of rooms has brass and oak furniture and hand-quilted floral bedspreads. Next door, in the Lindsay Room, the paper-white cutwork shams and bedspread stand in crisp contrast to the royal blue carpet; photographs of Orson Pratt, a counselor to Brigham Young, hang over the fireplace. The bathroom is tiny, but there's a large Jacuzzi tub in a separate room.

Creaking wicker chairs sit on the rustic porch of the weathered two-room Tolley cabin, which looks out toward the swimming pool. Inside, where a family of 13 once lived, are two simply decorated rooms, each with a fireplace.

Village founders Mark and Barbara Greene had to reconstruct the two-bedroom Morris House, originally located several blocks away: On moving day, the axle on the house trailer broke, and the two-story home suddenly became a pile of shattered glass, adobe brick, and broken door- and window-frames.

Breakfast, served in the garden room of the Bentley House, usually includes omelets, bacon, sausage, juices, and either pecan waffles, homemade bread, or croissants.

🏨 *62–78 W. Tabernacle St., St. George, UT 84770, tel. 801/628–6999 or 800/350–6999. Village: 3 double rooms; 2 triples, and 5 quads, all with baths. Off-site: 4 doubles and 1 quad room with baths; Greene House complex (house and carriage house), which can sleep 22. Telephone and TV in all rooms, kitchens in 2 rooms, fireplaces in 6 rooms, whirlpool tub in 4 rooms; pool, walking tour, off-street parking, 5-course dinners served Thurs.-Sat. by reservation. $50–$125; full breakfast, afternoon refreshments. AE, MC, V. No smoking, no pets; 2-night minimum for Greene House complex.*

Harvest House

When native Bostonians Steve and Barbara Cooper first visited Zion Canyon, they were determined to find a way to come back permanently. Barbara, a gourmet chef and former co-owner of Boston's Harvest Catering Company, also wanted to be able to use her culinary and decorating skills. Luckily for their guests, the Coopers found the ways and means to bring their plans to pass.

Just off Springdale's main drag, Harvest House is a modern, two-story ranch-style structure, built of mottled tan-and-brown brick and buttery stucco. Best of all, practically every window in the house lets in a personal slice of Zion Canyon.

Shades of black and gray dominate in the living room, including a nubby charcoal sofa and many black-and-white photographs; splashes of color come from a collection of cups and saucers and brightly painted wooden animals romping on the hearth. A stained-glass cactus bloom set above the front door sends prisms of light sparkling across the walls, and French doors lead to a flagstone patio.

The main-floor guest room sports lacy curtains on windows that have a view of the cactus garden Steve created; blue-and-green linens look refreshing, and Barbara's handmade paper collages accent the walls. Upstairs, one west-side room is done in stylish pink and black, with a wicker chaise longue for reading or dreaming. A snug love seat highlights another room decorated in rose and ferny green. Sunsets bathe both rooms in colorful light. The pastel-toned master bedroom has a wide window looking out on the apple orchard next door, which attracts deer each evening. On warm summer nights, the sound of the Virgin River is a soft counterpoint to conversations on the private deck.

Breakfast at Harvest House is both festive and delicious. Colorful place settings and butter sculptures formed in a collection of Victorian-era pewter molds are all part of the glamorous presentation of such entrées as poached eggs with basil hollandaise or cheese blintzes with rivers of fresh fruit topping. Fresh muffins, pastries or breads, and Steve's stout coffee help round out the morning meal.

🏠 *29 Canyon View Dr., Springdale, UT 84767, tel. 801/772–3880. 3 double rooms with baths, 1 triple with bath. Air-conditioning, TV, VCR, video library, wet bar in living room; outdoor hot tub, fish pond, off-street parking. $75–$90; full breakfast, afternoon refreshments. D, MC, V. No smoking, children by prior arrangement only, no pets.*

Nine Gables Inn

Jeanne Bantlin was visiting her brother in Kanab when she and her husband, Frank, discovered on an evening walk that the home they had been admiring throughout their stay was suddenly for sale. Both former US West Communications employees, the Bantlins promptly bought this 1890s, two-story ranch house and set about turning it into a bed-and-breakfast.

White stucco now covers the red sun-baked adobe brick, the building material used for most of the houses in the area. A pert white picket fence encloses a yard blooming with myrtle and vinca and a vegetable garden twined with perennial blooms.

The completely remodeled living room has shining new hardwood floors that reflect light from tall, narrow windows. Many of the furnishings in this room, and throughout the inn, are family treasures. But by far the most inviting common area is the upstairs sitting room, with its large circle rug, ceiling fan, rocking chairs, surprisingly comfortable dignified courthouse bench, wood-burning stove, and Victrola with a cabinet full of board games.

A small, sunny guest room at the front of the house has textured gray carpet and matte white walls; a first-edition Zane Grey novel on the nightstand is a reminder that the author was a guest in this home while researching some of his books. In a medium-size room down the hall are a honey-colored oak-slatted bed and the most comfortable chair in the inn: a reupholstered horsehair rocker found in an old milk house.

The long, quiet bedroom at the back of the house features a curly maple roll-top desk that invites letter writing; a firm bed covered with a blue-and-pink "Briar Rose"-patterned quilt; a framed crocheted collar and a colorful old Certificate of Baptism on the wall; and the trunk that carried Jeanne's grandfather's belongings when he emigrated from Norway.

Frank's breakfasts are served in what was once the front parlor; boasting the original bay window and a working fireplace, it's now a very pleasant dining room. Hot or cold cereal shares the board with pastries or muffins, juices, and fresh fruit. A summer treat to hope for is a bowl of huge raspberries from the backyard berry patch.

▥ *106 W. 100 North, Kanab, UT 84741, tel. 801/644–5079. 4 double rooms with baths. Air-conditioning and ceiling fans in all rooms, TV in common area; off-street parking. $60– $70; Continental breakfast. MC, V. No smoking, no pets; closed Nov.– mid-May.*

Seven Wives Inn

I n the heart of St. George's Historic District, two neighboring homes compose Seven Wives Inn, named for an ancestor of one of the owners, who indeed had seven wives. The larger two-story house, built in 1873, features a double-tier veranda and a wood-shingled roof projecting gables in three directions; its attic was the occasional hiding place of die-hard polygamists fleeing federal marshals after multiple marriages were outlawed in 1882. The adjacent President's House, a modified two-story Renaissance Revival cube built in 1883, often provided lodging for visiting presidents of the Mormon Church.

Innkeepers Jay and Donna Curtis and Jon and Alison Bowcutt are always keeping their eyes open for antiques to add to those collected in the parlors of both houses and throughout the guest rooms. Jon is a popular local artist and his pencil drawings and oil paintings hang in the inn's common areas.

In the main house, the Lucinda Room is a study in pastels, with an elaborate antique brass bed, soft, gray hooked rugs, a rose-colored velvet sofa and chair, and a green French ceramic stove; small children can be accommodated in a Murphy bed that descends from an antique armoire. The romantic, high-ceiling Melissa Room on the second floor has a lace minicanopy over the bed and a private balcony. The notorious attic room is brightened by a skylight and an art deco pewter chandelier; a high, floral-painted bed sits against a wall of exposed adobe brick.

The four rooms in the President's House are accessed by a steep, narrow staircase. The Caroline Room has dark green walls lightened by large windows, and a kaleidoscopic "Nine Patch" quilt on the bed. Spring is eternal in the small Rachel Room, where the walls are papered with pastel tulips. The furnishings are white wicker, and floral swags arch over white wooden blinds.

The high-ceiling dining room in the main house has tables set for two or four. In addition to homemade granola, breakfast choices might include German apple or apple pecan pancakes, bread pudding, sausage *en croûte*, or bacon, eggs, and cheese in a nest of hash browns.

▦ *217 N. 100 West, St. George, UT 84770, tel. 801/628–3737 or 800/600–3737. 10 double rooms, 2 triples, 1 single, all with baths (4 rooms can be combined as suites). TV and phone in all rooms, fireplaces or stoves in 4 rooms, private balconies in 4 rooms; outdoor pool, off-street parking. $55–$125; full breakfast. AE, D, DC, MC, V. No smoking, no pets.*

SkyRidge
Bed and Breakfast

kyRidge Bed and Breakfast is near the western boundary of Capitol Reef National Park. The house's design echoes territorial style, and the exterior is an unusual greenish brown—close in color to blooming rice grass, one of the native plants that surround the inn.

Owners Karen Kesler and Sally Elliot relocated from Mendocino, California, in 1993 to design, build, and decorate SkyRidge. Above all, the women wanted a visual feast. Seventy-five windows bring the outside beauty inside. Art furniture fashioned by Karen accents every room, and works by other local artists add visual interest and are available for purchase.

In the cozy living room, guests can relax around a central fireplace with a patterned facade made from more than 30 pounds of roofing nails. Built-in shelves are filled with books, from dog-eared Mother Goose to lush art tomes, and small pieces of African art. The walls here, as elsewhere in the inn, are hand textured and sponge painted neutral colors.

All of SkyRidge's guest rooms are comfortable and intriguing. On the first level, the Buffalo Berry Room mixes Oriental rugs with plump cactus-strewn pillows piled on the bed. Mannequin hands holding crystal door knobs further the room's funky feel. Across the front porch, the Tumble Weed Suite has antique walnut furnishings.

Upstairs, in the large Sagebrush Room, cream and jewel-toned quilts accent two beds perched on gray Berber carpet. Seven windows look across a valley to aspen-covered slopes. The Pinyon Room has heavily textured walls, a pitched roof line, and an oddly appealing jumble of furniture including a match stick four-poster bed, and an art deco floor lamp. A small hot tub is on an enclosed deck. From the high-back bed in the Juniper Room, a bay of six windows provides views of peaks and cliffs silhouetted against the sunrise.

In the main floor dining room, seven tall narrow windows share wall space with Mexican masks and a vivid canvas of a cactus in bloom. Sturdy wicker chairs provide comfortable seating for Sally's culinary specialties—croissant French toast, Mexican frittata with fresh tomatillo salsa, or apple spice pecan waffles—all accompanied by yogurt, granola, and fruit harvested from Capitol Reef National Park.

Box 750220, Torrey, UT 84775, tel. and fax 801/425–3222. 3 double rooms with baths, 1 quad with bath, 1 suite. Ceiling fans and individual heat controls in all rooms, TV with VCR in all rooms, video library, guest refrigerator; horseshoe pits, picnic area, barbecue, off-street parking, activity and trip planning. $68–$98; full breakfast. MC, V. No smoking indoors, children under 10 by prior arrangement and only in suite, no pets; 2-night minimum on holiday weekends.

O'Toole's Under the Eaves

It's easy to see why construction of this two-story mock-Tudor cottage, begun in 1935, took five years: Under the Eaves is made of buff sandstone blocks cut from the walls of Zion Canyon. Fronted by a lovely flower-filled square porch, the inn is a pleasantly incongruous sight on Springdale's motel-lined main street.

Owners Rick and Michelle O'Toole bought the already established property in the spring of 1993. Their first step toward making the guest house their own was to plant favorite flowers in the small backyard, a delightful oasis where pecan, almond, and fruit trees blend with flourishing perennials, lilacs, and lavender.

The parlor and dining room are filled with cozy, worn antiques, and shelves are stocked with books and games. Beyond the kitchen lie two guest accommodations. The cheerful south room has a polished hardwood floor and crisp country linens. The small blue-and-white north room is decorated with a springy handloomed rug and a simple ladder-back chair. Both rooms are illuminated by antique light fixtures taken from the "upstairs rooms" of an old saloon in Pioche, Nevada.

A popular suite nestled "under the eaves" encompasses the entire second floor. Its kitchen and sitting area overlook the gardens, and additional windows face Zion Canyon. A claw-foot tub adds an element of fun to the bathroom.

A separate Garden Cottage holds three small rooms. Two have fanciful linens and stained-glass windows in their compact bathrooms. A mahogany sleigh bed is the focal point of the antiques-filled third room, set in the large, well-lighted basement. This room also boasts a whirlpool tub.

Guests can enjoy sunrise coffee service on the front porch of the main house, and then eat family-style in the dining room. Breakfast highlights include fresh breads, egg-and-cheese casseroles with homemade salsa, and the occasional breakfast tostada with chilies and beans.

🏨 *980 Zion Park Blvd., Box 29, Springdale, UT 84767, tel. 801/772–3457. 3 double rooms with baths, 2 doubles share bath, 1 suite. Air-conditioning, kitchenette in suite; outdoor hot tub, garden gazebo, off-street parking. $60–$75, suite $125; full breakfast. D, MC, V. No smoking, no children under 10, no pets.*

Aunt Annie's Inn

In St. George's historic district, just down the road from Brigham Young's winter home, a cheerful yellow Victorian home (circa 1890) is now the domain of friendly innkeepers Bob and Claudia Tribe. Bob and Claudia, who moved from northern Utah in 1992 to open Aunt Annie's, have filled the bed and breakfast with beautifully restored antiques, some of which have been in their families for years.

The public areas and guest rooms, papered in tiny Victorian florals with brightly colored baseboards, moldings, and door frames, provide a perfect setting for the Tribes' treasures: a shiny brass commode from a turn-of-the-century railway car, say, or one of Bob's collection of antique phonographs.

All of the guest accommodations are impeccably period, right down to claw-foot tubs and authentic bathroom fixtures.

🏠 *139 N. 100 West, St. George, UT 84770, tel. 801/673–5504. 3 double rooms with baths, 1 triple with bath. TV in all rooms, fireplace in common room; off-street parking. $45–$65; full breakfast. AE, D, MC, V. No smoking indoors, no pets.*

The Blue House

Set off from the quiet highway that runs through Rockville, this mid-1980s New England-style home is bright blue, creating a contrast with the red cliffs behind it that is surprisingly attractive. Another nice surprise is the Blue House's economical rates.

Kelly and Anita Christensen operate this low-key, contemporary-style bed-and-breakfast, fronted by a large yard, spacious lawn, and a variety of fruit trees.

The main-floor Emerald Room has a comfortable oak bed, but its private bath is actually a claw-foot tub in the room and a screened toilet area. A brass-and-white king-size bed dominates the upstairs Wine Room, where a twin bed is tucked in a tiny alcove.

Breakfast is served just off the kitchen at a large oval table positioned in a bay window. An antique industrial coffee mill grinds fresh coffee daily to accompany Belgian waffles or muffins with homemade preserves and eggs, ham, or sausage.

🏠 *125 E. Main, Rockville, UT 84763, tel. 801/772–3912. 1 double room and 1 triple with bath, 2 doubles share bath. TV in common area; trampoline, outdoor patio. $50–$75; full breakfast. MC, V. No smoking, pets by arrangement.*

Bryce Point Bed and Breakfast

The ruddy tan exterior of this B&B echoes the cliffs of Bryce Canyon National Park, only minutes away. Guests are welcome in the remodeled, Depression-era cottage of Lamar and Ethel LeFevre, the friendly owners, but most prefer to sit on the wraparound porch or redwood deck of the guest annex and enjoy the fabulous views of Bryce Canyon.

Each of the guest rooms, named for members of the LeFevre family, has a 7 × 5-foot picture window facing the canyon. The peachy rose Clark and Stacey Room sports pretty teal-blue bedspreads, while the walls of the Lynn and Karen Room are a gallery for memorabilia from the former's aeronautics career. The Les and Dela Room has a fire-fighting theme, complete with bright-red linens.

Ethel's special breakfast is Seven-Up pancakes with apple cider syrup, but she also makes delicious oat bran muffins to accompany bacon and eggs.

The LeFevres grew up in this area and have entertaining stories and dependable recreation suggestions.

🏠 *61 N. 400 West, Box 96, Tropic, UT 84776, tel. 801/679-8629. 2 double rooms and 3 triples, all with baths. Ceiling fans and TV/VCRs in all rooms; outdoor hot tub, guest barbecue, off-street parking. $55-$65; full breakfast. MC, V. No smoking, no pets.*

Francisco's

You never know what will happen at Francisco's. Take the night that a guitar-playing guest teamed up with the neighbor from across the street for a little night music. Before long, there were 30 cars, a band on the porch, and a yard filled with people singing and dancing.

This modern log cabin on 10 acres isn't luxurious, but it appeals to those who enjoy sitting in an old church pew on a flower-filled front porch, and who appreciate such sights as the sun setting over Bryce Canyon or the mid-morning antics of wild turkeys strutting through freshly plowed fields. The large, plain guest rooms all have impressive views and a peek under the bedspread may reveal an intricately patterned handmade quilt.

Host Charlie Francisco recently retired from his job as a horse wrangler in Bryce Canyon National Park; his wife, Eva Dean, is the architect of huge breakfasts of pancakes, eggs, sausage or bacon, fresh or home-preserved fruit, and delicious sourdough or sweet breads.

🏠 *51 Francisco La., Box 3, Tropic, UT 84776, tel. 801/679-8721 or 800/642-4136. 3 double rooms with baths. TV in guest rooms, hot tub; farm animals, off-street parking. $45-$65; full breakfast. No credit cards. No smoking, no pets indoors.*

Grandma Bess' Cottage

Minutes away from the popular Brian Head Ski Resort, Parowan was southern Utah's first settlement, established in 1851. Behind a lilac hedge in the historic district sits Grandma Bess' Cottage, a 1920 brick rambler. The house is plain and unassuming, as is the warm welcome given to guests by the hosting Garrick family.

The common parlor is comfortable, with lots of children's books and family pictures. The small- to medium-size guest rooms have hand-painted ceiling borders, from twining flowers to a 1920s-era beach scene. The sunny Grandma Bess room has antique family photos and bright hats hanging on the walls. There's a roomy shower in the cedar-paneled bathroom shared by the three rooms.

Breakfasts of sourdough waffles and fresh fruit or biscuits and gravy are served in the adjoining dining room. In fine weather, guests can eat on the patio, where breezes carry the scent of backyard roses planted by Mormon settlers.

🏠 *291 W. 200 South, Box 640, Parowan, UT 84761, tel. 801/477-8224. 3 double rooms share bath. Air-conditioning in rooms, TV in common area. $45; full breakfast. No credit cards. No smoking, no pets, no alcohol.*

Morning Glory Inn

Surrounded by lots of trees and a grape arbor, this wood and stucco house less than a mile from the entrance to Zion National Park has a Spanish flair, and natural sandstone walkways and patios. It was built in the 1970s by J.R. and Mavis Madsen to accommodate their nine children. Most of the kids have moved away, yet staying here feels much like visiting interesting relatives—with a bit more freedom and privacy.

The living room has a cathedral ceiling and rustic stone fireplace. Full-length windows show off Zion's formations. Upstairs, three guest rooms cluster around a common area with a TV and VCR, a billiards table, and a quiet library nook. In the Rose Room, wreaths of dried flowers and floral bedding contrast with the rugged views of Zion Canyon from a private balcony. Next door, a smaller room with Southwestern-style rugs and pottery has an interesting built-in bed. Most mornings, J.R. plays the living room piano during breakfasts of granola, fresh fruit, and whole wheat pancakes, or "morning glory muffins" loaded with carrots, apples, pineapple, and pecans.

⚏ *25 Big Springs Rd., Springdale, UT 84767, tel. 801/772–3301. 2 triple rooms with baths, 1 quad with bath, 1 3-person cottage. Hot tub in cottage; volleyball, basketball, and badminton courts; playground equipment; picnic area; off-street parking. $60–$85; full breakfast. MC, V. No smoking, no pets.*

Paxman's Summer House

Popular with longtime attendees of the Utah Shakespearean Festival, just a short stroll away, this tan-and-rose brick Victorian farmhouse is large enough to provide privacy, but cozy enough that guests feel comfortable striking up a conversation. Three porches afford views of the quiet neighborhood and colorful flower beds shaded by mature ash and fruit trees. Karlene Paxman, a former home-economics teacher, has owned the home since 1963.

The front parlor has tall lace-curtained windows and a dignified upright piano. An upstairs sitting area with a blue velvet settee is surrounded by three guest rooms with sturdy antique beds and furnishings. In the Pine Room, a high, pioneer-era bed has the requisite bedside stool. A main-floor master bedroom with its own secluded side porch is popular in the summer.

In the dining room, a pump organ occupies a bay window nook. The breakfast menu varies daily, with treats like nutball coffee cake or homemade cinnamon rolls. Fresh peaches and cherries come virtually straight from the tree to the table.

⚏ *170 N. 400 West, Cedar City, UT 84720, tel. 801/586–3755. 3 double rooms, 1 triple, all with baths. TV in rooms; off-street parking. $65–$75; full breakfast. MC, V. Smoking on porches only, no pets.*

Smith Hotel

Wanting to escape the stress of her job as a computer analyst, Shirley Phelan was thinking about buying a B&B in Wisconsin when a friend visiting southern Utah saw this blocky white stucco hotel and persuaded her it was worth considering. She flew out over a weekend and ended up buying the place. Built in 1927, the Smith Hotel was one of the first in the area to accommodate tourists to nearby Zion and Bryce Canyon national parks.

The commodious sitting and dining rooms are largely ignored in favor of the casual comfort of the second-floor screened porch, which affords a view of the surrounding bluffs of the Virgin River valley. The hotel's guest rooms vary in size, but all host an informal mix of antiques and practical furnishings. One large room is furnished with a king-size bed and a handmade armoire.

Each day's Continental breakfast generally includes homemade fruit breads or hot muffins, toast, juices, and fresh fruit.

⚏ *Hwy. 89, Box 106, Glendale, UT 84729, tel. 801/648–2156. 6 double rooms, 1 triple, all with baths. Off-street parking. $40–$55; Continental breakfast. MC, V. No smoking, chil-*

dren by prior arrangement, no pets;
closed Nov.–Mar.

Snow Family Guest Ranch

Travelers to Zion National Park are
often distracted from the lonely desert
scenery by the oasis that is Snow Family Guest Ranch, a large, modern redbrick ranch house set on 12 acres of
lush green horse pasture divided by
crisp white-rail fences.

Hosts Steve and Shelley Penrose and
Clarence and Shirlee Snow have created a ranch environment with frills
and comforts that a real cowboy would
never dream of. The scrupulously clean
guest rooms are bright and airy with
tongue-in-cheek western decor: peeled
pine log beds and night stands, lots of
denim and bandanas, boots, and other
"cowboys and Indians" paraphernalia.
Most rooms have window seats plump
with colorful pillows to enjoy views of
grazing horses or the red rock formations that outline the valley.

Breakfast is served in the great room
complete with gleaming hardwood
floors and a soaring ceiling. Adjoining
are a cozy TV room and a conversa-
tion-perfect parlor decorated in warm
browns. The morning meal is a variety
of omelets, ranch-style hash browns,
and pancakes or French toast. For
those who prefer to get an early start,
a Continental breakfast of cereal,
muffins, and rolls is available early.

🏠 *653 E. Hwy. 9, Box 790190, Virgin,
UT 84779, tel. 801/635–2500 or 800/
308–7669. 9 double rooms with baths.
Big screen TV; swimming pool, outdoor hot tub, gazebo, garden pond.
$75–$105; full breakfast, afternoon
refreshments. MC, V. No smoking,
no infants, older children by arrangement, no pets.*

The Theater Bed & Breakfast

It's hard to miss this two-story bungalow, built in the mid-1930s. Most of the
houses on the quiet street (including
The Bard's Inn, *see above*) are varia-
tions on brown and beige, but The Theater Bed & Breakfast is stuccoed a
rich, lapis blue.

The interior is just as distinctive. Har-
man and Judith Bonniksen have filled
the common areas with artwork and
eclectic treasures from years spent in
Europe and Northern Africa. A main-
floor guest room has a carved high-
back bed from the 1870s. Two upstairs
rooms—one with a saddle from Har-
man's cowpoking days, the other with
a miniature Humpty Dumpty rocking
chair—are fresh and bright.

Breakfast, served in the flower-filled
backyard whenever possible, might
consist of fry bread, waffles, or French
toast served with lots of fresh melon,
berries, or other fruits.

🏠 *118 S. 100 West, Cedar City, UT
84720, tel. 801/586–0404. 1 double
room with adjoining bath, 2 doubles
share bath. Exercise equipment; off-
street parking, guest bicycles, ski storage, free airport shuttle. $50; full
breakfast Mon.–Sat., Continental
breakfast Sun. No credit cards. No
smoking, no pets, no alcohol.*

Zion House

A tri-level brick-and-wood rambler
with a shaggy wood-shingled roof and
ivy sneaking up the walls, Zion House
feels very much like home. Since it
opened in the early 80s it has provided
easy hospitality to guests from all over
the world who wouldn't dream of staying elsewhere when they visit the area.

Soft instrumental music plays on the
stereo in the large living room, which
has chairs designed for comfort. Host-

ess/owner Lillie Biardi maintains a library of current books and videos on Zion National Park for her guests. The ample guest rooms, with excellent beds and durable, if not unique, furnishings, all have stunning views of Zion Canyon.

Breakfast here is conversation filled, and a mirrored wall reflects the guests' animated faces. Morning menus are chosen the night before by consensus, but Lillie tends to favor fresh fruit salads, German pancakes with ham, and freshly baked muffins.

🏠 *801 Zion Park Blvd., Box 323, Springdale, UT 84767, tel. 801/772–3281. 1 double room with bath, 2 doubles share bath, 1 suite. Air-conditioning, kitchen and private entrance in suite; off-street parking. $58, suite $85; full breakfast. MC, V. No smoking, no pets.*

Zion's Blue Star

The terraced yard that leads from the highway up to this tile-roofed Spanish-style rambler hasn't fulfilled its promise, but the Frehner family, retired from a landscaping business,

has made it a personal project. And, in any case, both the tiled front porch and the living room windows look out onto the red mesas across the Virgin River.

Two guest rooms share an ample tan-and-ivory-tiled bathroom. One has an antique chest and dresser, a brass bed, and ivory-lace bedding; through its open windows, guests can hear the whisper of the wind in the willow tree and smell honeysuckle in the spring. Below the house, past a cactus garden and a gnarled 100-year-old cottonwood, is a no-frills cottage that can sleep eight.

Breakfast is hardy French toast, pancakes, omelets, and lots of homemade fruit preserves. Guests rarely leave the inn without being loaded up with fruit and nuts from the Frehners' trees.

🏠 *28 W. State Rte. 9, Virgin, UT 84779, tel. 801/635–3830. 2 double rooms share bath; guest cottage. Air-conditioning in rooms, kitchen in cottage, TV in common room, full meals by arrangement. $55, cottage $65; full breakfast. MC, V. No smoking, no pets.*

Southeastern Utah

Early explorers who charted the rivers and canyons of southeastern Utah filled their journals with superlatives and the margins of their maps with exclamations of awe. Modern writers such as Edward Abbey and Terry Tempest Williams built careers trying to find words to describe their responses to these landscapes. In many ways, this cataclysmic region—a vast, open area filled with solitary places—is still a wilderness waiting to be discovered.

The area wasn't without early settlers. The Anasazi people hunted and farmed here from roughly AD 400 to AD 1500, leaving evidence of their civilization in stone granaries and dwellings perched under cliff overhangs and in intriguing panels of rock art on canyon walls. Mormon pioneers and other hardy settlers who came in the mid to late 1800s left marks of their society beside the remnants of the early Native American culture.

Explorations of the rapids and placid stretches of the Green and Colorado rivers have changed a great deal since Civil War hero John Wesley Powell made the first recorded venture into the canyons in a wooden boat in 1869. These days, both Canyonlands and Arches national parks have paved, scenic drives and maintained day hikes, and some outfitters offer four-wheel-drive tours complete with gourmet meals.

This region's agelessness is evident not only in its rivers but also in its sandstone, eroded by wind and water and transformed into the 1,000-foot cliffs, bizarre needles, and serpentine mazes of Canyonlands National Park, and the arcing stone ribbons at Arches National Park. These parks have long been the showcase for the region, but, more and more, the acres of rolling dunes surrounding their boundaries are coming to be seen as a mountain-biking mecca, the slickrock—sandstone eroded by wind and slick with tiny grains—providing a particular challenge for bikers.

Moviemakers have appreciated southeastern Utah since John Ford's westerns immortalized it in the late 1940s. It was near Canyonlands' Island in the Sky District—not the Grand Canyon, as most people assume—that Thelma and Louise took their final leap, and it was in Arches National Park that a young Indiana Jones discovered the cross of Cortez in Indiana Jones and the Last Crusade. *Local artists have taken advantage of the stunning scenery as well: Each summer, ballet and opera performances are mounted along the Colorado River with sandstone boulders as their props and towering cliffs as their backdrop.*

In a few areas, small towns have rushed to accommodate the influx of visitors and new residents, sprouting subdivisions, motels, gift shops, and fast-food outlets with what seems like little zoning regulation. Other towns are proceeding with caution and waiting for visitors to discover them rather than clamoring to be found.

The B&B business, which began a few years back with residents informally taking visitors into their homes during the busy spring and fall seasons, has evolved to include much more upscale and elaborate properties. If the bed-and-breakfast experience here is still much more casual than in many parts of the country, that's in keeping with the nature of a region whose stunning backyard vistas couldn't be rivaled by even the finest amenities elsewhere.

Places to Go, Sights to See

Arches National Park (Box 907, Moab, UT 84532, tel. 801/259–8161). A 41-mile round-trip scenic drive leads visitors around many of the huge stone monoliths that were eroded from an ancient seabed, but Arches National Park is best experienced on foot. The park has a well-developed series of hiking trails, ranging from effortless walks to all-day explorations of canyons sheltering pristine arches and other formations. The park's most famous formation, Delicate Arch, rising 45 feet above a smooth sandstone basin, is reached via a moderate 1.5-mile march over buff-and-orange sandstone. A ranger-guided trip into the Fiery Furnace is offered daily in summer. The Arches Visitor Center is 3 miles north of downtown Moab, off U.S. 191.

Blanding. Situated on an enormous white sandstone mesa between the city of Monticello and tiny Bluff, Blanding mixes cowboy culture with a Native American heritage. Its *Edge of the Cedars State Park* (660 W. 400 North, tel. 801/678–2238) is an Anasazi ruin adjoined by a museum housing Anasazi artifacts. Several *pottery plants* clustered along Blanding's main street (U.S. 191) offer demonstrations of pottery crafting, decorating, and firing. The *Cedar Mesa Pottery Store* (U.S. 191, tel. 801/678–2241) also sells ceramics seconds at half price.

Bluff. On U.S. 163 across the San Juan River from the vast Navajo Reservation, Bluff was established in 1880 by an expedition of about 200 Mormon pioneers. At one desperate point during their trek, the determined settlers lowered their wagons through a cliff fissure to reach the Colorado River more than 1,000 feet below. The adobe brick homes built by members of this so-called "Hole in the Rock Expedition" still dot this little town. *St. Christopher's Episcopal Mission* (2 mi east of Bluff, tel. 801/672–2396), founded in 1943, has a school for Navajo students and a hogan-style chapel. In the middle of town, the *San Juan River,* one of the fastest-flowing rivers in the United States, is a particular favorite with river runners. A petroglyph panel depicting five images of Kokopelli (the mischievous hump-backed flute player from Pueblo Indian culture) is found at *Sand Island Campground,* 3 miles southwest of town.

Canyonlands National Park (2282 S. West Resource Blvd., Moab, UT 84532, tel. 801/259–7164) is a series of rugged landscapes in three distinct districts—Island in the Sky, Maze, and Needles—divided by the Green and Colorado rivers. Easily Utah's least developed national park, Canyonlands is best known for the solitude it offers; four-wheel-drive trails, popular with bikers as well, lead to the most rugged landscapes. In the Island in the Sky district, hikes are punctuated by panoramic vistas from atop a towering peninsula; the visitor center here has information on activities and attractions throughout the park. Treks through color-banded spires and pinnacles in the Needles section lead to overlooks, arches, and the ruins of ancient civilizations. The Maze portion of the park is serious backcountry, not to be explored without maps.

Green River. Settled in 1878 on the site of a centuries-old river crossing, this town is best known as a launch point for *rafting trips* on the Green River (*see* River Rafting, *below*). At the *John Wesley Powell River History Museum* (885 E. Main St., tel. 801/564–3427), a multi-image slide presentation matches the explorer's journal entries with the sights of a modern-day river expedition. Also known for the variety of melons it grows, the town holds a *Melon Days* celebration each September.

Moab. A Mormon settlement started near the banks of the Colorado River in 1855, Moab prospered from uranium mining in the 1950s and '60s. Now, the surrounding petrified dunes—especially popular with mountain bikers—are the town's major draw, challenged only by Moab's proximity to Canyonlands and Arches national parks. On the south end of Moab, *Arches Vineyard* (2182 S. U.S. 191, tel. 801/259–5397), Utah's only commercial winery, has a tasting room that allows visitors to savor the award-winning wines produced here. *Dead Horse Point State Park* (34 mi northwest of Moab, tel. 801/259–2624) is an isolated island

mesa with views of the LaSal, Abajo, and Henry mountain ranges; Canyonlands'
Island in the Sky District; and the lazy Colorado River, 2,000 feet below.

Monticello. Fifty-three miles south of Moab, the town of Monticello sits beneath
the Abajo Mountains, which appear a somber blue when viewed from a distance
(hence their local nickname, "The Blues"). It's lush compared to many of the
desert towns nearby, which is why a member of one of the founding Mormon
families, a native Virginian, named the town after Thomas Jefferson's home.
Abajo Scenic Drive, a U.S. Forest Service road, winds through 40 forested miles
from Monticello to Blanding; check with the Manti-LaSal National Forest (tel.
801/587–2041) for road conditions.

Mountain Biking. About a decade ago, southeastern Utah became a magnet for
"fat-tire" enthusiasts who wanted to test their mettle on the area's seemingly
endless supply of undulating rock; enthusiasts continue to claim the area as the
"mountain-biking capital of the world." *Bicycle Utah* (Box 738, Park City, UT
84060, tel. 801/649–5806) publishes a free directory of area trails. Among them
are the extremely popular *Moab Slickrock Bike Trail,* a 10.3-mile roller coaster
loop 4 miles east of Moab, marked only by paint slashes on the rock. Less intense
choices near Moab are *Hurrah Pass* in Kane Creek Canyon and the *Gemini
Bridges Trail* outside of town. One of the ultimate mountain-biking treks is the
96-mile *White Rim Trail* in the Island in the Sky district of Canyonlands National
Park. Off-road opportunities are not as plentiful in Arches National Park, but the
paved 41-mile road through the park makes a scenic full-day ride. Road cycling
is also popular on the *Colorado River Scenic Byway* (S.R. 128), part of Utah's
multi-agency-sponsored scenic roads program. West of Monticello, the *Abajo
Mountains* offer heat-beating Alpine rides. Blanding is a convenient starting
point for exploring the *Trail of the Ancients,* famous for rock art. Two good
choices for bike rentals, tours, and solid advice in Moab are *Rim Cyclery* (1233 S.
U.S. 191, tel. 801/259–5333) and *Poison Spider Bicycles* (497 N. Main St., tel.
801/259–7882 or 800/635–1792).

River Rafting. The San Juan, Green, and Colorado rivers, which traverse this
area, offer myriad opportunities for both white-water and float trips, including
stunning excursions through Canyonlands National Park. *Raft Utah* (153 E. 7200
South, Salt Lake City, UT 84047, tel. 801/566–2662) publishes a complete list of
outfitters that serve the region; additional information is available at the park
visitor centers and at the visitor center on North Main Street in Moab.

Restaurants

Although 3.2% beer and wine coolers are widely available in grocery and
convenience stores throughout southern Utah, restaurants in some smaller towns
may not have liquor licenses. When in doubt, call ahead or ask your server, who is
frequently able to serve (but not offer) alcohol to customers.

In Bluff, the **Sunbonnet Cafe** (tel. 801/672–2201) serves up Native American
specialties, including huge Navajo tacos, in a setting of gingham-curtain
simplicity. Popular with the river-running crowd, **Ray's Tavern** (tel. 801/564–

3511) in Green River has the best (and biggest) burgers in town; service may be slow but the food is worth the wait, and there are billiard tables in the back. Some standouts among Moab's many restaurants are the spare and modern **Center Café** (tel. 801/259–4295) for upscale pasta, chicken, and fish; **Eddie McStiff's** (tel. 801/259–2337), which offers good pizza and freshly brewed beer in a family dining area or a more rowdy lounge; and **The Sundowner** (tel. 801/259–5201), serving German fare in a building that looks like a western fort (it was originally a movie set). For people-watching and inexpensive spaghetti, try the lattice-covered patio at **Pasta Jay's** (tel. 801/259–2900). In Monticello, your best bet is **The Lamplighter** (tel. 801/587–2170), which has one of the few liquor licenses in town and passable steaks, chicken, and seafood served in a Victorian atmosphere.

Tourist Information

Moab and Green River Visitor Information (805 N. Main St., Moab, UT 84532, tel. 801/259–8825 or 800/635–6622). **San Juan County Multi-Agency Visitor Center** (117 S. Main St., Box 490, Monticello, UT 84535, tel. 801/587–3235 or 800/574–4386).

Reservation Services. There are no bed-and-breakfast reservation services in the area; write the statewide **Bed and Breakfast Inns of Utah, Inc.** (Box 3066, Park City, UT 84060) or the **Utah Travel Council** (Council Hall/Capitol Hill, Salt Lake City, UT 84114) for a free brochure.

Castle Valley Inn

Although it feels as though it's way out past nowhere, stunning Castle Valley is only about 20 miles from Moab; it's reached via S.R. 128, a designated Scenic Byway that winds along the Colorado River. A road marked by buildings ranging from a red rock-colored geodesic dome to a western movie set leads to the Castle Valley Inn, a wooden rambler home with a native-stone chimney and sparkling geodes set into the foundation.

When you arrive, you'll be surrounded by 360° of ragged-topped cliffs—and a lot of silence. There is a tendency to want to linger outside in the 11-acre yard and orchard, and innkeepers Eric and Lynn Forbes-Thomson have made this easy with balconies on bungalows, a large patio adjacent to the main house, lighted paths, and benches scattered about to take advantage of the vistas. A sheltered hot tub is magical at night.

Lynn is an archaeologist and Eric, a fine furniture maker. Both were Peace Corps volunteers in Africa and Asia, and the common areas of their house are a showcase for the exquisite artifacts that the two have gathered on their travels—among them a rice-winnowing basket, 1,000-year-old Asian ceramics, and Chinese pottery that Lynn excavated from a site in the Philippines. The pine-paneled main-floor living room has a stone fireplace and a mixture of modern furniture and pieces hand-crafted by Eric. Look for several signed Ansel Adams prints. In a common area below the first floor, low couches are surrounded by bright Asian carpets and basketry.

The main-house guest rooms, some upstairs, some down, are decorated in a simple, contemporary style, with striking color combinations such as variegated shades of lavender and green. Each bathroom includes a hair dryer, robe, and shower-massage head in a stall artistically tiled by Lynn. Three separate bungalows have private decks and porches. Baskets from Africa and a chest crafted by Eric decorate the Fremont Bungalow.

Breakfast, which might include green chili quiche, mango yogurt, muesli, and fresh-ground coffee, is served on the patio whenever possible. A fixed-price dinner is offered five nights a week, and "desert survival" lunches in coolers are available with advance notice.

🏨 *CVSR Box 2602, Moab, UT 84532, tel. 801/259–6012. 5 double rooms with baths, 3 double bungalows. Air-conditioning, kitchens in bungalows; VCR, video library in common room; outdoor hot tub. $85–$120, bungalows $145; full breakfast, afternoon refreshments. MC, V. No smoking indoors, no children under 12, no pets; 2-night minimum stay.*

The Grist Mill Inn

There was a lot of head-shaking among Monticello locals when Dianne and Rye Nielson announced their plans to gut a vacant mill and redesign and rebuild it, but doubt changed to admiration by the time the project was completed in 1988: More than 900 people showed up to tour the inn before its opening. Now a place worth staying in an otherwise passing-through kind of town, the Grist Mill Inn is also distinctive for its reasonable rates.

The portions of the huge three-story flour mill that were wooden clapboard when the mill was constructed in 1933 have been sheathed in light-gray aluminum siding. Bright blue tin roofs top both sections of the structure. The entire renovation is documented in a photo album.

A multicolored firebrick hearth in the lobby sitting room is the focal point for a conversation area, with plush purple wing chairs and soft lamplight. If you look up you'll see the driveshaft for a grain sacker that sits a few feet away—one of the many original pieces of mill equipment left throughout the inn. Other lovely common areas include the second-floor Blue Goose TV room (named after an old saloon in town), which also has a pump organ. A bank of high, square windows in the third-floor library provides sufficient light to enjoy reading materials ranging from magazines, remodeling books, and contemporary novels to a complete collection of Hardy Boys and Nancy Drew mysteries.

The Corbin Room, named for Dianne's grandfather, who owned the first telephone company hereabouts, has phones everywhere; one wall and the ceiling are horizontally paneled with rosy stained wood, and an antique armoire holds a Murphy bed. The three-level Bailey Room has two sleeping areas and several antique sewing machines; the bathroom sink is in a treadle machine cabinet. Behind the inn a wooden railroad caboose holds a snug Victorian-style bedroom and a kitchen; its observation tower has a sitting room.

Breakfast is served in the dining room; you can see the Abajo Mountains through glass doors and windows. The Nielsons' morning specialties include French toast stuffed with sweet peaches or served with a clove-tinged maple syrup, and scrambled eggs and cheese piled on cubed potatoes.

🏨 *64 S. 300 East, Box 156, Monticello, UT 84535, tel. 801/587–2597 or 800/ 645–3762. 8 double rooms, 2 triples, all with bath. TV in all rooms, indoor hot tub, gift shop. $46–$92; full breakfast. AE, D, DC, MC, V. No smoking indoors, no pets.*

Sunflower Hill

Once a bare adobe-brick farmhouse surrounded by nothing but crop land, Sunflower Hill was enlarged and renovated, and the crumbling adobe was fortified and covered with pale stucco. A separate cottage was added to the original late-19th-century structure and the farm field became a spacious wooded lot with a hedge of white roses lining the split-log fence.

The main common area, which doubles as the dining room, is as cheerful as innkeepers Aaron and Kim Robison. Mismatched antique chairs are pulled up to several small tables covered with blue-and-white-checked cloths; a century-old Austrian sideboard with dishes peeking through its heavy glass-pane doors sits between windows curtained in crisp white ruffles; and a tall umbrella stand and coat tree are topped with a bright-red hatbox. Across the hall, a small office area known as the Welcome Room contains copious information on the Moab area. An antique cash register is a reminder, perhaps, that this is where reservations are taken and accounts are settled.

The guest rooms are varied in size, but each has a distinctive character. In truth, there's not a bad choice among them. Accessed from the enclosed porch opposite the dining room door, the Sun Porch Room has been fitted with ceiling-to-floor windows covered in vertical miniblinds for privacy. Up a step is a painted metal bed; a woven sunflower throw draped on a quilt stand echoes a ceiling border blooming with golden sunflowers. The Rose Room has stenciled roses twining along the walls, a graceful four-poster bed, and an antique dressing table. The blue-and-white Morning Glory Room has a private garden entrance with morning glory vines growing around the door.

Across the yard, the Garden Cottage has a stenciled tulip border high on the sitting room walls. A whimsical flower garden is painted on the wall of the sunny bedroom.

Sunflower Hill's breakfasts are a variety of sturdy homemade breads, fruity muffins, yogurt, honey granola, and lots of fresh fruit, or hot entrées like fruit-filled pancakes, southwest eggs, or whole wheat waffles with tangy berry patch syrup.

🏠 *185 N. 300 East, Moab, UT 84532, tel. 801/259-2974. 3 double rooms with baths, 1 single with bath, 1 cottage suite. TV and air-conditioning in all rooms, outdoor hot tub, guest kitchenette; bicycle storage, barbecue. $67-$85, cottage suite $95; full breakfast. MC, V. No smoking, children over 8 only and by prior arrangement, no pets.*

Bankurz Hatt

Lana Coomer and her husband, Ben, stumbled into the B&B business when they decided to restore her grandparents' 1897 wooden clapboard foursquare, set in a sleepy neighborhood near the banks of the Green River. The result, Bankurz Hatt, is an incongruously sumptuous lodging in a river-rat town. Guests like to lounge on the tree-shaded front porch—perhaps because the elegant Victorian parlor and dining room seem to require them to be on good behavior.

Directly off the dining room, through discreetly curtained glass doors, a sage-carpeted master bedroom holds an 1850s-era mahogany bedroom set with intricately carved head and footboards, chairs, and a gentleman's chiffonier. The three sunny rooms upstairs are decorated with rose and green florals, antique beds, and elaborate window treatments; their shared bath has a massive shower.

Ben prepares huge breakfasts, say, lamb chops and eggs, quiche, or eggs Benedict, with fresh fruit from a neighboring orchard. Equally delicious dinners are served by reservation.

🏠 *214 Farrer St., Green River, UT 84525, tel. 801/564-3382. 1 double room with bath, 3 doubles share bath. Ceiling fans in rooms; outdoor hot tub, guest bicycles, off-street parking. $75, master bedroom $125; full breakfast. AE. No smoking, no pets; closed Jan.-Mar.*

Bluff Bed and Breakfast

Tiny Bluff, a gateway to Monument Valley and the huge Navajo Reservation, is super slow-paced, and the feeling of being in a time warp carries over to the Bluff Bed and Breakfast. The beige brick rectangular house, with a covered courtyard entry, is a Frank Lloyd Wright knockoff dating from the 1960s, and its well-built furnishings are the once-elegant artifacts of the same period.

Witty and articulate hostess Rosalie Goldman has eclectic interests and a passion for the adventure offered by the surrounding desert. The front and back walls of the inn's common area are composed entirely of windows through which a private canyon can be viewed; "don't-worry-about-the-mud" linoleum lines the floor. Books on the built-in shelves range from *Gray's Anatomy* to Erica Jong.

The larger of the two guest rooms offers 180° views and features a funky mosaic-tiled shower. Breakfast—consisting of anything guests want, from oatmeal to steak and eggs—is served in a dining area equipped with a piano (Rosalie counts on guests playing it to help keep it in tune) or on the backyard patio.

🏠 *Box 158, Bluff, UT 84512, tel. 801/ 672-2220. 2 double rooms with baths. TV in common area; off-street parking, hiking. $65-$75; full breakfast. No credit cards. No smoking, no pets.*

The Desert Chalet

You have to travel through a maze of mobile homes to reach the Desert Chalet, but don't worry—your destination is a whimsically decorated, dark-brown wooden cabin, easily the nicest address on the street. Owner Marsha Medford's sense of humor is evident from the moment you step into the vaulted-ceiling living room and are greeted by an assembly of wig heads wearing jaunty hats.

Among the simple but comfortable accommodations is the small Barn Room, with twin beds and walls paneled in—you guessed it—barn boards. A cedar-paneled master bedroom has exposed ceiling beams and hosts a queen-size waterbed as well as a twin bed. "Ralph the Movie Star," a reclining figure that Marsha salvaged from a film set and decked out in a party hat and Hawaiian leis, shares the loft with two twin beds; an adjoining room has a steeply slanted ceiling and knotty pine walls.

Guests enjoy a Continental breakfast buffet—bagels or muffins, cold cereals, lots of fresh fruit—on the patio or in the plant-filled dining area.

🏨 *1275 E. San Juan Dr., Moab, UT 84532, tel. 801/259–5793 or 800/549– 8504. 1 triple room with bath, 2 doubles and 2 triples share 2 baths. Ceiling fans in rooms, TV, VCR, and stereo in common area; outdoor hot tub; kitchen, laundry, and storage available; barbecue. $39–$75; Continental-plus breakfast. MC, V. No smoking, no children under 6, no pets; closed Feb.–Mar.*

Grayson Country Inn

Grayson Country Inn, a 1908 Victorian-style ranch house known formerly as the Old Hotel B&B, is a soothing place that guests revisit year after year.

Innkeepers Dennis and Lurlene Gutke bought the B&B in 1994 and promptly set about making it their own. A bay window with sheer lace curtains brightens the small living room where guests can try out a restored 1894 pump organ. An eye-catching selection of family antiques fills a nook above the stairway. Glider rocking chairs sit in several of the guest rooms, which are all individually decorated with brass beds topped by crocheted spreads, and accents like kerosene lamps, cowboy pistols, Native American pottery, and wreaths made of dried desert plants. Three rooms have stained-glass windows.

Breakfast, served in what was once the screened porch, generally includes homemade bread, a fruit cup, and granola.

🏨 *118 E. 200 South, Blanding, UT 84511, tel. 801/678–2388. 7 double rooms with baths. TV and air-conditioning in rooms. $32–$52; light breakfast. AE, MC, V. No smoking, no pets.*

Pack Creek Ranch

Sprawling across the foothills of the LaSal Mountains, nine wooden cabins with red roofs and stone porches are clustered around a lodge and dining room. It takes about 20 minutes to drive from Moab to Pack Creek Ranch on a road cut through scrubby pinion pine and juniper. Roll down the windows—the air is pungent with sagebrush.

Accommodating between two and five guests, the appealing rustic cabins all have kitchens, colorful rugs, and sturdy furniture; some have wood-burning fireplaces. The large Ranch House, available for conference groups, can sleep up to 12.

April through October, meals are served in the dining room, which has a massive bull elk mounted above the stone fireplace. Breakfast is a hot meal of the eggs-and-bacon variety, with juices and cereal available for those on the run. Dinner includes sophisticated entrées such as Cajun cream shrimp or French pepper steak. A lunch buffet for assembling sack lunches is set out each morning.

🏨 *LaSal Mountain Loop Rd., Box 1270, Moab, UT 84532, tel. 801/259– 5505, fax 801/259–8879. 9 cabins, ranch house (sleeps up to 12) with 1½ baths. Gift shop, masseuse, outdoor hot tub, pool, trail rides. $125 per person includes all meals; Nov.–Mar., $56 per person without meals. AE, D, MC, V. No smoking, no pets.*

Valley of the Gods Bed and Breakfast

Crouched between the tiny towns of Bluff and Mexican Hat on what locals call the Lee Ranch, Valley of the Gods Bed and Breakfast is in the proverbial middle of nowhere. It is the only habitable building within the Cedar Mesa Cultural and Recreational Management Area, and it is bordered on all sides by state and federal land. The inn's name comes from the nearby valley, which is filled with red rock spires and bizarre pinnacles.

Innkeepers Gail Goeken and Lee Dick, both Floridians, bought the ramshackle stone ranch house in order to escape the rigors of city life. Through restoration the men kept the structure's character, and its massive ceiling beams salvaged from an old oil derrick, but made it more liveable—solar power, a new roof, water cisterns, and a cellular phone link.

Antique furnishings, plush Oriental rugs, and miscellaneous objets d'art contrast nicely with rugged stone walls and the seemingly endless desert rangeland outside.

Breakfasts of hot sweet rolls and fruit or biscuits and egg casserole are served on a corner of the 75-foot porch in fine weather; otherwise, you eat in the common room. Dinners are by prior arrangement.

🏨 *Lee Ranch, Box 310307, Mexican Hat, UT 84531, tel. 303/749-1164 (cellular), fax 801/683-2292. 4 double rooms with baths. Raft trips, pack horse or llama trips and archaeological tours available by arrangement. $55–$75; full breakfast. MC, V. No smoking indoors, children and pets by prior arrangement.*

Directory 1:
Alphabetical

Directory 2:
Geographical

The Nagel House *160*
Schmidt Barn *160*
Settlers Crossing *155*
Glen Rose
Inn on the River *144*
Jefferson
The Excelsior House *139*
House of the Seasons *143*
McKay House *141*
Maison-Bayou *144*
Pride House *145*
Stillwater Inn *146*
Lubbock
Broadway Manor *168*
Post
Hotel Garza *167*
Salado
Inn on the Creek *153*
San Antonio
The Beckmann Inn and Carriage House *157*
The Bonner Garden *157*
The Bullis House Inn *157*
The Ogé House on the Riverwalk *154*
A Yellow Rose *161*
San Marcos
Crystal River Inn *152*
Stephenville
Oxford House *145*

Texarkana
Mansion on Main *144*
Tyler
Charnwood Hill *138*
The Seasons *146*
Uncertain
Caddo Cottage *143*

Utah

Blanding
Grayson Country Inn *199*
Bluff
Bluff Bed and Breakfast *198*
Cedar City
The Bard's Inn *178*
Paxman's Summer House *187*
The Theater Bed & Breakfast *188*
Glendale
Smith Hotel *187*
Green River
Bankurz Hatt *198*
Kanab
Nine Gables Inn *181*
Mexican Hat
Valley of the Gods Bed and Breakfast *200*
Moab
Castle Valley Inn *195*

The Desert Chalet *198*
Pack Creek Ranch *199*
Sunflower Hill *197*
Monticello
The Grist Mill Inn *196*
Parowan
Grandma Bess' Cottage *186*
Rockville
The Blue House *185*
St. George
Aunt Annie's Inn *185*
Greene Gate Village *179*
Seven Wives Inn *182*
Springdale
Harvest House *180*
Morning Glory Inn *186*
O'Toole's Under the Eaves *184*
Zion House *188*
Torrey
SkyRidge Bed and Breakfast *183*
Tropic
Bryce Point Bed and Breakfast *185*
Francisco's *186*
Virgin
Snow Family Guest Ranch *188*
Zion's Blue Star *189*

NOTES

NOTES

Fodor's Travel Publications

Available at bookstores everywhere, or call 1–800–533–6478, 24 hours a day.

Gold Guides

U.S.

Alaska	Florida	New Orleans	Santa Fe, Taos,
Arizona	Hawaii	New York City	Albuquerque
Boston	Las Vegas, Reno,	Pacific North Coast	Seattle & Vancouver
California	Tahoe	Philadelphia & the	The South
Cape Cod, Martha's	Los Angeles	Pennsylvania Dutch	U.S. & British Virgin
Vineyard, Nantucket	Maine, Vermont,	Country	Islands
The Carolinas & the	New Hampshire	The Rockies	USA
Georgia Coast	Maui	San Diego	Virginia & Maryland
Chicago	Miami & the Keys	San Francisco	Waikiki
Colorado	New England		Washington, D.C.

Foreign

Australia &	Europe	Madrid & Barcelona	Provence &
New Zealand	Florence, Tuscany	Mexico	the Riviera
Austria	& Umbria	Montréal &	Scandinavia
The Bahamas	France	Québec City	Scotland
Bermuda	Germany	Moscow, St.	Singapore
Budapest	Great Britain	Petersburg, Kiev	South America
Canada	Greece	The Netherlands,	Southeast Asia
Cancún, Cozumel,	Hong Kong	Belgium &	Spain
Yucatán Peninsula	India	Luxembourg	Sweden
Caribbean	Ireland	New Zealand	Switzerland
China	Israel	Norway	Thailand
Costa Rica, Belize,	Italy	Nova Scotia, New	Tokyo
Guatemala	Japan	Brunswick, Prince	Toronto
The Czech Republic	Kenya & Tanzania	Edward Island	Turkey
& Slovakia	Korea	Paris	Vienna & the Danube
Eastern Europe	London	Portugal	
Egypt			

Fodor's Special-Interest Guides

Branson	Fodor's London	Kodak Guide to	Walt Disney World
Caribbean Ports	Companion	Shooting Great	for Adults
of Call	France by Train	Travel Pictures	Where Should We
The Complete Guide	Halliday's New	Shadow Traffic's	Take the Kids?
to America's	England Food	New York Shortcuts	California
National Parks	Explorer	and Traffic Tips	Where Should We
Condé Nast Traveler	Healthy Escapes	Sunday in New York	Take the Kids?
Caribbean Resort and	Italy by Train	Sunday in	Northeast
Cruise Ship Finder		San Francisco	
Cruises and Ports		Walt Disney World,	
of Call		Universal Studios	
		and Orlando	

Special Series

Affordables

Caribbean

Europe

Florida

France

Germany

Great Britain

Italy

London

Paris

Fodor's Bed & Breakfasts and Country Inns

America's Best B&Bs

California's Best B&Bs

Canada's Great Country Inns

Cottages, B&Bs and Country Inns of England and Wales

The Mid-Atlantic's Best B&Bs

New England's Best B&Bs

The Pacific Northwest's Best B&Bs

The South's Best B&Bs

The Southwest's Best B&Bs

The Upper Great Lakes' Best B&Bs

The Berkeley Guides

California

Central America

Eastern Europe

Europe

France

Germany & Austria

Great Britain & Ireland

Italy

London

Mexico

Pacific Northwest & Alaska

Paris

San Francisco

Compass American Guides

Arizona

Chicago

Colorado

Hawaii

Hollywood

Las Vegas

Maine

Manhattan

Montana

New Mexico

New Orleans

Oregon

San Francisco

South Carolina

South Dakota

Texas

Utah

Virginia

Washington

Wine Country

Wisconsin

Wyoming

Fodor's Español

California

Caribe Occidental

Caribe Oriental

Gran Bretaña

Londres

Mexico

Nueva York

Paris

Fodor's Exploring Guides

Australia

Boston & New England

Britain

California

Caribbean

China

Florence & Tuscany

Florida

France

Germany

Ireland

Italy

London

Mexico

Moscow & St. Petersburg

New York City

Paris

Prague

Provence

Rome

San Francisco

Scotland

Singapore & Malaysia

Spain

Thailand

Turkey

Venice

Fodor's Flashmaps

Boston

New York

San Francisco

Washington, D.C.

Fodor's Pocket Guides

Acapulco

Atlanta

Barbados

Jamaica

London

New York City

Paris

Prague

Puerto Rico

Rome

San Francisco

Washington, D.C.

Rivages Guides

Bed and Breakfasts of Character and Charm in France

Hotels and Country Inns of Character and Charm in France

Hotels and Country Inns of Character and Charm in Italy

Short Escapes

Country Getaways in Britain

Country Getaways in France

Country Getaways Near New York City

Fodor's Sports

Golf Digest's Best Places to Play

Skiing USA

USA Today The Complete Four Sport Stadium Guide

Fodor's Vacation Planners

Great American Learning Vacations

Great American Sports & Adventure Vacations

Great American Vacations

National Parks and Seashores of the East

National Parks of the West